MODER

MODERN RUSSIA

A Volume in the Comparative Societies Series

MIKK TITMA
Tartu University

NANCY BRANDON TUMA
Stanford University

Boston   Burr Ridge, IL   Dubuque, IA   Madison, WI
New York   San Francisco   St. Louis
Bangkok   Bogotá   Caracas   Lisbon   London   Madrid   Mexico City
Milan   New Delhi   Seoul   Singapore   Sydney   Taipei   Toronto

McGraw-Hill Higher Education

A Division of The **McGraw-Hill** Companies

MODERN RUSSIA

Published by McGraw-Hill, an imprint of The McGraw-Hill Companies, Inc., 1221 Avenue of the Americas, New York, NY 10020. Copyright © 2001 by the McGraw-Hill Companies, Inc. All rights reserved. No part of this publication may be reproduced in any form or by any means, or stored in a database or retrieval system, without prior written consent of The McGraw-Hill Companies, Inc., including, but not limited to, in any network or other electronic storage or transmission, or broadcast for distance learning.

Some ancillaries, including electronic and print components, may not be available to customers outside the United States. This book is printed on acid-free paper.

1 2 3 4 5 6 7 8 9 0 FGR/FGR 0 9 8 7 6 5 4 3 2 1 0

ISBN 0-07-292823-9

Editorial director: *Phillip A. Butcher*
Sponsoring editor: *Sally Constable*
Marketing manager: *Leslie A. Kraham*
Project manager: *Kimberly D. Hooker*
Production supervisor: *Heather Burbridge*
Designer: *Pam Verros*
Compositor: *Shepherd Incorporated*
Typeface: *10/12 Palatino*
Printer: *Quebecor Printing Book Group/Fairfield*

Library of Congress Cataloging-in-Publication Data

Titma, M. Kh.
  Modern Russia / Mikk Titma, Nancy Brandon Tuma.
    p. cm.
    ISBN 0-07-292823-9 (softcover : alk. paper) (Comparative societies series)
    Includes index.
    1. Russia (Federation)—History—1991- I. Tuma, Nancy Brandon.
  II. Title. III. Series.
  DK510.76.T58   2001
  947.086 dc—21   00-036139

www.mhhe.com

"To ordinary Russian men and women, so long neglected, and still not yet masters of their own country."

In one of the early scenes of the movie *Reds*, the U.S. revolutionary journalist John Reed, just back from covering the beginning of World War I, is asked by a roomful of business leaders, "What is this War really about?" John Reed stands and stops all conversation with a one-word reply—"profits." Today, war between major industrial nations would disrupt profits much more than create money for a military industrial complex. Highly integrated global markets and infrastructures support the daily life of suburban families in Chicago and urban squatter settlements in Bombay. These ties produce a social and economic ecology that transcends political and cultural boundaries.

The world is a very different place than it was for our parents and grandparents. Those rare epic events of world war certainly invaded their everyday lives and futures, but we now find that daily events thousands of miles away, in countries large and small, have a greater impact on North Americans than ever before, with the speed of this impact multiplied many times in recent decades. Our standard of living, jobs, and even prospects of living in a healthy environment have never before been so dependent on outside forces.

Yet there is much evidence that North Americans have less easy access to good information about the outside world than even a few years ago. Since the end of the Cold War, newspaper and television coverage of events in other countries has dropped dramatically. It is difficult to put much blame on the mass media, however: International news seldom sells any more. There is simply less interest.

It is not surprising, then, that Americans know comparatively little about the outside world. A recent *Los Angeles Times* survey provides a good example: People in eight countries were asked five basic questions about current events of the day. Americans were dead last in their knowledge, trailing people from Canada, Mexico, England, France, Spain, Germany, and Italy.* It is also not surprising that the annual report published by the Swiss World Economic Forum always ranks American executives quite low in their international experience and understanding.

Such ignorance harms American competitiveness in the world economy in many ways. But there is much more. Seymour Martin Lipset put it nicely in one of his recent books: "Those who know only

---

*For example, whereas only 3 percent of Germans missed all five questions, 37 percent of the Americans did (*Los Angeles Times*, March 16, 1994).

one country know no country" (Lipset 1996: 17). Considerable time spent in a foreign country is one of the best stimulants for a sociological imagination: Studying or doing research in other countries makes us realize how much we really, in fact, have learned about our own society in the process. Seeing other social arrangements, ways of doing things, and foreign perspectives allows for far greater insight into the familiar, our own society. This is also to say that ignorance limits solutions to many of our own serious social problems. How many Americans, for example, are aware that levels of poverty are much lower in all other advanced nations and that the workable government services in those countries keep poverty low? Likewise, how many Americans are aware of alternative means of providing health care and quality education or reducing crime?

We can take heart in the fact that sociology in the United States has become more comparative in recent decades. A comparative approach, of course, was at the heart of classical European sociology during the 1800s. But as sociology was transported from Europe to the United States early in the 20th century, it lost much of this comparative focus. In recent years, sociology journals have published more comparative research. There are large data sets with samples from many countries around the world in research seeking general laws on issues such as the causes of social mobility or political violence, all very much in the tradition of Durkheim. But we also need much more of the old Max Weber. His was a qualitative historical and comparative perspective (Smelser 1976; Ragin and Zaret 1983). Weber's methodology provides a richer understanding of other societies, a greater recognition of the complexity of social, cultural, and historical forces shaping each society. Ahead of his time in many ways, C. Wright Mills was planning a qualitative comparative sociology of world regions just before his death in 1961 (Horowitz 1983: 324). [Too few American sociologists have yet to follow in his footsteps.]

Following these trends, sociology textbooks in the United States have also become more comparative in content in recent years. And while this tendency must be applauded, it is not enough. Typically, there is an example from Japan here, another from Germany there, and so on, haphazardly for a few countries in different subject areas as the writer's knowledge of these bits and pieces allows. What we need are the textbook equivalents of a richer Weberian comparative analysis, a qualitative comparative analysis of the social, cultural, and historical forces that have combined to make relatively unique societies around the world. It is this type of comparative material that can best help people in the United States overcome their lack of understanding about other countries and allow them to see their own society with much greater insight.

The Comparative Societies Series, of which this book is a part, has been designed as a small step in filling this need. We have currently selected 12 countries on which to focus: Japan, Thailand, Switzerland, Mexico, Eritrea, Hungary, Germany, China, India, Iran, Brazil, and Russia. We selected these countries as representatives of major world regions and cultures, and each will be examined in separate books written by talented sociologists. All of these basic sociological issues and topics will be covered: Each book will begin with a look at the important historical and geographical forces shaping the society, then turn to basic aspects of social organization and culture. From there each book will proceed to examine the political and economic institutions of the specific country, along with the social stratification, the family, religion, education, and finally urbanization, demography, social problems, and social change.

Although each volume in the Comparative Societies Series is of necessity brief to allow for use as supplementary readings in standard sociology courses, we have tried to assure that this brief coverage provides students with sufficient information to better understand each society, as well as their own. The ideal would be to transport every student to another country for a period of observation and learning. Realizing the unfortunate impracticality of this ideal, we hope to do the next best thing— to at least mentally move these students to a country very different from their own, provide something of the everyday reality of the people in these other countries, and demonstrate how the tools of sociological analysis can help them see these societies as well as their own with much greater understanding.

Harold R. Kerbo
San Luis Obispo, CA
June 1997

For centuries, Russia has intrigued and amazed outside observers, as well as frightened and perplexed them. Since its founding in the ninth century, Russia has been a land of enormous potential. Throughout history, Russians have used this great potential to achieve astounding results. Its major military accomplishments include the expulsion of Mongol oppressors in the fifteenth century; the creation of a vast empire covering much of the Eurasian landmass under the tsars in the eighteenth century; the defeat of Napoleon's army in 1812; the triumph over Hitler's forces in World War II; and the ascendance to one of the two major nuclear superpowers, dominating even more of the Eurasian landmass during much of the twentieth century.

But relative to other major countries in the West, Russia has been slow to develop socially and economically. It entered the twentieth century with a huge peasant population, a small industrial base, and a few merchants ruled by an autocratic tsar and his noble entourage. At the end of the twentieth century, a quarter of its population was still engaged in agriculture, far more than in any other industrialized country. Its industrial base has been much enlarged since the start of the twentieth century, but rarely can it compete on world markets due to its decrepit physical infrastructure, outmoded technologies in many industries, and inefficient work organization. With its tremendous natural resources and its highly educated population (one of the most beneficial legacies of the Soviet regime), Russia nevertheless remains a land of great economic potential.

Russia is distinctive also in the political paths it has taken. It retained an absolute monarchy much longer than any other European country. In wealth and political influence, the gap between its nobility and the masses was also far greater than in other European countries. As the twentieth century began, its ruling nobility was unwilling to relinquish power, even gradually. Then it lurched toward the political left in 1917 when a small group of Communist intellectuals mobilized the latent discontent of the masses to overthrow the tsarist regime and establish the Soviet Union, the world's first state based on Karl Marx's Communist vision. But Marx did not give a detailed blueprint for a Communist society. Consequently, the development of the Soviet Union's political system can be attributed largely to its early leaders, Vladimir Lenin and his successor, Josif Stalin. They were determined to build communism according to their own vision, no matter what people wanted. For most Western observers in the middle of the twentieth century, Russia symbolized totalitarianism and rule by force and fear. This political extremism did not last. Amazingly, the Soviet Empire crumbled from within. Its nuclear weapons could not protect it from its own internal weaknesses.

Today Russia is again immersed in a major transition. There is widespread hope that it is headed toward a market economy and democracy. There is an immense gap between where it is headed and the command economy and Communist party-state of its Soviet past. The process of change cannot be smooth or easy.

As the twenty-first century dawns, we are confident in predicting that Russia will continue to play a major role in world affairs, as she has for centuries. Her exact role is unclear, however. The possibilities are manifold; either optimism or pessimism can be justified. When relationships are not yet stable and institutionalized, seemingly small choices can have big consequences. In this situation, it is particularly important to understand both Russia's past and her present society.

People in America first encountered Russians who were exploring and trading in the eighteenth century, providing the outposts that allowed Alaska to be incorporated into the Russian Empire. Americans next had significant contact with the Russian Empire during the American Revolution, when some of the tsar's forces helped Americans gain independence. (Naturally this help was not sent out of the tsar's love of democracy but the desire to limit the power of the British Empire, a major competitor.) Toward the end of the nineteenth century, Americans met Russians in a new guise, as millions of Poles, Jews, and other suppressed peoples in the Russian Empire migrated to the United States. An enduring image of Russia began to be formed in the minds of Americans: a vast and mysterious empire with diverse suppressed peoples. The symbol of Russia as a huge, powerful, and often ferocious bear (whether white or brown) reached the shores of America from Europe where this imagery was already established.

Then came the 1917 October Revolution. The tsar was not only toppled but assassinated, and Bolsheviks with their radical, left-wing ideology took power. In the ensuing Civil War of 1918–1921, the United States, along with other Western powers, sent its navy and troops to fight the Communists. The rise of Hitler and his Nazi armies forced the United States into an uncomfortable but necessary alliance with the Soviet Union during World War II. This brief toleration of the Russian bear was soon followed by the decades-long Cold War in which Russia was viewed stereotypically as an evil empire and Russians were its sinister agents. Then, almost out of the blue, came a new and much more vigorous general secretary of the Communist Party of the Soviet Union: Mikhail Gorbachev. He recognized the Soviet Union's stagnation but had unclear ideas about how to make things better. He prescribed *glasnost* (openness) and *perestroika* (restructuring). All sorts of unexpected genies escaped from the bottle of the Soviet Empire. With surprising rapidity and relatively little violence, the Soviet Union collapsed from within.

Hope grew that Russia would become a democracy, develop a market economy, and be a peaceful partner in world affairs, perhaps even an ally of the United States and other Western countries. Russia's first elected head, Boris Yeltsin, initially boosted the image of Russia in the eyes of Western observers. For Americans, it looked as though Russia was quickly moving from communism to democracy and a market economy. But with every passing year, the image tended to revert to that of an old Russian bear: still huge, powerful (but less so than in the past), ornery, and cranky (if not quite as ferocious as before). Now that Yeltsin has resigned as president and there is a new president, expectations for change in Russia have been renewed. But will things get better or worse? Americans, just as Russians themselves, are hoping for the best; in any case, they want to know what will happen next in Russia.

This book is intended to serve as a guide to modern Russian society, politics, economics, and culture and thereby to open a window onto Russia's vast lands and diverse peoples. We hope our book will give readers a better understanding and appreciation of Russia, of both features she shares with other industrialized countries and ones that are unique. Only through such knowledge and understanding can outside observers help the mighty nation that is modern Russia achieve prosperity and stability and interact peaceably with the rest of the world in the coming decades.

We ourselves chose Russia as our scientific interest starting from very different beginnings. Mikk Titma lived most of his life in the Soviet Union. Though a native of Estonia, he lived in Russia for many years. For him, writers like Dostoevsky, Chekhov, and Solzhenitsyn were the fertile intellectual ground of Russian culture that gave him insight into the Russian soul and character. His early scholarly training occurred during Khrushchev's Thaw, which appeared to furnish a real opportunity to build a decent society based on socialist ideals. But the dismal era of Brezhnev followed, breaking all his hopes and ties to socialism. His cohort was of an age to play a leading role in Gorbachev's perestroika, but with a different agenda: to dismantle communism in the least painful way for ordinary people. Being politically active during this period gave him insight into the wheels of Soviet power and into ways to overcome it.

As a sociologist, the process of the transformation of the former state socialist societies began to be a scientific interest. In particular, how and why have some of these new countries been fairly successful while others have failed? Why has tiny Estonia succeeded, whereas Russia has not, despite its immense natural resources and great human potential? What is the reason? Is it something about the people themselves (e.g., their culture or heritage) or rather a consequence of the choices of their elites? In understanding the emerging variety of ways out of the Soviet Union, a tremendous help came from the ongoing longitudinal study, "Paths of a Generation." This project began in 1982 by surveying secondary school graduates in 15 different regions of the USSR. Some of these same people have been interviewed again in the late 1980s, in the early 1990s and yet again in the late 1990s. Colleagues in this project have expanded our insights into different regions of Russia and in other successor states of the USSR. Life itself as well as sociological research undergird Titma's approach to Russia and the Russian people.

In contrast, Nancy Tuma was born and raised in the United States' South, later lived in the Northeast, then the Midwest, and finally in California. Her youthful experiences in the South triggered an abiding interest in social stratification and inequality, while her subsequent moves within the United States and travels first within West and East Europe, and then within Asia and Australia, led to the realization that social, economic, and political differences within and between societies have enormous consequences for people's lives and the way they think. Her initial interests in social mobility within the life course of people within the United States expanded into interests in these phenomena in different societies. The striking differences between market-based democratic societies and state socialist societies with command economies first captured her attention in the late 1970s, but they became her major object of study only in the late 1980s. At that point, she began to do research first on China and then, in collaboration with Mikk Titma, on post-Soviet societies as a part of the "Paths of a Generation" project.

STYLISTIC NOTES

Our book contains a few stylistic guides for readers. Words in small caps, like THIS, are defined in the glossary. Many foreign words are *italicized* on first appearance in the text. (Following convention, titles of books, journals, and other major works are also italicized.) Foreign words rarely mentioned in English are in the glossary and identified in the text like *THIS*. Words or phrases in **bold,** along with major and minor headings, are intended to help readers keep track of major themes.

ACKNOWLEDGMENTS

Since "Paths of a Generation" has been so important in helping us to understand Russia and Russians by giving us firsthand information on how the Soviet Union and its successor states have affected ordinary people's thoughts and actions, we want to thank both our colleagues who have assisted with it and those who have supported it financially. With regard to the latter, we thank especially the Johann Jacobs Foundation, the National

Council for Eurasian and East European Research (contracts #812-10 and #813-01), the National Science Foundation (grants #SES-9212936 and #SBR-9710399), the Spencer Foundation (grants #09699 and #199800085), the International Research and Exchanges Board (for travel assistance), Stanford's Center for Russian and East European Research, and Stanford University. The university has also provided us with a stimulating intellectual environment. The Stanford undergraduate and graduate students in our various classes on topics related to this book have been an especially important and positive aspect of this environment. Their particular interests, questions, and occasional misunderstandings have helped us adapt our book to students.

On a personal note, we thank Harold Kerbo for inviting us to write this book, the editorial staff at McGraw-Hill for their patience and help, and Walter D. Connor and Philip Roeder for their very helpful comments on the first draft of this book. Gregory Marsden, a Stanford student formerly in one of our classes, gave useful suggestions on the second draft. Last but definitely not least, we express our deep gratitude to two students who took one of our freshman seminars on the transition from state socialism and then stayed on to give us extensive assistance with a wide variety of tasks involved in producing this book: Robert Person and Mark Silver.

TABLE OF CONTENTS

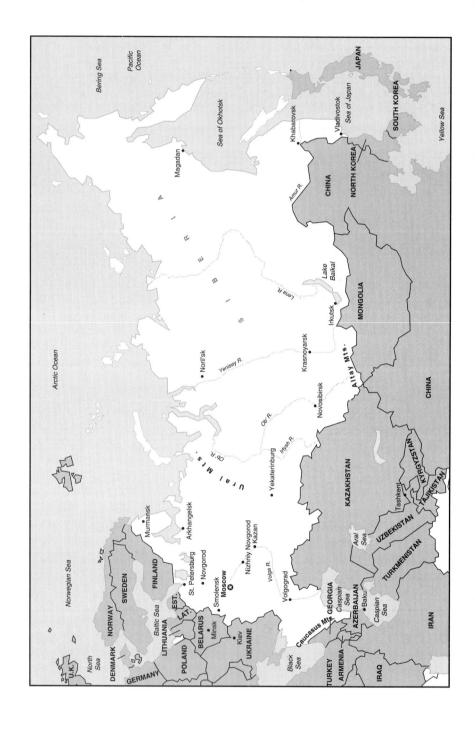

CHAPTER 1

The Place, the People, and the Past

1.1 THE PLACE

Russia! The world's largest country covers 11 time zones, nearly four times as many as the continental United States. Its size is truly continental, 6.6 million square miles, encompassing the largest part of Europe and all of northern Asia. Its vast lands cover an eighth of the area of the earth's populated continents. From west to east, Russia ranges 5,600 miles (9,000 kilometers) from the western port of Kaliningrad (formerly Königsberg) on Poland's border to the Bering Strait, a few hundred miles from Nome, Alaska. Though its northernmost parts extend well above the Arctic Circle, parts are also as far south as Boston, Massachusetts. From the north to the south, it ranges 2,500 miles (4,000 kilometers). Crossing this huge landmass takes 11 hours by air and roughly two weeks by train. For all practical purposes, it cannot yet be crossed by car.

Russia's emblem, the bear (white or brown), appropriately symbolizes the wild forests and harsh climate typical of most of this land. For Russia, Siberia is roughly like Alaska is for America, with one big difference: Siberia's winter, with temperatures far below zero degrees Fahrenheit, covers two-thirds of Russia's landmass and lasts more than half the year.

Almost every kind of terrain can be found in such an immense land. Europe's largest mountain, Elbrus, lies on its border with Georgia in the CAUCASUS in the south. Historically, mountain ranges have formed the natural border separating Russia and China. However, the primary internal barriers for Russians have been not mountain ranges, but large rivers, which divide the country and make internal communication difficult. Russia's share of the world's freshwater is even larger than its share of land, with Lake Baikal in Siberia alone containing a fifth of the world's freshwater reserves.

In tsarist Russia, only a few natural resources were exploited, in particular, the mineral resources of the Caucasus and the URAL region on the European-Asian border within Russia. The huge reserves of Caspian oil helped Alfred Nobel to make his fortune, allowing him to endow the Nobel Prizes given annually to the world's top scientific, literary, and political figures. Extensive exploration of natural resources began with the Soviets, who exported more oil, precious stones, ordinary metals, and rare metals than they consumed in order to fatten the Soviet budget. But the majority of these natural resources still lie untouched beneath Russian soil, promising the chance for future wealth to whoever can extract them. No other country comes close to Russia in the level of natural resources.

Russia's population is sizable, 145 million in 1998 (Interstate Statistical Committee of CIS 1999). Its population size ranks sixth in the world, well below the third-ranked United States' population of approximately 270 million people (Department of Economic and Social Affairs, Population Division 1998).

The population density of Russia is very low, 22.5 people per square mile, about a third of that in the United States (*Goskomstat Rossii* 1997–1999). Not surprisingly, vast areas of Russia are barely populated, and the large majority of its population lives in a relatively small, fertile triangle in southeastern Europe where agriculture can flourish due to favorable weather and soil conditions. The population density is much greater in European Russia than in Asian Russia. Still, roughly a fourth of its population lives east of the Volga River basin,[1] which lies in the middle of European Russia. A harsh climate and distantly spaced population concentrations are the living environment for a great many of Russia's people.

Historically and currently, Russia's plains have been the main areas where people live. Indeed, as in the United States, vast plains available for settlement were a major natural asset, providing opportunities for population growth. Russia's most populated area is the Central region around Moscow, followed by (in descending order) the Volga River basin, the North Caucasus, the Ural region (on the border of Europe and Asia), the Northwest (around St. Petersburg), Siberia, and the Far East (the area bordering on the Pacific Ocean).

The collapse of the USSR left about 25 million ethnic Russians living abroad in former parts of the Soviet Empire. It also left within Russia's borders roughly the same number of people whose NATIONALITY (or ETHNICITY, to use an American term) is not Russian. Ethnic Russians constitute only 120 million (roughly 80 percent) of Russia's 145 million people, with the remainder composed of diverse nationalities (e.g., Tatars,

---

1. All numerical estimates concerning the populations of Russia's regions come from Khrushchev (1997).

Bashkirs, Chechens). As we discuss later, ethnicity has long been an extra-ordinarily important factor in Russia. The Russian word ROSSIIANIN (meaning "Russian") may indicate a person's citizenship or civic status but not his or her nationality. Every ethnic Russian identifies his or her nationality as RUSSKII, whereas members of an ethnic minority identify their nationality as Tatar, Bashkir, Chechen, and so on (Khrushchev 1997).

The Russian Federation has nearly 90 different administrative building blocks that are analogous to states in the United States. The land areas and populations of these territorial units vary as greatly as do those of states in the United States. An important difference from the United States, however, is that many of the territories comprising the Russian Federation, like their analogues in the former Soviet Union, are based on the traditional homelands of various nationalities. In contrast, tsarist Russia carefully avoided nationality-based administrative divisions of its territory.

Russia has two metropolises: Moscow, with over eight million people, and St. Petersburg, with more than four million. Moscow, the historical center of the Russian state, is now both its capital and financial center. The huge concentration of economic and political power in Moscow roughly balances that of the rest of the country. Despite a harsh physical environment, St. Petersburg was the site chosen by the founder of modern Russia, Peter the Great (1689–1725), to serve as the country's capital, a role it fulfilled for two centuries. Sparked by Peter's interest in the West, Peter's new capital city developed a fairly European outlook that is still quite different from other parts of Russia. Today it is a city with ambitions and Russia's main window to Europe. But a third of its population is elderly, and it is the home of numerous closed factories, many of which were formerly in the Soviet defense industry. These two features are likely to make it hard for St. Petersburg to realize its ambitions.

There has also been a remarkable revival of Russia's regional centers, such as Nizhniy Novgorod and Saratov on the Volga River, Yekaterinburg in the Ural region, and so on. In Russia's EMERGING MARKET ECONOMY, multifunctional centers with a large surrounding hinterland are doing fairly well economically, compared with the country as a whole.

Approximately two-thirds of Russia's people live in urban areas (*Goskomstat Rossii* 1997–1999). Although large, economically diverse cities have fared relatively well in the 1990s, factory towns are deeply troubled. Many factories have closed, and alternate job opportunities are still limited. Small towns are, however, regaining their historical role as trading centers for large rural hinterlands, where the distances between neighboring villages can take a half day to traverse (more typically 1–2 days in Siberia). Consequently, small towns play a key role in cementing the Russian economy into an unified market.

Historically, Russia's **geopolitical location** was favorable for expansion (Billington 1970). There is no historical trace of the Slavic tribes who were the ancestors of modern Russians until the fifth or sixth century, unlike the ancestors of the peoples living elsewhere in Europe. In the sixth century, these Slavic tribes came from what is now Slovakia and Ukraine to the plains of eastern Europe, then the periphery of the European world. In the ninth century, the strong KIEVAN RUS state emerged after the Vikings (called *variags* by Russians) found a route from the Scandinavian peninsula to Constantinople via Novgorod, Kiev, and the Black Sea. This strong state was the basis for the expansion of the eastern Slavs to the northeast, where they established a Russian homeland near present-day Moscow. In this forested but fertile land, the basic activity was agriculture, which allowed the population to grow. Moreover, there was no strong ethnic or political unit to threaten the Russians.

The only real danger came with the invasion of the Tatars and Mongols in the thirteenth century, who imposed what modern Russians call the TATAR-MONGOL YOKE. This invasion was—and still is—a major event in Russian history and culture. But it was a significant danger only for the expansion of the nation and the Russian state. In the sixteenth century the Russians began to acquire superior European military weaponry and eliminated the Tatar threat. Thereafter, nothing blocked Russia's expansion to the east. Indeed, Russian explorers arrived on the western coast of North America before Captain Cook landed there in 1778, and Russia ruled Alaska until the United States purchased it in 1867.

In Asia, Russian expansion to the south was prevented by topographical barriers (e.g., mountains and deserts) and not by China's army. Significant expansion by Russia westward into Europe was limited by the well-developed states there. Russia's expansion to the southwest was constrained by relatively populated lands and the forces of the OTTOMAN EMPIRE. Russia's struggle to conquer surrounding territories is a major theme in much of Russian history.

Comparison to the United States

Russia resembles the United States in its large territory and general pattern of settlement. Both began with a large territory inhabited by scattered native populations; both acquired new territory by a fairly gradual expansion to bordering lands involving periodic clashes with neighboring states and with the earlier inhabitants of the bordering lands. Americans, however, purchased land from France and Russia, and even from some native American tribes. From the beginning, trade was a major tool used to expand the borders of the United States, and aggressive force was used less often, mainly when trade failed. Russia always used force first and tried other methods only if force did not succeed.

Superficially, the populations of Russia and the United States were also similar in their development. Like Americans, Russians ASSIMILATED many local populations. Both also killed a large portion of the native inhabitants of the territories into which they expanded. But there is a major difference. The territory of the continental United States was the homeland of roughly three million Native Americans. When Russia incorporated Siberia in the sixteenth and seventeenth centuries, its native population was roughly the same size. But the Russian Empire's expansion into areas other than Siberia occurred where sizable groups of non-Slavic peoples lived. These non-Slavic nations were forcibly incorporated into the Russian Empire. Their incorporation and assimilation was accomplished by political means (state power), not by economic integration (trade). Not surprisingly, even small nations fought hard for a continued existence in their historical homeland, and many have succeeded in achieving this. Chechnya, whose struggles with Russia in the 1990s have captured worldwide attention, is one such nation that has not only survived as a people but dared to seek independence.

Success in competing for living space is crucial for the survival of individuals, tribes, nations, countries, and states. German historians developed the study of GEOPOLITICS on the basis of the concept of geopolitical competition. The basic idea is that location among competitors is a major factor influencing the existence of every state or nation. This concept gave historians a deeper understanding of European history than did battles and historical personages. It also led to more sophisticated diplomacy based on geopolitical interests. (A good example is offered by American foreign policy when Henry Kissinger was President Nixon's secretary of state.)

A geopolitical perspective is also useful in sociology. Every specific analysis of America's population can be put in a broader geopolitical context. The United States is largely comprised of immigrants and their descendants. Geopolitical events help to explain why immigrants came from a certain part of the world at a specific time. Moreover, the functioning of the U.S. labor market depends on the world market, which also has a clear geopolitical structure.

Russia's geopolitical location among weak neighbors gave it immense advantages. Unlike Britain and France, Russia did not need to cross oceans to conquer and acquire new land. Wherever possible, Russia's rulers simply incorporated neighboring territories into the Russian state. This geopolitical factor made Russia very powerful in times when manpower mattered in warfare. From Ivan IV (the Terrible, 1533–1584) to Stalin (1924–1953), Russian rulers used Russia's manpower without giving any thought to the death toll in wars. Consequently, in the early nineteenth century, Europe was trembling before the Russian colossus represented by its huge territory and population masses. In the 1990s, Russia still has a large arsenal of nuclear weapons but is no longer a world power in other respects. Nevertheless, Russia has difficulty understanding its limited geopolitical role because its past importance still pervades Russia's image of itself.

1.2 FORMATION OF THE RUSSIAN PEOPLE

The **roots** of the Russian nation lie in the idea of a common Slavic homeland. The anthropological origins of today's Russians are mainly east Slavic tribes, as mentioned above. Ethnic diversity was first introduced into Russia when the agriculturally oriented east Slavic tribes moved into the lands of the Finno-Ugric people, whose descendants are now the major ethnic group in Finland. The latter group was incorporated into Russia rather than slaughtered because agriculture needed a lot of laborers. So the Finno-Ugric peoples furnished the second important anthropological element of modern Russians. Many Finno-Ugric names were retained, with the best example being *Moskva* (Moscow), the name of Russia's capital.

The next major addition to the population resulted from the Tatar-Mongol invasion already mentioned. Mongoloid features are very visible among Russians now living in the east. Russians integrated and intermarried with many small ethnic minorities dispersed throughout the east. As in every large nation, Russia's population is the product of multiple ethnic and cultural influences. Still, a Slavic physical appearance is very visible and predominates in all regions.

The integration of ethnic groups with distinctive cultural and religious backgrounds was not always successful. As the state religion, ORTHODOXY sought to convert the peoples of conquered lands. Religious assimilation was easy within the loose framework of non-Russian cultures and ethnicities. Nevertheless, in the very heart of Russia, the Chuvash, Mordva, Udmurts, and Mari people still exist as distinct nationalities, each with a population of roughly one million, and each living principally in its traditional homeland. Although all of these NATIONS have been integrated into Russian culture and now have Russian Orthodoxy as their religious faith, they still identify themselves as members of separate nations, and not as *Russkii*. These separate nations survive largely because their homelands have very cold climates and few economic opportunities to attract ethnic Russians.

Culturally unique characteristics and a Muslim background aided in the survival of Russia's largest minorities, the Tatars (6.5 million) and Bashkirs (1.5 million). Both nations live peacefully with Russians in the same areas. However, this is not the case for those forcefully integrated into the Russian people in the mountainous Caucasus region in the south of Russia. Bloody wars in the Caucasus occurred throughout the nineteenth century. Uprisings regularly recurred until Stalin resettled the entire populations of Chechens and Ingushes from the Caucasus and the Tatars from the Crimea in Central Asia. This forced resettlement caused many deaths and reduced the populations of these nations by at least a third.

The 1970 Soviet census revealed that ethnic Russians had begun to leave the autonomous republics in the North Caucasus in some numbers.

Furthermore, since the 1970s, local titular nationalities have actively sought to expel Russians throughout the Caucasus region; the Chechens are just the nation whose efforts have attracted the most attention in the West. All non-Russian nations in the Caucasus have high birth rates and could eventually make Russia a more multiethnic country with greater cultural and religious diversity. It remains to be seen whether this will happen, or whether these unruly nations will achieve political independence, as so many of their members hope.

The **population** of every country follows a certain growth pattern. With URBANIZATION, INDUSTRIALIZATION, and growing opportunities for individuals to control births, the numbers of births and of deaths tend to become roughly balanced, and the population size stabilizes. Russia reached this point in the 1980s. However, World Wars I and II, with their excess deaths and shortages of births, still cause the age structure of Russia's population to exhibit so-called DEMOGRAPHIC waves, in which age groups increase as well as decrease in size as age increases.

The harsh conditions caused by the transition from a communist past to a MARKET ECONOMY have taken a substantial toll on the population. Death rates have risen, and birth rates have fallen. In 1997 the birth rate was the lowest of any urbanized and industrialized country, 8.6 births per thousand people, or 1.4 million births. If births to Russia's national minorities were excluded, the birth rate for ethnic Russians would show an even more dramatic drop. With roughly 2.3 million deaths per year, the rate of growth of the population (the so-called rate of natural increase) became negative in 1992. In the mid-1990s, the population size was declining by 6 percent per year (*Goskomstat Rossii* 1998). If these patterns of birth and death rates continue, the size of Russia's population will decline substantially in coming decades. Such levels of depopulation in the absence of a major war or epidemic are new in the modern world.

Only re-immigration of Russians from its NEAR ABROAD (the lands once in the USSR but not now in Russia) helps to stabilize Russia's population. Re-immigration numbers are not known very exactly, but one can estimate that it increased Russia's population in the early 1990s by about a million people per year. Only America has ever had such a huge number of immigrants.

One internationally accepted indicator of a country's level of development is the life expectancy of its population—the number of years that a newborn can expect to live on average. In Russia, where the death rate is 1.6 times the birth rate, life expectancy is 59 years for men and 72 years for women (Interstate Statistical Committee of CIS 1999). It has fallen substantially for men since the Soviet collapse and was the lowest in Europe in 1998. The high death rate implies that the population has severe health problems. These health problems are aggravated by the fact that the health care system is moving toward a market economy where patients must pay for medical care. While long waits and low-quality care plagued the old Soviet health care system, treatment was both free and guaranteed. Although the current health problems are probably temporary, men have historically been a scarce commodity in Russia because Russian rulers have treated men as gun fodder.

Age is a crucial variable in populations living under hard conditions. The crudest categorization is usually based on a person's relation to the workforce: too young to work, old enough to work, and too old to work (retired). Not surprisingly in view of the low birth rate, only 22 percent of Russia's population was under age 16 in 1997, which is extremely low for an industrialized country. Another 22 percent of the population was retired. Given that retirement ages are lower than in most industrialized countries (age 54 for women, 59 for men), this percentage is lower than one would expect. The rest, 56 percent of the population, are of working age (*Goskomstat Rossii* 1997–1999).

The most crucial age-based difference within the Russian population is in living conditions, which are truly terrible in the case of retired people. Retired people have little support from the state and few savings, unlike those in the United States. So the elderly population must constantly struggle to live. Lacking economic resources, they also lack political power compared to those of working age. Because opportunities for work are scarce and localized, youth entering the workforce comprise another important disadvantaged group. The miserable living conditions experienced by so much of Russia's population are likely to change only when the Russian economy begins to grow.

Historically **gender** has been a basic division in Russian society; however, the Soviet state's efforts to emancipate women were fairly successful. By the 1980s, average EDUCATIONAL ATTAINMENT was higher for women than for men (*Goskomstat SSSR* 1989, 1990). Gender differences favoring women were especially substantial at the university level. These were real and impressive gains for women in comparison with the rest of the world.

Women also achieved access to the paid workforce by the 1950s, earlier than in most of other parts of the world. By the 1960s, full employment of women was commonplace. In the 1980s, women outnumbered men in the professions and in most other white-collar jobs.

Inclusion in the paid workforce gave women access to the world outside of the family and enlarged the scope of their life opportunities. Women's advances in the paid workforce cannot, however, be unambiguously interpreted as equalization with men. Women were clearly disadvantaged in their pay, which averaged approximately 60 percent of men's, a figure similar to that observed in Western industrialized countries (Flakierski 1993). As Russia moves to a market economy, women's gains in economic life are being threatened. Women are disadvantaged in the competition for jobs, and their earnings have fallen not only absolutely but also relatively to men.

Comparison with the United States

One helpful and widely used idea is the concept of American society as a melting pot, describing a country where immigrants arriving from different nations and at different periods acquire similar features through living in a common social environment and mixing with one another. In the most limited use of this term, it simply signifies identification as a permanent resident and possibly a citizen of the new country. That is, within a few generations, descendants of Anglo-Saxon, German, Irish, Italian, Jewish, Scandinavian, and Slavic immigrants came to regard themselves as Americans. Later, the term "melting pot" was used to characterize the process in which immigrants not only acquired a general identification as American but also were culturally integrated into America.

Using this concept in other countries is harder because historically based nations living in separate, traditional homelands are not easily fused into one nation, even in the civic sense. Soviet leaders definitely had the United States in mind in their attempts to assimilate everyone into a "Soviet [wo]man" and a Soviet identity. The Russian language was imposed on non-Russian peoples with this motive in mind. But Russians, who had one of the richest cultures and histories of those to be melted into a Soviet identity, suffered and lost a lot in this process of "Sovietization" (Roeder 1993).

To some extent, the process of Sovietization worked. But, as the Soviet regime became less oppressive, countervailing forces occurred, and nations began to behave more distinctively. When an opportunity arose in the late 1980s, many of these nations acted against the Soviet Empire that had been portrayed as their motherland. In the end, the idea of the Soviet Union as a melting pot did not fit very well.

1.3 RUSSIAN HISTORY[2]

History is a most controversial phenomenon. There are facts, but the interpretation of facts can vary widely and be very controversial. For example, nobody disputes the fact that World War II happened; we have all seen countless battles and heard endless chronicles of it in a seemingly unlimited number of films. But what World War II means to the people in a particular country varies widely.

For Americans, World War II was not a unique national experience. Other events rival and exceed its place in American history, in particular, the Civil War of 1861–1865. But for Russians, World War II was the

---

2. One of the best Russian authors on Russian history is Kliuchevsky (1994, 1997). Useful texts by Western authors include Billington (1970), Moss (1997), and Riasanovsky (1993).

GREAT FATHERLAND WAR. The tens of millions of casualties in it had never been experienced in any previous war, and the actual existence of the Russian state had not been seriously challenged for a great many centuries (though Napoleon's armies had entered the Russian heartland in 1812). Not only official historians but also the national consciousness of Russians hold this experience above all other events in the country's history. To those who contributed much to the victory in World War II, this war unquestionably was their life destiny.

Americans are proud of their founding fathers, but 200 years is not a lengthy history. The British look back to the Magna Carta, which established the rule of law in 1215, and also to the glory of the British Empire in the nineteenth century. Russia searches through its history for its own major events. Its two main memories in addition to World War II are the glory of the THIRD ROME (when Moscow claimed to replace Rome and Constantinople as the center of Christendom) and the menace of the Tatar-Mongol yoke (when Russia was ruled by the Tatars and Mongols from the thirteenth through the sixteenth century). The first symbolizes all the greatness of the Russian culture, and the other explains why so much went wrong. Problems start from the beginning of the Russian state (Riasanovsky 1993).

History tells us that states were often established by outsiders who conquered much larger entities than those they had previously possessed. Examples include China, ancient Egypt, and Rome. It is hard, however, for a large nation to accept that its state was founded by foreign invaders.

As with many nations with a long history, the beginning is explained not by hard facts but by arguments. Few in Britain dispute that William the Conqueror came from Normandy and introduced the Norman nobility as England's upper class. Similarly, historical evidence confirms that another branch of Normans (the Vikings, or *variags*, as Russians call them) established the Russian state and ruled it through the Rurik dynasty until the end of the sixteenth century. The difference is that this idea was unacceptable, not only within the popular Russian consciousness, but even for serious Russian historians (Kliuchevsky 1994, 1997). It could not be true: the Russian (or nowadays, the Ukrainian) state must have been established by Slavs.

In the beginning, **Kievan Rus** had a strong Viking influence because the major cities of Novgorod and Kiev were on the route from the Scandinavian peninsula to Constantinople. Kievan Rus acted essentially the same as the other warlike states established by the Vikings, and it was a mighty threat to Byzantium.

Appeasement of this formidable power in the north was a real success for Byzantium. Vladimir, Grand Duke of Kiev, was baptized into the eastern version of Christianity in 988 and had his subjects in Kiev baptized in 990. Their conversion to Orthodoxy had an enormous impact on the whole mood of Russia. Byzantium gained an ally instead of a formidable enemy. Previously time and resources had been wasted in raids on neighboring territories. The new Orthodox Church began to develop its own cultural INSTITUTIONS and to organize society internally. Byzantium existed as a model for development. There was rapid development of new cities and of the city of Kiev as a metropolis. By the end of the eleventh century, Kievan Rus under Yaroslav the Wise was a European power. Yaroslav even managed to marry his four daughters to kings in Europe. The Orthodox Church became a powerful spiritual base, which has helped to maintain the distinctiveness of the Russian people in the following centuries.

As elsewhere in Europe, the rapid development of towns in Kievan Rus dispersed power and created rivalries among Russian dukes and the topmost levels of the nobility. The ability of the Orthodox Church to unify Russia was limited because the Church was heavily influenced by Byzantium at that time. Power in Russia was increasingly dispersed among different centers. The most power lay in the hands of the dukes, who used the rapidly developing towns as their power base. Among these, the most powerful was the duchy of Vladimir-Suzdal, located less than a hundred miles east of Moscow.

The Kievan state unified people on the basis of language, religious faith, and territory. From Kiev in the south to Novgorod in the north, and from the Galician dukedom in present-day Slovakia to Ryazan on the Volga River, Slavic tribes began to unite. The infrastructure for the foundation of a state was developed. This development was accomplished by the Russian Church, trade, and the growing towns. It was cemented by a wide range of monasteries, which spread literacy and knowledge with a common ideology. Viking cultural influence was clearest in the life of the democratic city-state of Novgorod, but it was contested by the Byzantines' overtly dogmatic concept of Christianity and their rules of politics. However, all of these factors did not yet deeply affect people's lives or the organization of society. The Slavic pagan spirit and natural democracy of communal life absorbed and dampened these foreign influences and turned them into something acceptable to the people. The ready availability of land created opportunities for individualistic activities such as hunting, agriculture, craftsmanship, and trade.

Like elsewhere in Europe, medieval life in Russia was based on a network of towns that, purely by accident, lay between the powerful Mongol Empire in the east and the Frankish Empire, the Mongols' imagined enemy in the west. To challenge this imagined enemy, Genghis Khan sent 20,000 riders on a 2,000-mile reconnaissance trip in 1223. It dramatically changed Russian history and thought.

Tatar-Mongol Yoke

Russian dukes first heard from their enemy's *polovets* (nomadic people then living on the Ukrainian prairie) that strange people had appeared in their land and that they desperately needed the Russians' help. Soon the Grand Duke of Kiev saw the enemy across the Dnieper River, and with other Russian dukes, he started to pursue them. Suddenly two Mongol *tumens* (troops of roughly 20,000 men) confronted them on the Kalka River near the present city of Taganrog. A terrible slaughter of the Russian armies ensued, all but guaranteeing Russia's defeat by the invaders.

The real Mongol conquest of Europe began about 15 years later. Russia was conquered in 1237–1241 in the face of the Mongols' overwhelming tactical superiority. To a considerable degree, the Mongols' success resulted from their special horses, which could feed themselves by digging under the heavy winter snow, unlike ordinary horses in Europe. As a result, winter did not defeat the Mongols, as the Russians had come to expect would happen when they were attacked. One after the other, each town fell; no major battle ever took place. Soon the Russian dukes realized that it was better to surrender and cooperate with the invaders than to try to fight and defend themselves.

It is a pity that Alexander Nevsky, one of Russia's most glorified heroes, is respected for his military victories over German knights and Swedes rather than for saving Russia by his political acumen. Through clever maneuvering, he even obtained the title of Grand Duke of Vladimir for his cooperation with the invading Mongol army.

When Batu Khan, the Mongol leader, advanced to conquer the more western parts of Europe, Russian troops who had switched sides were the principal forces who put Kiev under Mongol rule in 1240. The superiority of the organization of the Mongol army was such that only the death of Great Khan Ogadai stopped the Mongols' advance in Europe. For 300 years, until the middle of the sixteenth century, Russia paid tribute to the so-called Golden Horde. This successor state of the Mongols was mainly populated by Tatars, which is why Russians refer to this period as the Tatar-Mongol yoke.

Tatars intervened in Russian society in two primary ways. First, they tried to divide internal power. Second, they collected taxes or booty. From time to time, both required the use of force, and they made brutal raids. The impact of this period on Russian consciousness is tremendous; much about Russia since then can be explained partly by this Asiatic influence.

In reality, things are more complex than they seem. First of all, the Russian nobility extensively intermarried with the Tatars. Intrigues, violence, absolutism, and pragmatic behavior against kin were common in medieval Europe and were not introduced by the Tatars, though these practices were certainly widespread during the Tatar-Mongol yoke. However, taxation of individuals was something new, and it made people's lives extremely hard. The burden was especially heavy because the Russian nobility as well as the Golden Horde demanded tribute. So life was definitely harder under Tatar-Mongol rule than previously. Moreover, the constant danger of raids by the Tatar cavalry definitely curbed the development of societal life and culture in Russia.

This period brought the RUSSIAN ORTHODOX CHURCH into the center of Russian society. Its distinctive faith and the spiritual strength of its monasteries saved the Russian nation. The key role of the Russian Church during the Tatar-Mongol yoke gave the Church immense moral authority. It even allowed its spiritual leader, Sergei Radonezky, to contest the rule of Ivan IV (the Terrible) later in the sixteenth century.

Muscovy

This small and unimportant duchy centered in present-day Moscow grew in power when Alexander Nevsky's heirs used it as the center to build a new Russian state. Located in the middle of the Russian heartland, it was a relatively safe place during the Tatar-Mongol yoke. Trade, the spiritual power of the Church, and military might made it the center of the unification of Russia. Adding one duchy after the other, its ruler Dmitri challenged the Tatars in 1480 in a major but inconclusive battle. Nevertheless, Dmitri's leadership in this battle boosted Moscow's authority among Russians. Since Moscow was already the center of the Russian Church, it soon established an absolute monarchy, a typical pattern in Europe in that period. This monarchy began with Ivan IV, Russia's first TSAR, the Russified word for "caesar."

The Tatar threat was crushed forever by Ivan IV, the Terrible (1533–1584). With no formidable enemy in the east after the Tatar-Mongol yoke was removed, he turned his might to the west, the first ruler of Moscow to do so. A new Russia with its own history was born. The land of Kievan Rus, whose population lived under Lithuanian-Polish rule from the thirteenth century, followed another destiny with an emerging Ukrainian identity.

The rise of Muscovy coincided with the fall of Byzantium. It gave a new and unexpected legacy to the emerging Russian state. The Orthodox Church's wealth, spiritual connections, theological assets, and huge numbers of followers became centered in Russia. The Russian Church's claims to be the center for all eastern Orthodox churches gave a special authority to Moscow, which was later developed into the concept of Moscow as the Third Rome. It gave Russia an historical mission beyond its boundaries. It came to see itself as the savior of the Christian faith and world. For this destiny, everything else could be sacrificed—the first of these being, of course, all ordinary Russian people. This gave the state and the state religion (Orthodoxy) enormous authority over its subjects. In this way its rulers also justified the conquest of the eastern lands and battles against Muslim enemies.

Muscovy's attempts to gain territory in the west were modest, but its expansion to the east was substantial. Resources were accumulated in this expansion, allowing the Russian state to build an empire.

Russian Empire

Growing up in a German suburb of Moscow, Peter the Great (1689–1725) discovered that knowledge gives power. Understanding that Westernization was the only way to realize Russia's huge potential, Peter undertook to revolutionize life in Russia. After winning a war with Sweden, a seventeenth-century superpower in Europe, Peter established St. Petersburg (later renamed Petrograd and then again renamed Leningrad in the Soviet era) as the new capital of Russia, thereby opening a window onto Europe. With the conquest of the Baltic region by Peter the Great, a Baltic German elite came to the new capital, and the real construction of the Russian Empire began. An effective state bureaucracy was developed, and the financial basis for an expansion policy was established. Russia had a huge army of conscripts ready to be turned in any direction at a moment's notice. The culmination was the entry into Paris of Russia's forces after the defeat of Napoleon in 1814. Russia became the dominant power in Europe. The main worry for the rest of Europe was how to stop the Russian colossus.

Westernization in Russia was, however, opposed by two powerful institutions: the nobility and the Russian Orthodox Church. The nobility was afraid of losing serfdom, which provided free labor and served as its economic power base. The Church not only supported the nobility on the policy of serfdom but feared the development of schools, literacy, and science. The nobility and Church succeeded in blocking the development of the basic institutions of a modern state. SERFS were freed only in 1861 and even then were not given any land. In the late nineteenth century, Russia was still backward relative to other large countries in Europe, and its status as a superpower declined.

After Russia's defeat in the Crimean War in the 1850s came its humiliation in the Russo-Japanese war in 1904–1905 and the 1905 revolution in Russia, which forced the tsar to create a constitution and the *Duma* (parliament), albeit ones lacking real teeth. The 1897 census of Russia's population revealed a ruinous picture: a rural country without roads and with more than 80 percent of the population illiterate, stuck in a preindustrial stage in which a tiny circle within the Russian court had total power and in which the state bureaucracy ran the state apparatus. The Russian Orthodox Church did not challenge this situation. In practice no institution within the regime provided protection for ordinary Russian people. The regime tried to cope with the lack of popular support through CHAUVINISM (extreme nationalism) and Jewish POGROMS (vicious and violent campaigns scapegoating Jews), by stirring up hatred toward "foreigners" (i.e., non-Russians) and "other believers" (i.e., those who did not share the Russian Orthodox faith). The Russian Empire entering into World War I was doomed to become a loser (Lincoln 1983).

Soviet Empire

It was not so much the strength of the BOLSHEVIKS (the Communist Party) as the total collapse of the tsarist elite and the desperation of ordinary citizens that made Russia the world's first Communist country (Hosking 1985). It does not mean that Lenin and his inner circle do not deserve credit for their victory. They skillfully took power and won the ensuing civil war. They provided the peasantry with land and reestablished order. However, from the beginning, there was an extremely elitist philosophy in Communist rhetoric and dogma. A few intellectuals were to provide the deprived masses with an ideology and to govern them on the path to a better life (Schapiro 1984).

No civil war is fought under established rules of war. Thus, it is not surprising that the Bolsheviks used brutal force against their enemies in the ensuing Civil War of 1918–1921: extreme measures were needed to win. The ruling circle of the Bolsheviks then faced the impoverished and uneducated masses that needed to be led to a better life. Here the use of repression was justified by the need to overcome the ignorance of the masses and to enforce the concept of society as the origin of a better life for people. This almost inevitably led to a totalitarian state based on the unlimited abuse of power. As someone who came from a culture not known for respecting the lives of individuals and who had learned to be ruthless in his struggles up from the bottom of society, Stalin did not shrink from establishing repression and brutal force as the basis of Soviet power.

Totalitarian rule can be extremely effective in carrying out changes in society and in confronting external enemies. It urbanized and industrialized an indisputably backward country and gave it the status of world power. Education was reformed, and the Soviet Union indeed produced highly educated people by contemporary Western standards. It also emancipated women, raising not only their level of education but also their position in the occupational hierarchy. But these accomplishments came at an awful price. Tens of millions died from starvation or were killed during the COLLECTIVIZATION of agriculture and in the purges of 1937–1938 (Conquest 1991). Four million prisoners in the *GULAG* (labor camp) system were a tiny fraction of the prewar victims. During and after World War II, they were joined by tens of millions of other victims (Solzhenitsyn 1973). Never before were Russians so afraid of the state and so obedient to state authorities as they were under this terror (Conquest 1991).

The greatest success of the Soviet regime came with the victory over Germany in World War II. The Russian Empire was never so large as after World War II, when Soviet troops occupied central Europe and aided in the creation of a Communist state in China. For the Russians, the price of this victory was immense. Some sacrificed their lives voluntarily to save the motherland, but most of the 28 million who died from this war had no choice and were pushed into death. The tremendous loss of Soviet lives may have been necessary to stop the Nazi war machine in 1941 and 1942, but the huge losses from 1943 onward resulted from a total neglect of people's lives. One of the most shocking examples occurred in World War II when three Soviet marshals competing for the honor of entering Berlin first lost over a half million of their own troops in a few weeks.

As the Soviet regime started to liberalize after Stalin's death in 1953, its effectiveness as an empire built on fear began to crumble. The defects of the COMMAND ECONOMY became more visible in the midst of the more peaceful economic competition and arms race of the Cold War that developed after World War II. Then came the humiliation of the Communist Party in the Brezhnev era when leaders were chosen like medieval popes: The oldest and weakest candidate was promoted to be the ruler with the expectation that this person was likely to die soon and was not likely to cause others any problems. It raised a question never asked in Russia before: Are people for the state, or is the state for the people?

Modern Russia

By the mid-1980s, Gorbachev and the Soviet intellectual elite saw that the Soviet economy could at best be described as stagnating whereas Western economies continued to grow. With fears of a possibly escalating nuclear arms race, it was clear that something had to be done to save the country.

The first step was GLASNOST: opening of society for discussion. Because the ruling Soviet elite had little imagination regarding how to transform the existing regime, political life was opened (e.g., by the introduction of elections with multiple candidates), and the use of force was restricted. Next, the implementation of PERESTROIKA (liberalization and reform) gave opportunities to various forces with the capacity to destroy the Soviet Union. Intellectual and political life was democratized: the media and the people began to ask openly and publicly about life in the Soviet Union. There were even political rallies.

The OUTER EMPIRE in Eastern Europe fell quickly. When the Soviet ruling elite failed to revitalize the power structures following the attempted COUP D'ETAT in August 1991, the Soviet Union also collapsed. Suddenly and painfully a Russian state was reborn, but without much of its former empire. Russia rapidly lost its superpower status as well as much territory perceived by Russians as their own land. Ukraine's emergence as an independent country hurt the most. Since Russia traces its origin to Kievan Rus, it is a major blow to have Kiev, Ukraine's capital, in another country. The fact that Ukraine is an important breadbasket and the home of 50 million people adds to the blow.

The collapse of the command economy and its transformation into a capitalist economy left the Russian state with few financial resources and brought immense pain to its people. In China, economic reforms were begun by Chinese peasants at the bottom, but in Russia, privatization started from the top. Even now, Russia still has COLLECTIVE FARMS (*KOLKHOZES*) and a thoroughly unsatisfactory system of agricultural production, despite possessing some of the world's most fertile soil. Not only have ordinary people been neglected, so have its cities and regions.

But something very important emerged from this mess. Russia's provinces have begun to assert their rights and to challenge the central government's authority. A real plurality of power has emerged on a level that is rather like democracy in America. The United States was founded by colonists who had declared themselves independent of England and then united their colonies to form a larger state while retaining many rights at their own level. Moreover, in the United States, counties as well as the 50 states have rights. Russia has moved toward democracy in a somewhat similar way, except that power has shifted downward rather than upward as in the United States. In particular, Russia's republics and regional centers are developing some political independence and their own political structures. The dispersal of power seems to be genuine and gives hope of a new and wealthy Russia in the future. It may even turn around the historical understanding on which all of Russian history is based: The state, the motherland, and even the local community has supreme value; individual life matters only as part of the larger collectivity.

Understanding of History

There are two opposing views of life (Gellner 1996). One, deeply rooted in Russia throughout history, is fatalistic, the understanding that historical development is predetermined. Not only individuals but also nations and societies are viewed as having a destiny. One's destiny can be seen as having divine origins. For instance, religious people are sometimes ready to be martyred, believing this is their destiny. There can also be an atheistic understanding of destiny. This is represented well by Karl Marx's theory about the primacy of the collectivity (society, motherland, nation) in human life and the inevitability of certain stages of societal development leading capitalism to be succeeded by COMMUNISM.

Another understanding was brought into social thought by French thinkers like Rousseau and Montesquieu and by the German philosopher Fichte. Unlike the Russian way of thinking, their views stressed the subjective source of social reality, politically emphasizing free individuals as the masters of the world. Nowhere is this understanding of society more deeply rooted than in America. This view also holds that every country builds its own history and is responsible for it. Present opportunities for countries as well as individuals have roots in the past, but new possibilities open up at every step. What Russia's leaders as well as ordinary Russians choose is crucial for Russia's future. The questions to be asked and answered by the new Russians are: Has individual life legitimacy? Or does individual life have meaning only when used to support some common, supreme goal: motherland, state, church, or ideology? Are individuals their own masters and responsible for their own gains and losses? Or do foreigners deserve praise for the good and blame for the bad that happens to Russia?

CHAPTER 2

Basic Institutions in Society

2.1 THE STATE

The state is a basic institution in every modern society. However, societies differ appreciably in the importance of the state relative to other basic institutions.

To foreigners, America's foremost symbols are the Statue of Liberty and Wall Street—signifying liberty and capitalism, respectively—not the American flag and the U.S. Constitution. Although the United States has a strong federal government, the market is the most influential institution in America. In contrast, social networks, especially kinship networks, dominate most other institutions in every developing country (e.g., Somalia, Afghanistan, Lebanon). Throughout history, the state has been the dominant institution in Russia.

Legacy of the State

From 1922–1991, Russia was part of the USSR, the Union of Soviet Socialist Republics, which had a Communist regime. For the first four decades, the USSR was a dictatorship ruled by one individual, first Lenin and then Stalin. After Stalin died in 1953, it was transformed into a PARTY-STATE. This strange term needs explanation. The party-state's key feature is the top-down bureaucratic control of state structures by the corresponding party apparatus at the same level. The Soviet party-state was a phenomenon in which the apparatus of the Communist Party of the Soviet Union (usually abbreviated as the CPSU) was integrated into the state structure at every level and dominated it. A party-state penetrates the state far more deeply than in other types of states where a single party rules.[1] Thus, the supreme decision maker in the

---

1. McAuley (1992) gives a good insight into Soviet politics.

USSR was the CPSU's Politburo, not the government or the Supreme Soviet (the USSR's parliament). The dominant executive power was also in the CPSU's apparatus.

The transformation from a personal dictatorship to a party-state after Stalin's death is remarkable, in view of the open and extensive abuse of state power by repressive institutions in Stalin's era.[2] After the 1950s, the state was still repressive and totalitarian, but it had clear institutional arrangements that established the rules under which power was exercised. There still was no freedom of speech and no organized opposition, however. The party-state controlled every activity, and the unauthorized existence of any institution was beyond imagination. Even the independence of the economy, which is typical in most dictatorships, was effectively abolished under the state-commanded economy.

When Russians in the 1990s think of the state, they automatically think of the state in the Communist period. But describing the role of the state only in terms of the situation during the Soviet period is an oversimplification.

Russian Empire

In the sixteenth century, every major country in Europe had an absolute monarch as the head of state (Beissinger 1995). Thus, it was normal that Ivan IV, the Terrible (1533–1584), finished his construction of the Russian state by establishing an absolute monarchy. Absolute monarchy in Russia and elsewhere in Europe differed greatly, however. Ivan commanded not only the Russian state, but also the Russian Orthodox Church. England was the only other country whose monarch was also the head of the church. Ivan was much more powerful than most other absolute monarchs in Europe at that time.

Indeed, Ivan was more powerful than the King of England. In England, the king's power was partly limited by the Magna Carta (the agreement in 1215 between King John and the English nobility specifying their mutual rights and obligations) and a fairly sophisticated legal system. In Russia, the tsar's will was the law. In England, a king who wanted things to be different at least took the trouble to change the laws to suit his will. But in Russia, both the tsars and modern-day rulers have ruled by decree and have not felt the need to bother changing the laws to suit their wishes.

Throughout Russia's history, law has never played a major role. Russia's rulers frequently abused their legal powers and ignored existing laws. In the beginning of the twentieth century, for example, Tsar

---

2. The breadth of control of the repressive institutions is illustrated by the fact that the KGB (the Soviet secret police) directly managed science and industry within its own organization. In particular, the entire atomic-weapons program was managed within the KGB's own organization.

Nicholas II (1894–1917) not only treated the DUMA (the parliament) as a nuisance but also paid scant attention to the formal legal system and legal institutions.

To the Russian people, the state has long been a repressive institution that dominated society through orders and obligations that it imposed upon them. Until 1861, nearly 90 percent of Russia's population was comprised of serfs and conquered populations with limited rights. Consequently, only a tiny part of the population in tsarist Russia had any possibility to contest state power. State power dealt only with groups (e.g., serfs), regions, and whole populations (e.g., of conquered territories). As far as an individual was concerned, state power was unlimited. The state's neglect of ordinary people's interests was total. For example, a soldier's term of duty lasted 25 years, and most soldiers never returned to their homes after they had been conscripted. The state never considered that a soldier might have some right to do with his life what he would like. The church offered no protection because it acted as an arm of state power.

In small towns and villages, life did proceed fairly independently from state directives, and CIVIL SOCIETY existed and functioned. This mainly happened because small places were too unimportant for the tsarist state to pay much attention to what happened in them. The vast eastern parts of the Russian Empire also lived outside the reach of the central power of the state and had their own way of life, simply because of their remoteness. The Baltic region even had a fairly sophisticated legal system in which peasants had certain rights.

The tremendous increase in both the size and actual power of the civil service (i.e., of state bureaucrats) was the most important development in the Russian state in the nineteenth century. The bureaucracy's power began to balance the might of the army and even contested the power of the ruling nobility.

The Communist State

After gaining power, the BOLSHEVIKS began by abolishing the division of power and the few existing institutional arrangements that allowed different political actors to influence the tsarist state. The Soviet state was built by a fairly small circle of Communists who did not hesitate to use brutal force against all other political and social actors. By the end of its first decade, the Soviet state had developed into the personal dictatorship of Stalin. Even the Communist Party lost much of its power, and the country was ruled by repressive institutions that had total control over the population. All powers (especially economic and political powers) were in the hands of the totalitarian STATE APPARATUS, where repressive organs dominated. At the center of Stalin's dictatorship were the Politburo and secretariat of the Communist Party and the OGPU, which was the predecessor of the KGB. These bodies operated outside of existing laws and without any fixed rules. They practiced terror against members of the Communist Party and of other loyal groups, as well as against enemies of the Communist regime. This terror made the lives of individuals unpredictable and totally dependent on the regime. Under Stalin's dictatorship, the characteristics present in all modern totalitarian societies were developed:

1. Repressive organizations, such as the OGPU and later the KGB, had total control of mass and personal communications. Fear of repression acted to atomize people, that is, to make each individual behave as a solitary person.

2. There was an attempt to form a new Communist mentality by endangering people's existence as well as by directly indoctrinating them.

3. There were efforts to control the socialization and education of new generations by undercutting the family's role and by using schools to implement Communist values.

4. Every activity in society, even one as minor as bird-watching, was controlled by some state organization.

After Stalin died in 1953, a more bureaucratic and less tyrannical state gradually developed. First, the concept of the party-state was officially incorporated into the Soviet Constitution, giving the dominant role of the CPSU apparatus some legal foundation. This change formally divided power between the CPSU apparatus and state organizations. Eventually the government and state organizations gained the power to run the economy. These changes were concentrated in the executive organizations, but law enforcement and even the KGB came partly under the control of the party apparatus.

In the early 1980s, the Politburo, and not the general secretary of the CPSU, was de facto in charge of the USSR (see the sketch of the political structure of the USSR in Figure 2.1). This collective body, which included the heads of all important ministries, controlled the Council of Ministers, the apparatus of the CPSU, the KGB, the army, and all other organizations responsible for defense and security. Executive power over the command economy was in the hands of the economic ministries. The powers of the CPSU apparatus were limited to ideology and to the appointments of key figures. At the level of republics (and smaller regions), the first secretary of the CPSU in the republic (or in the region), had the real power. However, the strongest central ministries issued and implemented directives within their own domain without even consulting local party heads. This system of political power operated without any clear legal foundation and was based instead on customary practices. As the party-state weakened over time, loyalty to immediate superiors and to organizations rather than to some higher political authority became increasingly common. All of these developments increased the complex-

FIGURE 2.1

Soviet State: Institutions and Power Relations in the 1980s

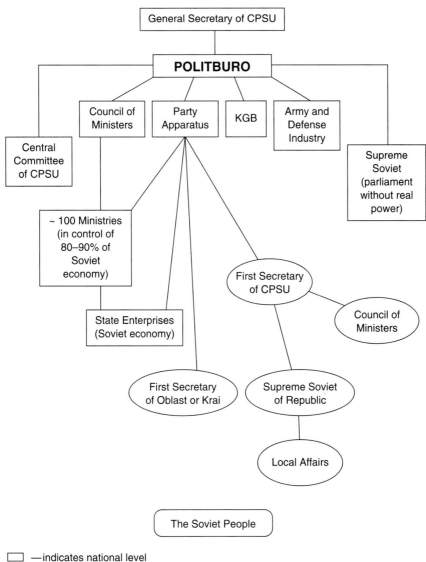

☐ —indicates national level
◯ —indicates local level

ity of the Communist party-state; it became more bureaucratic and administratively more effective. But individuals still had no protection against the abuse of power by the party-state apparatus.

All legislative bodies (from the Supreme Soviet to local soviets) just rubber-stamped decisions made by the party-state apparatus. Members

of legislative bodies were not accountable to the people, only to their superiors. Elections were held, but they were a sham because the Communist candidate was the only one in the running.

The New Russian State

All of the Soviet Union's successor states, including Russia, inevitably
have certain similar characteristics because of their previous common history. Many of these new states have repeated numerous past mistakes,
one of the most important being only to change the personnel and organization at the top of the state bureaucracy and otherwise to incorporate the
former state apparatus of the USSR almost entirely. As a result, many old
habits and institutions of the Soviet state apparatus continue in the new
Russian state, as well as in many other Soviet successor states.

Democratic states have three distinguishing characteristics (Linz
and Stepan 1996). First, they divide power; the state's executive, legislative, and judicial branches are separate. Second, they have civil services
rather than state bureaucracies; civil servants owe their loyalty to the
state, not to those who hold power at any given moment. Third, in democratic states, the mass media are a so-called fourth power. Does the
new Russian state have these features?

Starting in 1992, Russia's top leaders did try to build a new democratic state by separating the economy from the state. They proceeded
with the American model in mind. Privatization of property and reform
of the command economy was done from the top downward using the
SHOCK THERAPY that was highly recommended by Western economic experts, such as Swedish economist Anders Åslund and Harvard economist
Jeffrey Sachs.[3] This approach rapidly created a few immensely rich people
and left the large majority of the population in even greater poverty than
in the Soviet era. The separation of economic and political powers was indeed a crucial step needed to control the abuse of political power. But the
manner in which it was done—shock therapy—quickly led to a situation
in which a relatively few private capitalists (bankers and industrialists)
became powerful in all spheres of public life and acquired extensive influence over a large part of Russia's state apparatus. Many former Soviet industrial ministries de facto, if not de jure, became semiprivate monopolies
(e.g., GAZPROM, LUKOIL). The continuation of social networks from the Soviet state apparatus enabled the new economic elites to influence their
former colleagues who are still in the state apparatus.

For the first time in Russian history, a constitution was approved
by the people in a popular referendum in 1993. This constitution has
been taken by both Russia's political elite and the people as a serious

---

3. For a critique of the shock therapy and citations to the relevant literature, see Murrell
    (1993).

document, not just as a piece of paper describing the rulers' intentions. However, the new constitution was drafted in a manner that was very reminiscent of the past. In particular, it was crafted to give Yeltsin powers that exceed those of American and even French presidents (Colton 1995). As a large and diverse country, Russia undoubtedly needs a state with a strong executive power. But, the new Russian constitution gives the Duma weak, consultative legislative powers, similar to those of the Duma under Tsar Nicholas II early in the twentieth century. The Duma's weak legislative powers are not sufficient to counterbalance the enormous executive power in the hands of the president, who has not yet acted much differently from the former tsars. A major weakness of the new Russian state is that it lacks institutions that can guarantee a smooth transition of power from one president to the next. A state that is unable to change leaders smoothly faces an uncertain and difficult future.

This brings us to the third component of the state: the independence of the judiciary. This basic principle of a democratic state is not yet a strong feature of the new Russian state. The abuse of law is commonplace in business (e.g., arbitrary privatization of property, widespread avoidance of taxes, illegal transfer of money abroad), the state apparatus (e.g., bribes, open corruption, sale of public property), and civil life (i.e., in adjudicating disagreements between neighbors). Since Russians are accustomed to ignoring the law, the abuse of law is not surprising. Changes in the legal system are likely to take a long time. Courts and modern law enforcement systems can be transferred gradually from their entrenched positions within the executive branch to new institutions allowing them to be independent of the executive branch.

Change especially takes a long time when there is a long tradition of state bureaucrats running the state. There has long existed a thick layer of state bureaucrats between the Russian people and their rulers (the tsar, the GENERAL SECRETARY OF THE COMMUNIST PARTY, the president of the Russian Federation). The state bureaucracy has its own way of life and interests. The top leaders of every state wants to use the state bureaucratic apparatus to achieve certain political aims. But will the state bureaucracy implement these aims? Ironically, the transition to a market society has eliminated some constraints on the state bureaucracy that existed in the Soviet party-state. In Soviet times, different ministries had powerful institutional interests and tried to pursue them; however, they were tightly controlled by the apparatus of the CPSU. The new Russia has had almost the same bureaucrats in essentially the same institutions. Suddenly they found themselves in charge—a party apparatus was no longer watching over their actions. Consequently, the rise of a FREE MARKET SYSTEM has, among other things, given state bureaucrats substantial ability to use (and abuse) their positions for personal or institutional gain. Bureaucrats in every institution in the new Russia have begun to sell their services quite openly. One may call it "corruption" or just "private business on the side." The label is not very important. The key fact is that state bureaucrats are wonderfully able to benefit from their official position when the legal system does not work, and this has effectively crippled the new Russian state.

A news report on Russian television provided a good example of this corruption. The camera showed a completely empty railway terminal in a major port city on the Pacific coast. A chief railroad executive explained that rail traffic from Asia to Europe through Russia ceased after customs officials introduced more than 20 forms to complete and imposed heavy official and unofficial fees. The state bureaucrats' greed killed the golden goose—the economic potential of this key port.

The road to democracy began with Russia's first national elections to the People's Congress of the Russian Federation in 1990. These free elections were largely contests between individual candidates who had no affiliation with an established party. As is common in newly emerging democracies, the majority of voters chose candidates declaring democratic ideals. Building new political parties takes considerable time and effort, but this process had begun by the 1995 parliamentary elections.

The 1996 presidential election in Russia was odd. For most Russian voters, their choice was between bad and worse candidates. Here we come to the fourth power in Russia: the mass media. Yeltsin won the 1996 presidential election partly with the aid of the mass media, which helped him by portraying Zyuganov, Yeltsin's main opponent, as someone who intended to return Russia to its Communist past, which Zyuganov himself vigorously denied. By putting this spin on Zyuganov's speeches, Yeltsin's team achieved victory despite Yeltsin's very low ratings in public opinion polls (McFaul 1997).

The most basic and important actor in a democracy is the citizen. Free elections are definitely a major step forward in giving some power to citizens. In the United States, most state offices are publicly contested in elections. In Russia, only a very small fraction of state offices are filled through elections. This is not surprising because a citizenry trained in democracy only emerges gradually through experience. Elections in Russia are still far from being an expression of voters' knowledgeable choices. But the progress made in less than a decade is impressive, and the importance of public opinion to state officials is gaining ground, thereby increasing citizens' control of state officials.

Comparison with the United States

The American state developed fairly smoothly into an institution in which people are represented by two main political parties contesting for power in free elections. Only once, during the Civil War of 1861–1865, were political differences not solved by democratic means or by the division of powers within the state as an institution. This lengthy democratic tradition in the United States gives the state tremendous authority as an institution that represents the American people. In contrast, the Russian state had an even longer history as the predominant institution and tool of the empire. Power was in the hands of a very few, and the people never had any say about the people who governed them or how they were governed. The bloody Civil War of 1918–1921 brought to power the small circle of Communist ideologists who built a new state that created the first modern totalitarian society.

The state was the tool used to exercise total control over people, not the people's representative. Consequently, the new post-Communist Russian state has little legitimate legacy from past history. For this reason, the founders of the new Russian state looked abroad to try to overcome the lack of a positive political heritage from past states in Russia. At the same time, all founders of the new state, and especially the bureaucrats in the new Russian state, came with past experience in the Soviet state. They inevitably kept some old habits and practices. Building an effective state in Russia that represents the will of its people is a long and hard process, especially because its previous political systems have been so hostile to democracy.

2.2 THE RUSSIAN ORTHODOX CHURCH

The Russian Orthodox Church was the state religion of Russia for centuries, and it still tries to keep this position. To understand the Church's position in the new Russia, we must consider its origins and history.

Its Origins[4]

Like most pagan European countries, Kievan Rus could have accepted Christianity from Rome or from Byzantium. When Constantine moved the capital of the Roman Empire from Rome to Constantinople in 330, he took most people living in Rome with him, leaving the city with only a tiny population. Although Charlemagne attempted to reincarnate the Roman Empire in western Europe in 800 and tried to overcome the influence of Byzantium, Rome's popes were not the undisputed leaders of Christianity in the tenth century. When Vladimir, Grand Duke of Kiev, adopted Christianity in 988, he chose the religion of Byzantium, a more familiar and impressive place than Rome at that time. His choice made geopolitical sense because Kievan Rus was fairly near Byzantium and far from the Roman Catholic, western part of Europe.

After Vladimir accepted the Orthodox Church, Orthodox churches and monasteries were established in Kievan Rus. The basic liturgy was the same as in Byzantium, and church leaders came from Byzantium.

---

4. For an overview, see Pospielovsky (1998). For more details on the Russian Orthodox Church, see Alberigo et al. (1996).

There were considerable efforts to keep church power in the hands of Greeks, who ruled both the Byzantine Church and Empire. Because the monasteries recorded the chronology of events in the country, the Cyrillic alphabet and writing were developed on the basis of the Greek alphabet and writing. But the Slavic language became dominant in the monasteries. Gradually local Russian priests and monks began to run the church in Kievan Rus.

Tatar-Mongol Yoke and the Church

The Tatar-Mongol yoke was the darkest period of Russian history, the one when the Russian Church established its role as the soul of the nation. Since political leaders were brutally killed at once if they resisted the Tatar-Mongol invaders, they were obliged to bend to these foreign rulers. Consequently, resistance to these invaders was subtle rather than open. It was concentrated in the monasteries and churches. During this period, being a church leader or monk in Russia was too dangerous to be very attractive. Hence, the Church hierarchy, formerly dominated by Greeks, was taken over by Russians, and the Church's headquarters were moved from Kiev to Moscow. In those days, a real church of the people emerged. Priests grew close to the people through their common cultural heritage, their manner of living, and the sharing of danger. Monasteries assumed military as well as religious functions.

As the fight for political independence proceeded, the Russian Church backed the political forces that successfully united Russian lands. The dukes from Moscow and the metropolitan of Moscow (the head of the church in Moscow) ruled hand in hand. This practice peaked in the sixteenth century when Moscow became the center of the Russian Empire. Consequently, independence from the Tatar-Mongol yoke also led to the establishment of a separate Russian Orthodox Church that was independent from the Byzantine Orthodox Church.

Moreover, after the collapse of the BYZANTINE EMPIRE in 1453, the Russian Orthodox Church gave the Russian state a right to claim to inherit the role of Byzantium—an impressive position in European history. Adopting the role of the Byzantine Church, the Russian Church claimed to be the representative and defender of all Orthodox churches. To maintain a grip on this claim, a substantial fraction of the Byzantine elite was incorporated into the Russian Church and nobility. The tsar even married a member of the last ruling family of Byzantium.

In the sixteenth century, during the reign of Ivan IV (the Terrible), the Russian Orthodox Church acquired the status of "state church." Concomitantly, the Russian state adopted the role of defender of Orthodox Christianity. This led both to the creation of a large Church hierarchy and to a political alliance between the Church and all levels and components of the Russian imperial state. The tsar was the defender of the Church, and the Church defended the tsar.

One practical consequence was that wherever the feet of Russian soldiers stepped, a church or monastery was built. With the expansion of Russia's territory, conversion of conquered peoples to the "right faith" began. Not surprisingly, the official state church had little tolerance towards other faiths: Religious dissent is a form of political dissent when there is a state church.

Antagonism to other faiths made it hard to modernize the Russian Orthodox Church. Maintaining the purity of the Orthodox dogma was a major task, and numerous schisms were crushed. Many activities that were typical of Protestants in the west and that led to the partition of the Catholic Church in western Europe ended up differently in Russia: with a state declaration of anathema (heresy) and submersion into the official church. Thus, the Russian Church was a conservative force in society that resisted all kinds of changes. It was the main spiritual defender of one of the most backward absolute monarchies in Europe until early in the twentieth century.

The Church's role in fostering Russian patriotism and hatred of people of other faiths (INOVERTSY) and foreigners (INOZEMTSY) was especially notorious. Jewish pogroms at the end of the nineteenth century and the beginning of the twentieth century got scant attention from the Orthodox Church. The mass slaughter of Central Asians, adherents to Islam, by the tsarist army and by mobs also occurred with the blessing of the Russian Orthodox Church. Only local Russian priests who worked with conquered peoples tried to defend minorities against chauvinistic repression.

The Soviet Period

On the eve of the Bolshevik Revolution of 1917, the monarchy and the hierarchy of the Orthodox Church were closely linked and distant from people's real lives. After the tsar, the Russian Church was the largest owner of land and property; its income was also second only to the tsar's. It is no wonder that the tsarist state and the Church were viewed similarly when the Bolshevik Revolution of 1917 began. Though local priests had contact with the masses, leaders of the Church hierarchy had lost this connection long ago, and the official church was viewed as an alien phenomenon. Even the language spoken in church services, Old Slavonic, was not understandable by ordinary people. For national and religious minorities and for the masses of peasants, the Orthodox Church provided very little spiritual, let alone practical, support.

This situation made it easy for the Bolsheviks to turn people against the Russian Church. The destruction of the Russian Orthodox Church was a major ambition of the Bolsheviks, second only to crushing the tsarist elite. Marx's famous statement that "religion is the opium of the people" was used as a guideline for the Bolsheviks' policies toward churches. First the organization of the Russian Orthodox

Church was destroyed, and all of its property expropriated. Next the religious elite were sent to the GULAG, the string of concentration camps established by Stalin in remote regions of the country. Then the Bolsheviks began a campaign against religion, which had consequences for anyone publicly showing any signs of religious sentiments. All religious rituals marking life's significant events (birth, marriage, death) were taken over by the state and replaced with atheistic rituals. Special atheistic marriage and burial rituals were developed to replace traditional religious rituals.

The Soviet state crushed the Russian Orthodox Church and put it under firm control. A political need for religion arose during World War II when the heritage of the Russian Orthodox Church was used by Stalin to unite the people behind him in this Great Fatherland War. But this tolerance for the Church was just a brief interlude. When the Church's help was no longer needed, the state returned to a policy of overt hostility to it and to religious practice. By the end of the Soviet era, the Russian Orthodox Church had lost all real importance. By 1989, shortly before the 1,000-year anniversary of Christianity in Russia, only one monastery and a few hundred Russian Orthodox priests remained. Society had become essentially atheistic, and the Orthodox Church and religious faith were not very relevant to most people's lives.

Its Reemergence

Of all political leaders in the Soviet Union, Yeltsin was the first to link himself openly with the Russian Orthodox Church. It is hard to know who found whom, but in the spiritual vacuum following the moral and political collapse of Communist ideology, it was a smart political move to align with the spiritual heritage of the Russian people. The Byzantine Orthodox Church had brought Christianity to Russia at the end of the first millennium. The Russian Orthodox Church had brought enlightenment and literacy to the elite and formed the basis of Russian culture. It had been a major spiritual force supporting Russians' resistance to the Tatar-Mongol yoke. As the Third Rome, it had provided a mission for the Russian state and had been the spiritual backbone of the Russian Empire. No other ideology had a comparable legacy to offer spiritual shelter in the period when the Soviet Union was collapsing and when the state and people's lives were in disarray. The Russian Orthodox Church was somewhat tainted by its close support of the tsars in earlier centuries, but after 70 years of Communist rule, this aspect of its heritage did not seem too important to most Russians.

Not surprisingly, the weak, reemerging Russian state sought spiritual help from the remnants of the Russian Orthodox Church. Relying on its historical legacy and the support of the new state, the Russian Orthodox Church was revived.

Russian Orthodox Church overshadowed by a modern high-rise on the New Arbat.

The first objective was to restore the whole richness of the Russian Orthodox Church as an institution. Reviving it created a tremendous need for educated priests and its own theological centers, as well as the need for preachers able to bring God's word to people. With the exploding need for people to spread the word of God, there was an urgent need to ordain many new priests, often without first testing their beliefs, let alone their knowledge. This situation created problems within the hierarchy of the Russian Orthodox Church as well as in the hierarchy's relations with ordinary believers.

The new existence of the old church is not easy because the world has changed tremendously. The rebuilding of the Russian Orthodox Church is occurring in an entirely new environment. The Church must not only deal with Russia's recent history of atheism but also compete with many different religious organizations, some of which are not connected with major world religions. A historical legacy does not help much when people no longer share a common religious faith. From the viewpoint of religious freedom, it is worrisome that the Russian state is openly helping to reestablish the undisputed spiritual power of the Russian Orthodox Church. A 1997 law giving advantages to established world religions is controversial. Even if the intention is to guard people against various kinds of religious charlatans and entrepreneurs speculating in religious faith, this law restricts people's religious freedom. Faced with tough competition from other religions as the Orthodox Church tries to reemerge from obscurity, its leaders still yearn for the privilege of being the state religion. But modern democratic states almost never have a state religion. Only winning the souls of people by their voluntary commitment can ultimately give the Russian Orthodox Church the leading role that it seeks.

There is a surprising new tendency in the Orthodox Church itself. Local priests have organized independent, national Orthodox churches. This has happened not only in Ukraine, but even in tiny Estonia. It could end with every nationality within Russia eventually establishing its own Orthodox Church, despite the absence of any apparent theological differences. Unlike the Roman Catholic Church and most Protestant churches, the Orthodox Church has had national (ethnic) churches (Greek Orthodox, Armenian Orthodox, and so on). These national Orthodox churches tend to encourage as well as to be supported by national, ethnic divisions.

Public opinion polls report favorable, but not overwhelming, support for the Russian Orthodox Church. It does not yet signal victory for the Church, but its revival is promising. The Orthodox Church was clearly not as powerful an institution in the heart of Russian society in the late 1990s as it was until the end of the nineteenth century. Its status as the faith of everyday life, forming the character and basic habits of the Russian people, was its glorious past—and it may yet be its future.

Comparison with the United States

From the beginning, the United States had a plurality of churches and religions. Despite competition and some occasional open conflicts of varying intensity between religious faiths, American democracy has always presumed a plurality of religious faiths. The state has never supported one specific church and tried to suppress others. It lends legitimacy to democracy. In Russia, the tradition of a state religion and a state-sponsored church was deep, but the Communist regime erased it. The new Russia began without an established religion. The Russian Orthodox Church is rebuilding in competition with other religious faiths. Churches acting for the people can succeed in a democratic religious terrain. So after huge human, religious, and cultural losses, faith in God and institutions supporting this faith are established in Russia on the basis of individual choice. If this effort succeeds, it could make it easier to build other aspects of a democratic society.

2.3 COMMUNITY

In the past, the majority of Russian writers, and almost all famous ones, wrote about the Russian peasant community. Some authors mercilessly described the autocratic rules of life in those rather closed communities. Others glorified them as the carriers of an old, pure, and sincere morality. At the onset of the twentieth century, when the Industrial Revolution was at its peak and Henry Ford was already thinking about how to provide cars to millions of Americans, it was not strange to have a different vision of Russia's future, one grounded in the peasant community (Bartlett 1990).

No one surpassed Count Leo Tolstoy, one of Russia's most famous writers, in making the peasant community the essence of his philosophy. Tolstoy's vision of the future portrayed a peasant society viewed through the lens of the communal life in a Russian village community. After writing several famous books (*War and Peace, Anna Karenina*) while living on his own estate, Tolstoy "discovered" the Russian countryside. At the time, over 80 percent of Russians lived in villages, and few peasants lived outside of a village community. Compared with the rest of Russian society, village communities had simple but well-established NORMS and values. The harshest side of life was absent in the uncommon villages where counts (like Tolstoy) had given land to peasants. So the village community provided fertile ground for a moral thinker like Tolstoy.

The impact on Russian culture of the village community was wider and deeper than is exemplified by Tolstoy's philosophy. Even at the end of the Soviet era, there was an influential group of writers called "villagers" *(derevenshchiki)*. Although unproductive *kolkhoz* villages did not offer their inhabitants a bright future by any normal standard, there was widespread nostalgia for the village community as the provider of something basic and good (Denisova 1995).

The roots of almost all cultures, even America's, lie in an agricultural society. Most people obtained their livelihood through agriculture, even in the middle of the nineteenth century in Europe. The organization of society emerging from agriculture can, however, be very different.

Farmers, as individual entrepreneurs, are one way that agriculture can be organized. This pattern tends to emerge on soil that provides small parcels of fertile land. Historically it occurred in northern areas like Scandinavia and elsewhere in hilly land with small arable plots. Under such conditions, a farmer was able to support himself and his family on his own separate farm.

Danger, especially from other people, was a factor that forced some rural people to settle together in villages. A village provided a formidable defense against outsiders. This is a reason why so many cultures have roots in village communities. The first settlers in America lived in villages, but the main centers of life in America were towns, as they were in most of western Europe, too, where a belt of towns linked villages together, even in medieval times. A similar pattern began to develop in Kievan Rus but was interrupted by the rise of serfdom. When the nobility owned people and the land, there was no need for towns to link villages together. Because the land-owning gentry lived in cities, everything commercially usable was transported directly to cities, and villages were left to live and to manage as best they could. The Russian gentry did not begin to think about owning estates for economic gain until the second half of the nineteenth century. So for at least six centuries, a separate village life shaped Russian character.

Because individuals had a very limited ability to influence their environment in the face of the overwhelming power of the village community, fatalism was predominant in this social landscape. This fatalism has had a deep impact on the Russian soul.

A totally different organization of social life emerged in the border lands. Ukraine literally means "on the border" *(u kraina)*. In the border lands, serfdom was never established, and the Russian state encouraged the formation of free people, whose help was used to expand the empire. Such people were known as the COSSACKS. The spirit of the frontier land is well known from Hollywood films about the Wild West. The Cossacks had the same free spirit, and their communities were ungovernable by the central authorities. They provided a Russian character through a different type of experience: a community of freelancers with a spirit of adventure and a willingness to endure high risks. This side of the Russian soul and character is linked especially with Siberia and the area around the Don River in southern Russia near the Black Sea, but it occurred elsewhere, too. In 1957, during the period known as KHRUSHCHEV'S THAW, the

spirit of freedom emerged in an uprising in Novocherkassk, the historical center of the Cossacks. Although the Soviet authorities brutally suppressed this uprising, it is evident that historical roots do matter.

A third type of village community emerged in Siberia. People settled in Siberia to avoid the power of the state (e.g., to have religious freedom, to escape serfdom). Settlers usually established new villages and
tried to cut off all contacts with the outside world. These communities
did not trust the state, the church, and most other outsiders. Famous
"one-family villages" were established in Siberia in this manner. As the
story is told, Ivanov came with his wife, and they had children. Over
time, the Ivanovs multiplied. If later fresh blood came from outside, the
village might acquire two family names.

Thus, even crude accounts tell of very different types of village
communities in Russia. The impact of these types on Russian character
and culture is not one dimensional. The real communal life and cultural
roots of Russia were certainly even more complex.

At the beginning of the twentieth century, farmers as individual entrepreneurs were developed as a social force by one of Russia's most vi-
sionary prime ministers, Pyotr Stolypin. This innovation was especially
successful in the part of Siberia where newly arriving, free settlers were
given their own plots of land. These settlers in Siberia eventually became
wealthy farmers by producing wheat for export. Indeed, in the early part
of the twentieth century, Russia was the biggest exporter of wheat to Europe. These farmers did not back the Bolsheviks and were among the
first to suffer under the Communist regime.

To recover from the disasters of the civil war that followed the Bolshevik Revolution of 1917, Lenin introduced the NEW ECONOMIC POLICY
(NEP) in 1921, which gave peasants land as private property, as the Bolsheviks had previously promised. The NEP also allowed private production and trade. The NEP succeeded in restoring the country to order after
the chaos of the 1918–1921 Civil War and enabled the ruble to be a fully
convertible hard currency in 1923. But by creating numerous successful
though small entrepreneurs, the NEP also created many enemies of communism. Stalin concluded that millions of these enemies needed to be
killed. In the late 1920s, he abandoned the NEP and began **collectivization** of agriculture. Additional millions died from starvation in the transition from a highly productive, export-oriented system of agriculture to
the Soviet system of "industrial agriculture," which became famous for
its chronic inability to produce the agricultural yields needed to support
the Soviet people.

The only constructive attempts to overcome the impact of the vil-
lage-based community on Russian character were two economic policies:
Stolypin's and the NEP. Within most industrialized societies, farmers
have been the important entrepreneurs breaking down the restrictions of
village life through villagers' competition with one another. Another

way to do this is to introduce a very different way of life. The Soviet state did this very effectively through collectivization, which also succeeded in destroying village life.

In the Soviet era, Russia's communal past was converted into an ideological phenomenon. The Communist Party proclaimed the supremacy of the community over the individual as a basic principle of life. This principle is called COLLECTIVISM. It is to be contrasted with INDIVIDUALISM, which elevates individual rights over those of the community. Nourished by centuries, the "village community" was given another meaning by Communist ideology: The individual had value only as a part of a larger community (e.g., a village, factory, or society as a whole).

Existing village communities were destroyed during the campaign to collectivize agriculture. The poorer peasants were used to crush the more successful ones, and kolkhozes (collective farms) were organized as analogues of industrial plants with a complex division of labor involving a high degree of specialization, though not necessarily high levels of skill. For example, the kolkhoz had tractor drivers, dairy workers, agricultural laborers, bookkeepers, agronomists, and a kolkhoz manager (and so forth) rather than unspecialized farmers/peasants who did the entire range of tasks necessary for agricultural production. The collectivization of agriculture had devastating effects on both the character of social life and the quantity of agricultural output. In addition, the destruction of peasant communities created a vast pool of labor, which was needed to achieve rapid industrialization. The old communal psychology was transformed into the supremacy of the labor unit over the individual. As the essential spatial bases of village communities vanished, people migrated in masses to the cities and towns. Behavior oriented around the collectivity was shifted from people's living places (villages) to their places of work (factory, kolkhoz). Moreover, "community" was transformed from a fact of everyday life to an ideological principle.

Now that communism has collapsed and the village community has vanished, Russians are at the crossroads insofar as community as a basic institution is concerned. A communal psychology has deep roots in Russia and still widely influences behavioral patterns. But most people in Russia now live in cities, which have an anonymous environment. Moreover, the ideological basis for communal behavior vanished with the Soviet Union and communism. Under current market conditions, collectivism as the ultimate moral foundation for life has little support. The ideology and practice of individualism emerges with markets in which individuals compete with one another for scarce resources and goods.

2.4 FAMILY

Every culture, religion, and state declares the family to be a basic institution in society. But the nature of the family that they have in mind varies considerably. Historically, men have been more engaged in the public domain, and a paternalistic family has been generally accepted as the ideal. To varying degrees, different religions advocate it as the ideal, too. The Russian Orthodox Church definitely supported the paternalistic family. The father was the undisputed head of the family, and every family member was supposed to obey his orders. A woman's job was to raise the children and to satisfy the (male) head of the family.

In most agricultural societies, families were production units, and the status of women depended greatly on their share of the labor. Because Russian women shared in all jobs in the fields, as well as fed the animals, the status of women in the Russian family was fairly high. Moreover, men tended to have shorter lives and were not infrequently in short supply in village communities because tsarist Russia was continually at war and village men were used as gun fodder. By virtue of their numbers and experience, older women usually were at the core of the moral life of the village community. Consequently, though the public status of women was low, their actual status in the family was higher than is often portrayed. Men and women were certainly not equal, and the rough peasant culture offered women little protection, especially after the male family head died. But the same was true in most agricultural societies.

The historical roots of Russian family life have little effect on the nuclear family as it exists now. The major influences on family structure in modern Russia derive from the Soviet era. As an institution, the family changed radically during the Soviet era. Initially the Soviets tried to put the family under the fairly direct control of the state. For one thing, state education was begun shortly after a child's birth in order to eliminate the family's backward influence. To achieve this goal, the state created a comprehensive system of nurseries, kindergartens, and schools, often intentionally located outside the area where parents lived. This plan was successful and destroyed a fundamental element of the family.

Another blow to the family came from the state's program of female emancipation. State authorities intended it to raise the status of women, not to damage the family as an institution. They simply did not foresee the consequences of female emancipation for the family. Emancipation of women, as we noted earlier, was one of the main ideological slogans of the Communist Party that was actually implemented and that had clear results (Lapidus 1982). It started with the naive introduction of rules intended to equalize men and women. There is a crucial difference, however, between feminism and female emancipation. Feminism is a movement of women to free themselves from masculine domination in society. Female emancipation is an ideology worked out by wise men to raise women to the level of men.

The Bolsheviks, whose leaders were male, practiced female emancipation. They began with sincere simplicity. Since all marriages were

Modern family life in Russia starts with the bride and groom leaving the House of Weddings.

registered in the Church and were supposedly for life in tsarist Russia, the Bolsheviks changed this. The Soviet state not only abolished religious marriages but also made marriage and divorce easy formalities done in local government offices. Instead of liberating women, however, civil marriage with easy divorce procedures liberated men, leaving divorced women to struggle to support themselves and their children.

This approach to female emancipation was soon canceled and reversed. From the 1930s until the late 1960s, it was almost impossible in the Soviet Union for a married couple to get a divorce, though marriage continued to be easy. The difficulty of divorce in this period is shown by the fact that for every 100 marriages there were 4 divorces in 1950, in contrast to around 40 in the 1990s.

The real success story was the equalization of men's and women's educational opportunities. The gains in female literacy rates were especially impressive. By the end of the Soviet era, women were more educated than men on average. The 1994 Russian microcensus reports that among all age groups younger than 50 years old, the average educational level is higher for women than for men. Women's educational gains had a big impact on family life because skills and knowledge became more equally distributed between spouses.

Another blow to the family resulted from the inclusion of women into the paid workforce. It created a public life for women and gave them access to social relationships outside the family, other than those with their immediate neighbors. This weakened ties among family members.

Another crucial influence on the family was the destruction of village communities through collectivization and industrialization. These diffuse social processes indirectly and gradually destroyed the paternalistic peasant family. As private property confiscated by the state from peasants was gathered in collective farms (kolkhozes), the male head of the family lost the underpinnings of much of his power and authority, and the peasant family lost much of its force as a social institution. In the countryside, fertility—and with it, family size—fell sharply with the disappearance of economic incentives for a rural couple to have many children. In 1926, rural families had an average of 5.6 members and urban families 3.9 members. In 1989, the average family had 3.2 members.

Urbanization created huge waves of migrants from rural areas to cities. This rural-urban migration eradicated the large extended family based on rural life. Since the 1960s, the small nuclear family has predominated among urban Russians. According to the 1989 Soviet census (*Goskomstat SSSR* 1990), families with five or more members were 13 percent of the population, with the level rising to 16 percent in rural areas. Most of these large families were in Russia's republics, which are the homelands of its national minorities. In Russia's rural heartland, the average household size was 2.45 but as low as 2.25 in some regions. The 1994 microcensus reported that the average number in a household was 2.84 (*Goskomstat Rossii* 1995). This means that families with children are relatively rare.

Migration also disrupted family and kin ties and shattered the generational unity of families. The same thing happened in the United States as it industrialized, but for rather different reasons. In the United States, the rising standard of living enabled older couples and their adult children to live separately and independently. This was impossible under Soviet conditions. Living standards rose only slightly in the Soviet period, and severe housing shortages meant that younger generations had to dream and work for many years to obtain separate apartments and to live independently from their parents. In the USSR, the ties between generations were broken instead by the abolition of private property (which thereby reduced inheritances to insignificance) and by the spatial distance between parents and children.

In addition, state authorities inadvertently reduced marriage opportunities by creating schools with imbalanced sex ratios and by making certain parts of the economy female-dominated and others male-dominated. Among the best known examples of this practice are what people jokingly called "cities of grooms" (predominantly male cities) and "cities of brides" (predominantly female cities). Regrettably, the two types of cities were rarely close enough to each other for their residents to find mates in the other type of city. Official statistics also reveal an amazing imbalance in the sex ratio of the rural population. Girls were especially likely to move away from villages, leaving behind young men without potential partners. As a result, women under age 50 are in short supply in rural areas. The individual-level data from the 1994 Russian microcensus reveal that in rural areas, males outnumber females among all those younger than 50 years old, whereas females outnumber males among people older than 50.

The abolition of private property struck a more fundamental blow to family ties between generations and also between spouses. The intergenerational transmission of property acts as cement between parents and children. Old and weak parents are often respected and treated well, not because of love, but because of an anticipated inheritance. Abolition of inheritable private property removed the main material incentive for strong family ties. It is hard to hold a family together for many years purely through romantic love. Without accumulation of property over the life span and the mutual responsibility of spouses for one another, the probability that a marriage dissolves is much higher than in a typical Western society where private property and shared commitments secure the family as an institution.

In the newly emerging Russia, families are struggling with multiple problems. First, they must adapt to a situation in which the meeting of basic needs cannot be taken for granted. Because most families come to a market society without any property in a situation in which the state refuses to guarantee a minimal existence, the foremost goal of the family as an institution is survival and building an adequate material basis for the family's existence.

2.5 SUMMARY

Modern societies differ substantially in the importance placed on various social institutions. In Russia, the economy has never been the major institution. Historically it was always less important than the state, the community, and (with the exception of the Soviet period) the church or family. A new institutional structure is emerging in Russia from this historical context. In periods of transition, all institutions are vulnerable. With Russia's striking losses in people, material resources, and imperial territory and with its ideological uncertainty, all societal institutions are in disarray. The hierarchy of basic institutions is a problem that modern Russia has yet to solve. It is an open question to what extent the historical pattern of the relative importance of different institutions will reemerge in the renewal of Russian society (North 1991).

Another important problem for modern Russia is the distinctive meaning and reality of its societal institutions. Americans are accustomed to the state being under the control of the people. The American people elect officials to almost all important political offices, from the president to members of Congress. In Russia, people have never controlled the state; rather, the state has always dominated the people.

A new Russian state is emerging from the past with great pain. But what will be its character? The Russian state has never had a real division of powers among the legislative, executive, and judiciary branches. Moreover, the Russian state has sought the freely given support of the Russian people only in great wars. At other times, people have tried to live their lives while avoiding contact with the state as much as possible. The state was only rarely a tool in the people's hands; rather, the opposite was true, as illustrated by the fact that Russian rulers managed to have the largest standing army in the world from the eighteenth century until the 1990s. Ironically, the new Russian state is not strong enough to solve the immense economic and social problems facing the country. In order to become an effective democracy and to have a flourishing market economy, the Russian state and its political institutions need to become strong enough to protect its population from organized crime, the abuse of power by the state bureaucracy, and the enormous economic power of a few wealthy individuals.

Spatial and Ethnic Diversity

3.1 SPATIAL ORGANIZATION

Naturally, a vast country like Russia (more than twice the size of the United States, excluding Alaska) is divided into smaller territorial units for purposes of administration and governance. The Russian Federation is comprised of 89 distinct territorial units that are officially called the "subjects of the Federation." Each territorial unit has substantial powers not contested by the central federal government. Importantly, for the first time in Russian history, each of these basic units is headed by freely elected executive and legislative bodies. This development is arguably the most important step toward democracy in Russia: At last people in Russia are able to influence their lives locally.

In this aspect of its spatial organization, the Russian Federation resembles the United States, which is composed of 50 states. There is an important difference, however. The 50 states in the United States are formally equally to one another; they have the same legal rights and powers under the U.S. Constitution. In contrast, the 89 subjects of the Russian Federation are not formally equal. Although the legal rights and powers of the various territorial units were made relatively equal by the Russian Constitution of 1993, subsequent bilateral treaties between the federal state and the individual territorial units have created variability and inequality in the rights and powers of the various territorial units. Indeed, the rights and statuses of the 89 units not only differ but are still being debated.

Russia's 89 territorial units include (in approximate order of decreasing rights and powers) 21 republics, six *krais* (border lands), 49 OBLASTS (regions), two federal cities (Moscow and St. Petersburg), one autonomous oblast, and 10 autonomous *okrugs* (national districts).[1] As

---

1. All data on Russia's regions comes from Khrushchev (1997).

a general rule, territorial units organized around a particular nationality, especially the 21 republics, have many more legal rights and powers than the six krais and the 49 oblasts. As 2 of the 89 "subjects of the Russian Federation," Moscow and St. Petersburg have a special status.

Russia has had a long-standing **rural-urban cleavage.** Nearly three-fourths of Russia's people live in cities, mainly in European Russia. In total, Russia has 1,092 cities, of which 650 are centers of regions or subregions. At the top of the urban hierarchy are 13 "million-cities"—the Russian term for cities with a million or more inhabitants. The 13 million-cities are the home of 24 million people, a fifth of Russia's urban population and nearly a sixth of its entire population. Russia's economic power is mainly situated in its million-cities.

Moscow, the capital, is Russia's foremost city. The city proper has a population of more than eight million, and Moscow oblast (the political-administrative territorial unit surrounding the city, roughly analogous to a state in the United States) has roughly seven million citizens. Thus, greater Moscow has more than one-tenth of the population of the entire country—a huge fraction given Russia's vast expanse.

St. Petersburg, the former capital under the late tsars and the second largest city, has a semi-official status as the second capital. It has 4.2 million inhabitants and is an important economic center, second only to Moscow in economic power and wealth.

On the other side of the urban-rural divide is the countryside, comprised of enormous plains, seemingly limitless forests, and vast frozen wastelands. Although much of Russia's plains has been put into cultivation for agricultural production, people are few and far between, living mainly in scattered villages. As any Russian can tell you, city and countryside are worlds apart in life style and in well-being. Almost all advantages lie on the side of cities.

As in most other countries, Russia's rural population began to shrink when industrialization began. This decline accelerated after World War II. Since the collapse of the Soviet Union, however, the rural population has been relatively stable at around 40 million, or 27 percent of the total population. This number is not very large when one considers the size of Russia's land area.

Most of Russia's very large territorial units are not economically viable. The economically vulnerable territories include not only the lands in the far north, which were inhabited by only small native populations (similar to America's Eskimos) before the Soviet period, but even the southern part of Asian Russia, which is inhabited by ethnic Russians, where the average distance between villages is roughly 50 miles. During the winter, the only means of communication within these regions are radios and cellular phones, both of which are rare. The infrastructure needed for economic activities (e.g., ground transportation, basic utilities) simply requires more resources than local governments in these large, sparsely settled territories can afford.

As market forces develop in Russia, migration is reshaping the location of its population. People are rapidly leaving Asian Russia and other parts with inhospitable climates and few economic prospects. Between 1993 and 1995, some northern areas of Asian Russia lost a third of their populations (*Goskomstat Rossii* 1995). It would not be surprising if they lost another third by the year 2000. Economic and climatic conditions are, however, favorable for growth in the southern region of the Pacific coast and also in the southern part of western Siberia.

3.2 THE EMPIRE AS AN ORGANIZER OF TERRITORY

The territorial organization of modern Russia has historical origins. It began in the thirteenth century with tiny MUSCOVY, whose territory was about the combined size of Massachusetts and Connecticut (15,000 square miles). In the heyday of the Soviet Union, in which Russia was the leading republic, its empire officially encompassed 8.6 million square miles. Moreover, its "outer empire" also included Mongolia and most of Eastern Europe, making its effective spatial domain even larger. Its territorial expansion, occurring gradually over seven centuries, is unrivaled.

Although the British Empire encompassed a larger land area at its peak, Britain's colonies were never incorporated into Britain itself. The only comparable empire in terms of territorial size was China. But China has had nearly the same borders for the last 600 years, whereas Russia's borders were continually shifting—mainly expanding. Russia is unique in that the **ideas of empire and territorial expansion** were fundamental modes of life for centuries.

Few countries ever admit that they are expanding their territories. Rather, they (and their historians) say they are defending themselves: their borders, their interests, their culture. Russians were no different in this respect. To outsiders, Russia's expansion is likely to appear assertive, if not actually aggressive; but to Russians themselves, Russia was defending itself. More land just happened to be acquired in the process of its self-defense.

The mentality of conquest and expansion had an enormous impact on the development of Russia as a state and Russians as a people. Most empires that have tried to digest substantial territorial gains have been unable to do so successfully and have eventually collapsed. In contrast, aside from minor setbacks, Russia succeeded in absorbing all acquired territories gradually. This success came at great cost, however. Because the state was continually focused on territorial expansion, it used available resources primarily for this goal, leaving few resources for developing the kind of infrastructure that is normal in European countries.

For a striking comparison, consider the Netherlands, where Tsar Peter the Great, Russia's greatest reformer, learned many ideas that he later implemented in his own country. In the late 1990s, Russia has only one modern freeway: the Moscow Ringway. A highway allowing high-speed motor-vehicle traffic does not yet span the country. In contrast, every place in the Netherlands has been accessible by various modes of transportation since the seventeenth century. The elaborate transportation network in the Netherlands allowed every innovation to spread rapidly throughout the country. But in Russia, the typical province lived for centuries isolated not only from the outside world but also from the capital and other provinces. Russian culture also developed in isolation from the country as a whole, with merchants transporting goods acting as the main conduit of information and culture through Russia's provinces.

As a country, Russia never concentrated its resources on the development of a **social and cultural infrastructure.** In contrast, Holland's dense population in a small land area led to the development of institutions that allowed society to work effectively, even in the fourteenth and fifteenth centuries. Every kind of social activity and every locality sought to create institutional arrangements for dealing with all types of situational problems arising from disagreements about rules, values, and goals. These arrangements included, for example, provisions for handling the hardships of winter, the establishment of laws and courts, etiquette for families to get along with one another, and neighborhood regulations. This process created a sociocultural infrastructure in the Netherlands that allowed most problems to be solved through negotiation and without open conflict. Murder, suicide, and even bank robbery, not to mention a criminal underworld and open political conflicts, became rare in the Netherlands because of these subtle, implicit social contracts. This highly developed social life allows the Netherlands to be effective in the world economy, despite its small territory, on the basis of only one major resource: human beings.

Like every other country at some point in its history, Russia had a simple, basic rule: Whoever had power was right.[2] The Russian state routinely used brutal force to solve problems so that its resources could be directed on external expansion. For centuries the principle of absolute

---

2. This "might makes right" philosophy does not mean that a rather advanced sociocultural infrastructure never developed in some places, but such exceptions always disturbed the Russian state. Revolts against this philosophy are exemplified by the democratic city of Novgorod (which Ivan IV, the Terrible, suppressed in a bloodbath), the free Cossack communites, various religious groups in tsarist Russia, the Seventeenth Communist Party Congress's 1936 votes against Stalin's brutality, and Soviet DISSIDENTS, such as Andrei Sakharov (1975) and Aleksandr Solzhenitsyn (1963, 1973), who protested human rights' abuses.

power and an authoritarian state controlled by a small governing elite has been the primary way to solve problems in Russia. Norms, values, and institutions challenging a ruling group's supreme power rarely sprang up, and when they did, they were eventually eliminated. The development of legitimate institutions for solving internal conflicts was invariably temporary in Russian history. This institutional void was the price of territorial expansion. The new Russian state has not yet begun to fill this void.

Administering Russia's space after Muscovy's conquest and incorporation of different dukedoms in the fifteenth century was not a problem for its rulers. In the first systematic organization of Russian territory, introduced by Tsar Peter the Great in 1708, the basic units were the *guberniia* and the *volost*. The Soviet administrative system replicated guberniias and volosts but adopted a new, overarching principle based on the dominant nationality in a region. For the purposes of world revolution and the fulfillment of tactical needs, the Russian Empire was reorganized into the Union of Soviet Socialist Republics (USSR) in December 1922, and all member states formally belonged to this Union. Russia, as its largest, most populous, and strongest member, determined the territorial organization of the USSR. Almost all of Russia's numerous nations were incorporated as some kind of autonomous unit: as a republic, autonomous republic, autonomous oblast, or okrug. The 1936 Soviet Constitution instituted by Stalin fixed the status and rights of every national territory. Although this constitution was intended to be purely symbolic, it cemented the borders between national territories within the Soviet Union.

This arbitrary setting of borders had an enormous impact on the collapse of the USSR and the formation of post-Soviet states. First, the new Russian state accepted the 1991 borders of the Russian Soviet Federated Socialist Republic (RSFSR); with a few minor exceptions, these were the borders established by the 1936 constitution of the USSR. In accepting these borders, Russia excluded many territories where the majority of the population was Russian (not the titular nationality), creating a Russian DIASPORA. These excluded territories have come to be called Russia's "near abroad" by its people. Second, the new Russian state recognized all Soviet-established national territories as separate territorial entities. Specifically, it recognized every former Soviet republic as a new country, and it retained former autonomous republics within the RSFSR as separate administrative units within its own borders.

3.3 CAPITAL VERSUS COUNTRY

The capital city dominates most countries, not only politically but in every other way, including economically, financially, and culturally. The United States is among the few exceptions. Through a separation of economic and political powers and activities, it managed to develop without any one city dominating the rest. In the United States, Washington, DC, is the political capital, but the financial capital has long been New York City. Industrial power has shifted from region to region and become widely dispersed as the West and South have developed.

Throughout history, Russia's rulers have concentrated all forms of power in the capital. This concentration in the capital was normal during the era of absolute monarchs in Europe. Economic power, wealth, the arts, and learning naturally gravitated to the place from which the monarch ruled. Market forces operate differently and tend to diffuse economic power through space. Many other forms of power spread, too. A democratic ideology also tends to equalize the development of various regions of a country and to curb the dominance of a country's capital.

Until the eighteenth century, Moscow was not only Russia's capital but its only real city. Until then, Russia had some towns, but most of them were essentially trading posts. Some were sites where a limited amount of manufacturing was done. But every substantial economic center that competed with Moscow was eliminated, one way or another.

After the fall of the Byzantine capital of Constantinople to the Turks, Ivan III married the niece of the last Byzantine emperor in 1472. With this union of the two imperial dynasties, Moscow replaced Constantinople as the center of Orthodoxy and the spiritual capital of Russia. Numerous new churches were built, and Moscow began to rival Constantinople in the beauty and grandeur of its architecture. All of Russia's resources were targeted on developing this new world capital. Indeed, Moscow became the hub of political power in Russia. In 1589, the Russian Orthodox Church declared that it was headed by the Patriarch of Moscow, who contested the leadership of the Patriarch of Constantinople. Moscow became known as the Third Rome, as the Second Rome (Constantinople) declined as the religious center of Orthodoxy.

For centuries, the Church was the primary institution of education in Russia. It provided the nobility with religious instruction in numerous monasteries around Moscow. Russia's educated elite and its foreign compound were located solely in Moscow. The upper gentry (so-called *boyars*) also lived in the capital and governed their vast, remote estates through supervisors. Over time, *belokamennaia* (literally, "white stone") Moscow became the Russian center of political power, religion, wealth, and beauty.

As a nation becomes increasingly urban, the capital is often contested by other cities. In Russia, Moscow's primacy was challenged by Tsar Peter the Great, who wanted to institute sweeping reforms. He decided that his reforms could not last unless he moved the capital from Moscow because the elite and major institutions (such as the Church) in Moscow opposed his innovations. With the help of many foreigners, Peter rapidly built a new capital that he immodestly named St. Petersburg. The new Russian

Red Square. This is the most famous place in Russia. The photo shows the famous onion domes of St. Basil's Cathedral (left), as well as Lenin's tomb (center), and the Kremlin Walls before the huge square.

elite easily incorporated these foreigners because many members of the historically rooted gentry preferred to remain in Moscow and were slow to move to Peter's new capital.

Moscow remained officially the second capital and became the coronation site of every new tsar. The Russian Orthodox Church also continued to have Moscow as its official headquarters. Moscow also had the largest concentration of merchants in Russia until the twentieth century.

But power and wealth began to be concentrated in St. Petersburg. It became the center of science and learning in Russia. From the outset, it was culturally linked with Europe, and its architecture echoed the building styles of other modern European capitals. The army, the most important organization in tsarist Russia, had its main headquarters in Peter's Baltic capital. It was also the center of Russian industry in the pre-Soviet period. For all of these reasons, St. Petersburg was the main powerhouse in Russia in the nineteenth century.

St. Petersburg's power is the reason why the Bolsheviks so easily gained control of Russia after they seized control of the city in the October Revolution of 1917. In practice, the entire Russian Empire was controlled by this city of nearly three million people in 1917.

The Bolsheviks understood that they needed to move the capital back to Moscow in order to disassociate themselves from the tsars and establish their new regime. Unlike Peter the Great, the Bolsheviks were not oriented toward the West. Rather, they were focused on controlling the entire country. Moscow was ideally located for this task because it is in Russia's heartland, a highly advantageous site for dominating Russia's more populated hinterlands. In addition, it was the historical capital, which gave legitimacy to moving the capital back to Moscow.

The **Soviet system** was unique in its concentration of power in the center. The power hierarchy was constructed from the top downward to the localities rather than from the bottom upward to the capital. All top-level Soviet institutions were concentrated in Moscow, even if they dealt with a region seven time zones away, such as the special unit overseeing the Far East. Moscow was the headquarters of every ministry and administrative subunit, even the ones in charge of agriculture and the Arctic. The head office of every organization, from the union of chess players to the GULAG (the Stalinist system of labor camps), was in Moscow. Such concentrations of powers in the capital have existed elsewhere only in absolute monarchies.

This pattern came about as a result of the absolute and unlimited power of the apparatus of the Communist party-state. To maintain absolute power, the party-state apparatus needed the top levels of every organization and their subunits to be located in Moscow.[3]

Since all political and economic resources were channeled through the budget to the state apparatus annually, Moscow benefited in the following ways:

1. Ministries and departments had absolute control over their resources, and they naturally allocated considerable resources to their headquarters in Moscow, where their top officials had their offices.

2. It was easy to lobby for and get extra resources for the capital because central organizations were more likely to grant resources to other organizations in the same city where they themselves were headquartered.

3. Because the administrative organization in the territories was negligible compared to the ministerial apparatus that governed activities within the territories, the wealth that the state bureaucracy accumulated from the entire country flowed toward the capital.

4. Since Moscow was the capital, it had a special budget. This budget legally allowed developments in Moscow that greatly exceeded those elsewhere.

---

3. Members of the Communist Party had little power. Even members of the Communist Party's CENTRAL COMMITTEE rarely had any say on important matters, and ordinary Party members never did. The top leader of the Communist Party was never elected by the party's Central Committee.

5. Goods and services were invariably in chronic shortage in the former Soviet Union because no market existed. State organizations distributed all resources (goods, food, and services) on the basis of roughly 10 ranks of settlements. As the capital, Moscow had the top rank, which gave Muscovites benefits that far surpassed salary differences linked with different kinds of jobs. Every day at least two million people came from surrounding areas to shop in Moscow, recognizing it as offering a cornucopia of food and consumer goods, relative to the pitiful quantities sold near their homes.

Since the Soviet system was organized from the top downward, every activity done in Moscow was supposed to represent the best in the country. For example, it was considered a disaster if Moscow's teams did not win the country's championship in soccer and hockey. It was not only intolerable but impossible that some university, clinic, or scientific institute outside Moscow could have greater prestige than those in the Soviet capital. Hence, roughly half of the leading scientific teams (top research centers, top scientists, and so on) were located in Moscow, and approximately a quarter of the university students in the Soviet Union studied there. All of the above resulted in the unchallenged supremacy of Moscow in all developed areas of culture and science, as well as in power and wealth. The concentration of the best theaters, artists, dancers, scholars, and scientists in Moscow was quite harmful to Russian society as a whole because it deprived the rest of the country of their important benefits.

As a result of the capital's supremacy, Muscovites were recognized as a special category of Soviet citizens. As early as the 1930s, special rules were introduced to restrict migration to Moscow from elsewhere in the country. Nevertheless, Moscow was the most rapidly growing city in the USSR. The highest upward social mobility for people was to move to the capital. Most Soviet citizens saw Moscow only through the lens of a camera or television; the city itself was beyond their reach. But over a million people were always on the waiting list to register to live in Moscow officially, that is, to obtain a Moscow *propiska* (the legal document that named someone's official place of residence). It typically took 25 years or more to gain the legal right to live in Moscow. After officially becoming registered to live in Moscow, a person then got on the next waiting list for the right to have a permanent dwelling in which to live.

Because Soviet leaders realized that the control of remote, economically unimportant areas yields almost no benefits, remote regions and distant villages were very neglected as a general rule. As late as the 1970s, more than 50 years after the October Revolution in 1917, there still existed localities whose inhabitants lacked an internal passport, the essential document identifying a person as a legitimate Soviet citizen.

As the **new Russia** moves to a market economy, Moscow is developing on the basis of patterns developed in the Soviet era. It still dominates the country politically, economically, and culturally. Indeed, it may be moving even further above the rest of the country on the spatial hierarchy.

As the capital of the new Russia, Moscow has effectively used its previous advantages to reach a standard of living four times higher than that of the rest of Russia. This was not hard to achieve because the whole notion of how to create a market economy was very traditionally Russian: from the top downward. The macroeconomic approach advocated by Western economic experts and adopted by Russia's new leaders focused most changes within Moscow, leaving other places to scramble for scraps. Decisions in the new Russia have been made in Moscow by and for the few, just as in Soviet times.

3.4 FROM PROVINCES TO REGIONS

As noted earlier, Tsar Peter the Great divided Russia into guberniias, large regions that usually matched historically developed territorial boundaries. As the distance from Moscow rose, the size of a guberniia tended to increase, mainly because the tsar's information about resources and populations in more distant, thinly populated territories was less accurate. The hazy ideas of the tsar's inner circle concerning remote territories explains why Alaska and all of eastern Siberia were in the same, huge guberniia. The European part of Russia was politically more important and known more thoroughly; hence, guberniias there were smaller. A conquered territory, even one as important as Poland, was routinely split between different guberniias, ignoring its previous status as an independent state.

The guberniias had little real power under the tsars, but they did develop some limited authority to administer local areas outside the absolute rule of the nobility over their serfs. With the abolition of serfdom in 1861, the guberniias became more powerful because a majority of the population became formally free people, no longer the subjects of a feudal lord. Economic life based on markets started to develop. But this economic development ended with social conflict between peasants and workers on one side and the nobility (still the dominant political force) on the other. The guberniias had very little say in such conflicts.

The Soviet administrative system was modeled on the tsarist system of guberniias but was completely restructured. In particular, separate units for the homelands of many nationalities were created. Soviet leaders also reshaped the territorial distribution of the Russian population. Three main processes affected the territorial organization of the country in the Soviet era:

1. Industrialization under the command economy allocated the industrial power of Russia to specific economic sectors.

2. A new, state-directed process of urbanization created Russia's current urban structure.

3. Huge migration waves redistributed the population throughout the country.

Industrialization was a major aim of the Soviet party-state, made even more urgent by the relative backwardness of Russia, as evidenced by its devastating military defeat in World War I. The Bolshevik leadership realized that survival of the USSR depended on industrializing the country. Indeed, a famous slogan of Lenin was "Communism means electrification of the country," showing the importance that the Bolshevik leaders gave to industrialization. All of Stalin's FIVE-YEAR PLANS allocated abundant resources to develop gigantic industrial enterprises. The command economy was specifically designed to concentrate resources on such kinds of efforts. A huge dislocation of the population resulted from industrialization. Russia's eastern territories were rapidly populated and industrialized during this process.

Collectivization of agriculture, manifestly intended to industrialize agriculture, completely changed the Russian countryside. The rural population was moved from small, dispersed villages to large, central villages. Many peasants were forced to abandon homes held for generations. In the 1980s, four- and five-story buildings were built in the countryside, and rural Russians were given apartments instead of houses, despite an abundance of vacant land. Because agriculture and rural life offered even fewer opportunities after collectivization, youths were continually trying to leave the villages where they were born. There was a mass migration from rural areas to urban centers. On the whole, collectivization failed to fulfill its goals of greater agricultural productivity and more effective organization of farm work. It succeeded only in obliterating the traditional pattern of peasant life that had evolved over centuries.

One of the most noteworthy consequences of industrialization was the rapid increase in the urban population, and especially the settlement of large groups of people in factory towns and cities. In other countries, a network of towns gradually developed along trade routes and was further extended by industrialization, with some new population centers arising near newly discovered natural resources, such as coal or iron. Market-based industrialization did not occur in Russia. During the Soviet period, historically developed towns lost their importance, and trade no longer served as the basis for population centers. When the countryside underwent economic devolution during collectivization, the historical Russian towns that had traditionally supplied goods to rural areas lost their main function and their populations drifted (or were sent) away.

Urbanization in Russia was definitely a process planned from the top downward, not a slow, natural development from the bottom upward. The biggest beneficiaries of this planned process were great re-

Trains are still the main way most Russians get from one distant place to another.

gional centers, such as Novosibirsk, Yekaterinburg, Khabarovsk, and Omsk, which grew very rapidly. Also benefiting were industrial centers that mushroomed from small towns to million-cities, such as Chelyabinsk, Perm, and Volgograd. But Soviet planners neglected Russia's historical heartland surrounding Moscow. Within this part of Russia, the only new city that grew into a million-city in the Soviet era was Nizhniy Novgorod.[4]

Urbanization had another important aspect. For strategic military purposes, many factories were put in "closed towns"[5] in empty places, either outside existing populated areas or, worse, in places with harsh climates. Examples include Norilsk and Murmansk, two very large cities above the Arctic Circle. Many other closed towns were strung along the Trans-Siberian railway.

Population **migration** in Russia during the twentieth century has far surpassed that in any other country in Europe. The GULAG system of penal labor camps was designed initially to hold purported enemies of the Soviet state but later also to force people to move to new areas of Russia where labor was needed and living conditions were so harsh that

---

4. See Andrusz et al. (1996) for a description of the consequences of marketization.
5. Closed towns were ones that people were allowed to enter and leave only with special
   permission and documents. They were not even shown on maps or mentioned in
   public documents, such as census statistics.

voluntary migration would never have furnished enough laborers.[6] As a result, more than 30 million people were living in the Asian part of Russia in the 1990s. If one adds the northern part of European Russia, almost 50 million people are living in severe, wintry conditions. In a market economy, mining is the only economic activity that can be profitable in such a climate. But modern methods of mining cannot support the large majority of people who live in these difficult conditions.

A comparison of two major mining towns, Dawson in Canada's Yukon Territory and Norilsk in Russia's Krasnoyarsk *krai*, illustrates the stark realities and results of the Soviet system. Mining production in the two towns is very similar. Yet Dawson has a population of about 10,000 people, whereas Norilsk has roughly 200,000. Thus, the number of people involved in extracting the same amount of ore is roughly 20 times greater in Norilsk than in Dawson. Clearly, Norilsk is overpopulated for its level of economic output. As Norilsk develops a market economy, its population will almost surely shrink substantially.

In the Soviet Union, no one ever questioned the exorbitant cost of mining coal in Norway's Spitzbergen Islands, which Russia has a legal right to mine according to a nineteenth-century treaty with Norway. Soviet decision makers regarded the military benefits of access to Norwegian soil worth the economic cost. The same rationale cannot apply to the greater Murmansk area, where a million people live in very harsh polar conditions and cannot be sustained by a market economy. Only a command economy could force so many people to live and work in such inhospitable places as these. Most work done by the 50 million people in Russia who live in very harsh climates is unprofitable and could be done profitably by fewer people living under more humane conditions.

As Russia leaves the twentieth century, the geographic distributions of both its urban centers and its people are radically different than they were when the century began. As a market economy starts to force Russia to live under the rule of economic profit, millions of its people will again be forced to leave where they have been living in order to survive.

3.5 PRINCIPAL REGIONS

The regions of Russia differ widely in their terrains, soils, climates, and populations, and therefore in their economic conditions and prospects. These various features of Russia's regions form an important backdrop for Russian society and its evolving political system. There is no single,

---

6. Russia's most famous contemporary writer, Aleksandr Solzhenitsyn, was awarded the Nobel Prize in literature for *One Day in the Life of Ivan Denisovich* (1963), an account of the harsh life in Soviet penal labor camps based on his own personal experiences.

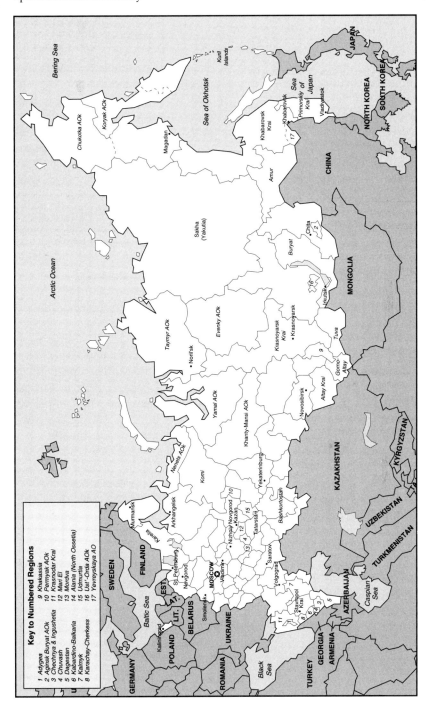

Key to Numbered Regions

1 Adygea	9 Khakassia
2 Aginsk Buryat AOk	10 Permyak AOk
3 Chechnya & Ingushetia	11 Krasnodar Krai
4 Chuvash	12 Mari El
5 Dagestan	13 Mordva
6 Kabardino-Balkaria	14 Alania (North Ossetia)
7 Kalmyk	15 Udmurtia
8 Karachay-Cherkess	16 Ust'-Orda AOk
	17 Yevreyskaya AO

agreed-upon division of Russia's regions; we describe the main regions identified by the Russian Statistical Bureau (*Goskomstat Rossii* 1998).

Russia's **Central Heartland** has 30 million people, 84 percent of whom live in urban areas. It includes 12 oblasts, plus the city of Moscow, as members of the Russian Federation. Half of its population lives in Moscow or in Moscow oblast. Except for Moscow and its surrounding oblast, the population of most oblasts in this region has been steadily decreasing since the 1950s because the Soviet central government did not devote many resources to them. This heartland is a relatively stable agricultural and living area with a climate fairly similar to Wisconsin's. A market economy is more likely to develop in this area than in most other parts of Russia, partly because of its proximity to Moscow.

The most fertile agricultural land lies in the central **Black Earth** region, so named for its rich, black soil. It contains 7.7 million people living in six oblasts and has no noteworthy cities. With 40 percent of its people working in agriculture on the most fertile soil in the world, this area could easily feed all of Russia. Unfortunately, the state and collective farms created in the Soviet era prevented efficient agricultural production, and the rural areas in this region lost nearly half of their population in the last 30 years of the Soviet era.

Historically, the Russian homeland also includes its **Northwest,** with 8 million people and St. Petersburg as Russia's second-largest city. The climate there is very severe: St. Petersburg is the northernmost city in the world with more than a million inhabitants. Since this city is a major shipping port at the end of the Baltic Sea and serves as Russia's most accessible port to Western Europe, the prospect of future economic development keeps people living in this area, despite its unpleasant climate.

Russia's **North** has six oblasts covering a huge area reaching beyond the Arctic Circle. It is very important militarily because it is Russia's only western route open to the ocean. (St. Petersburg has access to the sea, but its sea route is easily blocked by neighboring countries.) This region had six million people in 1998, but its population is rapidly decreasing because mining and military facilities are about the only activities that can be sensibly located in this region.

A similar story can be told for the **Volgo-Vyatka** region, except for its southern rim. Although this region contains Nizhniy Novgorod, Russia's third-largest city, and had eight million people in 1998, its population is likely to shrink because a market economy brings the recognition that many of its enterprises are not economically viable. The historical homelands of three sizable national minorities, the Chuvash, Komi, and Mari, lie in well-established republics in this region.

The Volga River links the Volgo-Vyatka region to the **Volga** region, which has good prospects for economic development. This region has a stable continental climate and tolerable living conditions. With 16 million people, its population is the fourth largest. It has grown rapidly, experiencing a 25 percent increase in population since the 1960s. It contains six oblasts and two republics. One of these republics, Tatarstan, represents the 5.5 million Tatars, the second most numerous nationality in Russia (after the Russkii). The Tatars trace their ancestry from the Volga Bulgars and Tatars from the thirteenth and fourteenth centuries.

The **North Caucasus** is the region with the best climate, but it also has many indigenous non-Russian people fighting over control of the region. It is roughly as far north as Maine, but it gets less rain and therefore more sun in the course of a year, giving it a climate similar to that of Colorado. This region was conquered partly by Peter the Great and entirely subjugated by the end of the nineteenth century. Its population of 18 million people grew by a third between 1960 and 1990. The region's national minorities, many of which are Islamic, have the highest birth rates in Russia. In the future, the North Caucasus could become the region with the most rapidly growing population, only partly because of the high birth rates. With the best climate in Russia and with easy access to the rest of the world via the Black Sea, it could attract investors hoping to turn its favorable economic prospects into economic realities, if its political conflicts could be resolved. Migrants from other regions of Russia might then follow.

The URAL region has 20 million people in an area roughly the size of Western Europe. Many of its people are descendants of the GULAG prisoners and semiforced laborers who arrived in the early Soviet period. This highly urbanized region has two republics and five oblasts. It contains three cities with populations exceeding a million people, the most famous being Yekaterinburg, where the last tsar, Nicholas II, was killed by the Bolsheviks. Although the Ural region was the powerhouse of Soviet industrialization, marketization is creating immense problems. It has many gigantic industrial enterprises employing hundreds of thousands of people. Such huge enterprises are not profitable in a modern economy. Moreover, many of its factories were part of the military-defense industry in the Soviet era and cannot easily be converted to produce other, marketable goods. The climate in the Ural region is too severe for it to develop much of a service industry. The only primary production activities in the Ural region that are potentially profitable in a market economy are mining and some aspects of heavy industry. Consequently, many of its factories are likely to close permanently. Because factory towns are the economic foundation of this region, every closed factory creates a growing number of ex-workers who then turn into a flood of migrants.

The region of **Western Siberia** encompasses land from the Arctic Ocean to Russia's border with China. Its 14 million people live in two republics, one krai, and five oblasts. With extensive natural resources (including a major diamond field), this region has great economic potential but a harsh climate. It is only habitable in its southern part, the site of its two million-cities, Novosibirsk and Omsk. Even in Novosibirsk, winter temperatures regularly drop to –40 degrees Fahrenheit. Since maintaining satisfactory living conditions in such a climate is very costly, it would not be surprising if half of its population were to move away in coming years.

Sustaining the population of **Eastern Siberia** is the greatest challenge. The development of heavy industry around the cities of Krasnoyarsk and Irkutsk in the 1970s and 1980s led this region's population to rise to nine million people. But the growth pattern reversed after the Soviet Union collapsed. Only its mining areas are likely to continue to be developed. The rest, including the vast expanses bordering Mongolia, are likely to continue to depopulate as the central government's financial support of northern territories contracts.

The fate of Russia's largest region, the **Far East,** is uncertain. From 1950 to 1980, its population nearly doubled to almost eight million people due to the construction of the Baikal-Amur railway across Siberia. The native population in its largest republic, Sakha (formerly Yakutia), continues to increase, but elsewhere the region is losing people and the capacity to exploit its substantial natural resources. Since the Soviet collapse, more than a million people have left. The population of its two northern oblasts has declined by almost a half. Primorsk krai, very near Korea and northern China, has the greatest economic potential. This gigantic territory is, however, at risk of unwanted immigration from China.

For the most part, **major regions** of Russia are more geographical than functioning social units. From the Ural region to the Far East, regions exist only as lines on maps and as administrative units. In these regions, people's lives are extremely localized, and access to other places, even within the same region, is very limited. The sociopsychological climate is distinctively individualized in each local area. Moscow has very little influence on local life in these parts of Russia.

Even the Central region, which has the largest population and the most extensive economic development, lacks an effective transportation system, except to and from Moscow. After its only major land route is closed by winter snows, the immense Sakha republic in the Far East has effectively no overland routes to the rest of Russia. Economic ties among regions are even less developed than the transportation system. Attempts to build larger, consolidated market-based subunits of the country have failed so far, even in the highly industrialized Ural region. Time is needed to develop a clearer picture of regionalization, for the market to establish profitable linkages, and for the development of an adequate infrastructure that permits these linkages to function effectively.

Vast, economically inviable areas will undoubtedly continue to depopulate so that Russia's population increasingly becomes concentrated in selected subregions with good economic potential. The Central region,

North Caucasus, and the Volga basin are the most promising regions to develop. New technologies offer the prospect of linking the whole country together through one communication network, which television partly does even now.

3.6 RUSSIANS AND MINORITIES

Nationality is invariably a major problem in empires, and the Russian Empire is no exception. Many of Russia's nationality problems were solved in the collapse of the Soviet Union.[7] By recognizing the former Soviet republics as new states, the Russian Federation avoided many potential nationality problems since most former Soviet republics had been incorporated into the Russian Empire since the seventeenth century and were not yet fully assimilated or accepting of their incorporation. Within the new Russian Federation, only the autonomous republics in the North Caucasus region had been incorporated into the Russian Empire as recently as the nineteenth century. All other national territories of Russia have been within the Russian Empire for many centuries.

The imminent breakup of the Russian Federation into smaller national states has often been discussed. Is breakup really likely? A look at the map suggests that some republics may break away. But breaking away is not the same as the breakup of the Russian Federation.

Let us consider the Russian regions that might want to break away. Russia's largest republic in land area is Sakha (formerly Yakutia) in the Far East with almost two million square miles and a million people, of whom more than half are Yakuts, the titular nationality. This huge northern territory lacks any internal infrastructure and depends heavily on Russia, despite its enormous natural resources. Eastern Siberia contains three republics with large territories: Buryatia, Tyva, and Altay. Buryatia has a relatively agreeable climate and a million inhabitants, of whom more than half are Buryats, the indigenous nationality. With their higher fertility rates, these indigenous people could constitute a majority of the population in the future and might desire to break away. The Tyva and Altay republics are not likely to try to break away from the Russian Federation because relatively few of their inhabitants belong to their titular nationalities (most of their populations are Russians).

The Volga region does contain several nationalities with large populations, including Tatars, Bashkirs, Chuvash, Mordva, Udmurts, and Maris. However, all of these nationalities have lived with Russians for centuries and are extensively RUSSIFIED. Forming a successful separatist or independence movement based on these nationalities would be very

---

7. See Beissinger (1995), Drobizheva et al. (1996), and Szporluk (1994) on Russia's
   nationality problems.

hard because they lie in Russia's heartland.[8] Even in Tatarstan, Russia's most populous republic, located in the heartland of Russia, Russians comprise nearly half of the population. Substantial autonomy given to Tatarstan, historical linkages to Russian culture, and widespread usage of the Russian language, quite aside from strong economic ties to Russia, make its secession very unlikely.

National, cultural, and religious differences are sufficiently strong to be the basis for secession from Russia in one region: the North Caucasus. The small nationalities in this area were conquered by the Russian Empire in the nineteenth century, and their peoples were subjected to mass slaughter many times. The declaration of independence of CHECH-NYA in 1991 was the first clear sign of potential breakaway in this part of Russia. A similar movement in the adjoining republic of Dagestan could happen in the future, but it is likely to depend on how the situation in Chechnya develops. It should be noted that relations between the Chechens and Dagestanis have long been tense, so Chechnya and Dagestan are unlikely to act as allies in a move to break away. Since the landlocked republic of Alania (formerly North Ossetia), also in the North Caucasus, has long been a close ally of Russia, it is even less likely to break away (cf. Drobizheva et al. 1996).

The minority nations in the North Caucasus can be kept in Russia by only two means: brutal force or major economic incentives. In Chechnya, Russia's leaders chose force. After the blood that has been shed there, offering economic incentives to Chechnya would have little chance to succeed in keeping it within the Russian Federation. All of the subregions in the North Caucasus, except Ossetia, contain Muslim majorities, whose population growth is so great that they have been pushing out Russians since the 1960s. Any move toward real democracy in this region must eventually give these nations independence.

Thus, there is a real risk of separation from the Russian Federation in the Northern Caucasus, but not elsewhere. Realistically, two or three republics in this region may press to secede from the Russian Federation. But overall, Russia faces little danger of disintegrating into numerous small states. Although 20 percent of Russia's population is non-Russian, only a third of its minority nationalities live in areas where they predominate. So a democratic Russia should be able to retain most minority nationalities within its geographical borders and political system. As long as the Russian government treats minority nationalities as Russian citizens rather than as conquered peoples and territories, major conflicts focused around issues of nationality are not likely to emerge.

---

8. The Tatarstan republic has been particularly assertive of local rights. For Tatarstan the main issue may not be leaving the Russian Federation but governing itself with a fair degree of autonomy, especially in economic and cultural spheres.

Russia is, however, unlikely to become a **melting pot** like the United States, where people of all nations and races come from around the world and become "hyphenated Americans" within a generation or two. The United States and Russia have one fundamental difference: In the United States, the only indigenous people are Native Americans, who comprise less than 1 percent of the U.S. population. All others (or their ancestors) came from some other country. The British, Germans, Irish, Chinese, and Mexicans in America originated in another country where their nation still has its own home and national identity.

In contrast, Russia's minorities have their homeland within Russia's borders. If they become assimilated as Russians, their entire identity, culture, and history can be lost. This fact works against assimilation. Historically the Russian Empire operated as a melting pot in places where Russians were numerically dominant. The more than four million Ukrainians and one million Belarusians living in Russia will almost surely be assimilated by Russians in the future. A similar process of assimilation can occur with most other nationalities living in predominantly Russian areas. As market forces start to operate, migration can be another factor promoting a melting pot.

There are two plausible scenarios for minority nationalities that remain within the Russian Federation, other than cultural assimilation. Distinctive subcommunities of minority nationalities may develop in major cities. In addition, minority homelands may acquire some degree of political and cultural autonomy.

The first scenario is the formation of what Americans call **ethnic ghettos.** Most big cities in the United States have a "Chinatown," where many Chinese live in an immigrant community that has a distinctive culture and occupies a certain economic niche. Such ethnic communities typically have a high degree of internal communication and internal trade but also furnish certain specialized goods or services to the larger society.

A similar phenomenon already exists on a modest scale in Moscow. A foreign visitor to a food market in Moscow might be amazed to see non-Russians stationed at almost every trading post; they are mainly Moscow-based Azeris from the Caucasus. Many large Russian cities may eventually come to have settlements of distinctive minority communities operating in certain niches of the market. It is unrealistic to imagine that war-devastated Chechnya can become a prosperous country any time soon or that densely populated Dagestan can feed all of its people. Scarcity of resources and limited communication with the outer world will make economic development in these areas very slow. Consequently, many members of smaller nationalities are likely to migrate to predominantly Russian regions and establish immigrant communities. Since such communities in Russian cities could maintain close ties to their national homeland, assimilation into Russian culture is likely to be

A private market (rynok) *where people can buy fresh fruits, vegetables, meat, cheese, and so on. Markets like this one were one of Russia's earliest steps toward a market economy.*

resisted. However, sooner or later, migration of individuals (in contrast with migration of whole national communities) leads to assimilation.

The second scenario consists of **minority homelands** within Russia. In such homelands, relations among nationalities will develop in distinctive ways due to historical, cultural, and economic differences. In Russia proper, relations between peoples who differed in nationality, religion, or culture were usually tense within the elite and professions being contested by minorities. After the Baltic nations were added to the Russian Empire, Germans were an important part of the Russia's elite. Competition between Russians and Germans was common, with Russians in the elite stirring up anti-German sentiments. Competition became more vicious when open RUSSIFICATION of minorities began at the end of the nineteenth century.

Anti-Semitism arose in Russia in an entirely different way. With Russia's conquest of parts of Poland and Lithuania, which had large Jewish populations, major areas of Jewish settlement in Europe were incorporated into the Russian Empire. The Russian elite, feeling pressure from potential Jewish competition, introduced the famous "pale of settlement" for Jews: Jews were allowed to live on one side of the line and not on the other side, which was in Russia proper. The typical imperial tactic of dividing conquered peoples and setting them against one another was employed. The Jews became the scapegoats for Russia's harsh policy toward Ukrainians, Belarusians, and Poles in the nineteenth century. When a

Russification policy was openly declared, anti-Semitism was a significant part of it, and the infamous pogroms against Jews were semi-officially initiated. These pogroms triggered a massive emigration of Jews from Russia to America at the turn of the twentieth century.

During Russia's Civil War of 1918–1921, the so-called White Russians supporting the tsar used anti-Semitism to combat the Reds because many Jews had joined the Bolshevik Revolution.[9] (Not only Marx, but Lenin, Trotsky, and many other famous Bolshevik leaders were Jewish.) Years later, the Stalinist leadership employed anti-Semitism by introducing quotas for Jews in government offices, in the educational system, and in some professions. As a result, anti-Semitic feelings were raised and used later against intellectuals and other opponents to the Communist regime. Once again many Jews emigrated, especially to Israel or the United States. The Jewish population of Russia decreased significantly during the Soviet period, falling to around a half million in 1998. In the late 1990s, Jewish emigration from Russia has amounted to roughly 20,000 people per year. The massive exodus of Jews from Russia has virtually eliminated an influential segment of Russia's cultural, literary, and scientific heritage and decimated an important part of its human resources.

In sum, nationality matters in everyday life in Russia, but the same is true in most Western countries. Nationality can be the basis for different treatment in government offices, the professions, and business corporations. But although nationality is still important in social relationships in Russia, at last no one can officially demand to know a citizen's nationality. The new Russian passports do not contain the infamous "fifth line" (*grafa*) in Soviet passports, which reported nationality.[10] It is a major step toward creating an open civil society.

Russians abroad present a new problem for Russia and in some sense for Russians (Chinn and Kaiser 1996). More than 20 million Russians and at least 10 million other former Soviet citizens who are not members of the titular nationality live in the "near abroad," the territory formerly in the Soviet Union that was previously in the Russian Empire. This number is 10 times greater than the number who left in any previous out-migration of Russians. The number of elite emigres in tsarist Russia and of White Russians after the Civil War in 1918–1921 was modest in comparison. The 20 million "Russians abroad" comprise nearly a

---

9. Those called "White Russians" in the Civil War of 1918–1921 should not be confused with Belarusians, the people living in Belarus. The prefix *belyi* indicates a white color in the Russian language.

10. It is interesting to note, however, that some national republics, such as Tatarstan, insist on listing nationality in their passports so that they do not lose their national identity.

fifth of all Russians in the world. The widespread territorial dispersion of Russians into the homelands of other nations resulted from the Soviet policy of trying to create "homo Sovieticus"—Soviet [wo]man. The Soviet leadership hoped to establish a melting pot in the Soviet Union, similar to the one in the United States. Both before and after World War II, the Slavic population was directed to national republics through organized labor migration. In this way, the Russian language (which was obligatory in every school, though it existed only as the language of secondary and higher education in most republics) was supposed to integrate titular nations into a Soviet identity through constant contact with ethnic Slavs who spoke the language. This policy was not successful. In most cases, birth rates were much higher for the titular nations than for the ethnic Slavs. Gradually, all non-Slavic titular nations began to push Russians out, even in the Soviet era.

After the collapse of the Soviet Union, Russians living in non-Slavic territories found themselves in an entirely new situation: formerly the chief representatives of the Soviet Empire, they were suddenly a national minority with an uncertain future. When new nation-states emerge or countries change their borders, population demographics always change. But for Russia, massive return migration of expatriates to their former homeland is a major problem. According to official statistics, from 1992 to 1996, roughly 4.5 million people immigrated to Russia from the successor states of the Soviet Union, and about a quarter of these were refugees seeking asylum. This pattern of return migration to Russia from its near abroad can be expected to continue for some years.

3.7 SUMMARY

With its vast territory, the Russian state has always been worried about how to integrate distant parts and diverse populations. As different territorial units gain more power, the former provinces of the central state become regions of the country controlled by local people. Power once centrally held in Moscow becomes spatially diffused and at least partly decentralized, thereby fostering democracy. The 89 subjects of the Russian Federation have become 89 actors added to Russia's economic and political life. This diffusion of power outward and downward is an ongoing process reshaping the entire economic, social, and political landscape in Russia. Different people are beginning to be major organizers of this landscape—no longer only a few central authorities as in the past.

Russia's territories vary tremendously in the sizes of their populations and territories, in their natural resources, in their economies and level of economic development, in their access and openness to other parts of Russia and to the rest of the world, and in the nationality (ethnicity) of their inhabitants. The primary historical legacy of Russia was that as an empire, it incorporated numerous different nationalities and their homelands, which it has claimed to be the Russian homeland. In most cases, nationality problems are regional in character because most members of the various nationalities are not widely dispersed but still live mainly in their traditional homelands. In principle, regionally based nationality problems can be solved democratically. The use of force only adds to the grievances over the historical injustices done to small nationalities in Russia. Chechnya is just one of the most vivid examples of how regional nationality problems can, however, become a major problem with international consequences.

A new problem for Russia—the millions of Russian nationals living in Russia's near abroad, the other successor states of the USSR—may eventually help Russians to become more tolerant of members of other nationalities than in the past. In any case, return migration to Russia of this Russian diaspora is a painful process with a multitude of consequences, few of which are clearly positive.

CHAPTER 4

Power and Politics

4.1 EMERGENCE OF THE NEW STATE[1]

Although the Russian nation has a 1,000-year history, the new Russian state is among the world's youngest. Since its political system has undergone substantial change in recent years, the next few decades will surely bring further, significant political change at a greater rate than in old, established states, such as the United States. In such a politically dynamic situation, it is useful first to review the key events and processes that have contributed to Russia's political system existing when this book was finished in the first days of the year 2000.

The fall of an empire in the absence of any military defeat or natural catastrophe represents a highly unusual historical event. What precipitated the collapse of the Soviet Union, one of the world's two great superpowers? How did the Soviet Empire collapse so rapidly and without force? Two basic factors contributed to its fall: a slow downward spiral in economic productivity, and the loss of faith in Communist ideology among the Soviet elite. The second was not independent of the first. Abandonment of communism as an ideology occurred precisely for reasons foreseen by Lenin: "Communism will win when it provides a higher standard of living than capitalism." Since the social system built by the Bolsheviks did not do this, Communist ideology was doomed. The question was how long the Soviet party-state could last after faith in communism was lost.

Did Russians want Russia to be a separate country or to lose the Soviet Empire? Few ordinary Russian people ever imagined it could happen. The match was ignited when the newly elected CONGRESS OF PEOPLE'S

---

1. For a good account of politics in the new Russia, see Urban et al. (1997).

66

DEPUTIES of the Russian Soviet Federated Socialist Republic (RSFSR) of the Soviet Union declared Russia to be a sovereign state on June 12, 1990. It was only a matter of time for the fires of independence to spread and for the USSR to vanish from the map. Thus, the new Russian state emerged within the old Soviet Union.

Yeltsin's team, which masterminded the events that led to the new Russian state, may not have foreseen the outcome of their actions. His team had a limited goal: to oust Gorbachev from his position as leader of the USSR. In a clever move, Yeltsin ran for president of the RSFSR in the June 1991 election and won with 71.5 percent of the votes. He thereby became the first person in history to be elected to the top office in Russia. As ideological doubts and internal conflict became widespread among the top echelons of the party-state cadres, Yeltsin was increasingly able to separate the government of the RSFSR from the government of the USSR.

A key event was the coup d'etat in August 19–21, 1991, organized by a handful of top Soviet leaders but also supported by much of the apparatus of the CPSU. This move was aimed at stopping Gorbachev from changing the Soviet Union to a federation of states, which he was on the verge of doing in order to try to halt the loss of the Soviet "inner" empire. Yeltsin's electoral success two months earlier gave him the legitimacy to block this coup d'etat. Gorbachev kept his leadership position, but his political power was seriously weakened. Actual power within Russia was in Yeltsin's hands.

After the thwarted coup d'etat, the central apparatus of the CPSU was in a daze. Anti-communism, though it arose as a viable movement only at the tail end of the Soviet era, managed to dismantle the party-state system with amazing speed. In December 1991, only months after the failed coup d'etat, Mikhail Gorbachev resigned as the head of the USSR, and the Soviet flag over the Kremlin was lowered. With a simple radio and television announcement by Gorbachev, the USSR had ceased to exist.

The **modern nation-state** of Russia had begun to exist officially and to gain international recognition as a new and independent country. Soon all other Soviet republics were independent and internationally recognized countries, too.

In March 1992, the Russian Federation Treaty was signed by most of the autonomous republics within Russia. Bilateral treaties with the Russian Federation gave these republics considerable autonomy and lay the foundation for a more decentralized, if not yet democratic, Russian state.

Yeltsin, as the father of the new Russian state, had the nearly complete support of the people in the beginning. Although Russia still had most of the political structures and features of the old RSFSR of the Soviet Union, Yeltsin installed a government headed by reformers who wanted democracy and a market economy. Initially no one openly challenged the notions of democracy and a free market as the key elements of the ideological foundation for the new Russian state.

At first Yeltsin's team recruited new members to important political positions from various sources. Not surprisingly, however, people who had no previous experience in government administration (some of whom mainly gave lip service to democratic slogans) turned out to be ineffective builders of the new state. Soon opposition to Yeltsin's new government developed, and a large majority of the members of the Supreme Soviet of Russia (the parliament at that time) began to block actions of President Yeltsin and his government.

In October 1993, the situation came to a head when Yeltsin ordered troops to storm the White House where the Supreme Soviet sat. This brief but bloody conflict was a struggle for power among Russia's top political elite. Few external pressure groups were involved. Further, in 1993 most people in Russia were in a desperate situation; survival was their main concern.

At that time, economic conditions of ordinary people were desperate due to the "shock therapy" that Yeltsin's team had introduced, and hatred of his government was understandably widespread. Nevertheless, Yeltsin's power remained very strong because his opponents were unable to organize an effective movement to oppose him. His team drafted a new constitution for Russia, which established a new political regime with an extremely strong president. The draft was approved in a popular referendum in December 1993. However, convincing evidence that Yeltsin's team doctored the vote later came to light (White et al. 1997).

In the same election, people chose the members of a new Federal Assembly, which replaced the Supreme Soviet, which Yeltsin had dismissed after his troops had stormed the White House. The Federal Assembly was created to exist for only two years until the Duma, the lower house of parliament established by the new Russian Constitution, came into being. To the astonishment of most political analysts, the political bloc supporting Yeltsin failed to win a majority of the seats in the new Federal Assembly in the December 1993 election. The main winner was Vladimir Zhirinovsky, whose nationalistic Liberal-Democratic Party (LDP) got the most votes, 23 percent. The LDP did much worse in the 1996 election of the Duma, indicating that its success in 1993 largely represented a protest vote against Yeltsin's government, and not a vote for Zhirinovsky and his CHAUVINISTIC platform.

Yeltsin's confrontation with the Supreme Soviet in 1993 began an important change in the electoral process. When the USSR collapsed, there were no organized political blocs or parties (except the Communist Party), and the electorate voted mainly for the names and faces of familiar individuals. But after the White House was stormed in October 1993, power groups began to organize and become consolidated. The basis of these groups varied.

The ideological backbone of democratic and market reforms came from the INTELLIGENTSIA, who strongly supported Yeltsin's team in 1991. Political newcomers from the intelligentsia soon withdrew their support from Yeltsin, however, as they became disillusioned with his authoritarian political ways and with the hardships resulting from marketization. A popular saying among the intelligentsia was: "Everything the Communists said about communism was false, but everything they said about capitalism turns out to be true."

The **forces supporting reforms** in the late 1990s are largely new groups created by marketization. Foremost are those who have benefited from marketization. The new class of owners and businesspeople is a small but formidable force with extensive resources and substantial power (Colton 1996; McFaul 1997). Within only a few years, marketization in Russia has led to an enormous concentration of private capital in the hands of banks and a few tycoons. These wealthy organizations and individuals have emerged as major independent actors backing reforms. In 1996, Yeltsin managed to be elected to a second term as president only with their support. Initially members of this group aimed for a weak government and a society with few regulations, but soon their primary interest and goal became stability. Stability and political power would protect their newly won gains and statuses. Indeed, members of this group participated in the 1999 parliamentary elections and won seats in the Duma.

A second force supporting reforms is the state bureaucracy. This group, crucial throughout Russia's history since Peter the Great, was put in a very vulnerable position by the collapse of the Soviet Union. Yeltsin's team quickly realized, however, that a modern state cannot be run without experienced and effective bureaucrats. Consequently, much of the former Soviet bureaucracy was gradually incorporated into the new Russian state. Because state bureaucrats survived as a group, and not just as individuals, they not only adapted easily to the new situation but actively began to use it to their own advantage. In a sense, they were the group closest to the property of the Soviet state and were in a nearly ideal position to use the state apparatus to their own advantage. The ability of state bureaucrats to act collectively and to serve their own self-interest had been severely limited by the Soviet party-state because their counterparts in the CPSU were constantly looking over their shoulders and were ready to criticize them for any wrongdoing. In contrast, the bureaucrats in every institution in the weak, emergent Russian state, with its new ideology of profit maximization, readily found ways to make money from their official positions, and no longer was there an institution that closely watched and controlled what they did. Thus, self-interest has prompted state bureaucrats to be one of the driving forces behind marketization and privatization in Russia.

Russia's regional administrative units are a third force supporting democratization and marketization. For the first time in Russian history, the leaders of Russia's republics and oblasts are in charge of their own localities. Since they are represented in the upper house of Russia's parliament, the FEDERATION COUNCIL, their political voice is even stronger than would be true if they governed only their own localities. As part of the parliament, they have a chance to champion regional interests at the highest level of the Russian state. As an organized state institution, they are a potent political force. Some members of this force (e.g., the leaders of Moscow, St. Petersburg, Sverdlovsk and Nizhniy Novgorod oblasts, Tatarstan republic) are very influential because they represent many people and formidable economic power. In addition, in the election of named individuals to the Duma (half of its seats), members of local elites gained more than half of the individual seats in 1999. A few OLIGARCHS, such as Abramovich and Berezovsky, managed to buy voter support of the elites in areas occupied by small nationalities. But overall it was an important change as compared with the situation in the previous elections of the Duma, when most candidates were able to ignore local elites.

A fourth force is comprised of small businesspeople and others employed in the private sector who are doing relatively well and have a higher standard of living than in Soviet times. It is the largest and most rapidly growing segment of the population supporting marketization.

But there are also two important **forces against market reforms.** One consists of the people who have lost a great deal and whose life strategy is survival. These unfortunate and unhappy people are a target for manipulation by various chauvinistic and conservative actors.[2] It is incorrect to imagine that restoration of communism is the basic goal of the Communist Party in the Russian Federation. Rather, the Communist leaders want to use malcontents as the political base for their party. This constituency pushes them to be less socialist. In reality, most Communists in the Duma would gladly change their party's name and champion a socialist platform if it would help them regain more of their former power. They are well integrated into Russia's political establishment and want to remain there.

A second and much more dangerous group is the defense establishment, including the corps of military officers and the managers of enterprises in the defense industry. They, in addition to Russians returning to Russia from the other Soviet successor states, are a strong force that favors restoration of the previous empire. A Russian nation-state is neither big enough nor powerful enough to satisfy them. They are influential not only because of their political and material resources but also because of the ideals they offer to people: Many Russians remain nostalgic about belonging to a grand and imperial state.

All of these interest groups are contending with one another in a difficult and uncertain terrain. In such a volatile situation, all rational actors seek short-term gains that fit their immediate interests. Russia is a country where short-term gains are overvalued, and very few consider long-term success. Thus, the political process in Russia is dominated by group interests and has little sense of the general welfare as a common cause.

---

2. In the new Russia, "conservative" means a preference for the old Soviet system.

4.2 THE NEW STATE: DEMOCRACY OR NOT?

In December 1993, a new Russian Constitution was approved by Russia's voters. It established Russia as a federal republic with a president as head of state. As mentioned in Chapter 3, substantial powers are granted to Russia's 89 smaller political-administrative units: its 21 republics, six krais, 49 oblasts, two federal cities, 10 okrugs, and one autonomous oblast. In the United States, the people delegate powers to the federal and state governments. But in Russia, it is the other way around: The central government grants powers to localities and people. The division of power between the center and regional subunits is an important way that democracy is starting to develop in the new Russia. De facto this sharing of power between the center and regional subunits had already begun in the last days of the Soviet Union. The 1993 constitution and subsequent bilateral treaties of the Russian Federation with regional units established this division de jure. As a result, the heads of local areas are elected by and responsible to their local constituencies.

Is the New Russian State a Democracy?

Political science uses three main criteria to decide if a state is democratic. First, are key officials elected by the people? Second, are political powers divided, especially among the executive, legislative, and judicial branches of the state? Third, are laws supreme? By these criteria, neither tsarist Russia nor the Soviet Union was even faintly democratic. The new Russian state has taken important steps on the road to democracy, but it does not yet meet all three criteria.

The introduction of elections into Russia's political system has been very successful. Not only Russia's top leaders, but also heads of major cities, are elected to their offices. The election of leaders of republics and oblasts by their populations represents a revolutionary change in the character of the Russian state. Under both the tsars and the Soviet regime, provincial heads were chosen by and represented central authorities. Although many fewer public officials are elected to office in Russia than in the United States, the electoral principle has been widely introduced and readily accepted by the Russian people. This innovation is crucial to the development of democracy in Russia.

The new Russian state does not satisfy the second criteria for a democracy nearly as well as it does the first. It misses being democratic because of the character of the 1993 constitution as well as its implementation. This constitution officially establishes three separate branches of the state (executive, legislative, and judicial), but it does not balance their powers. For the drafters of the 1993 constitution, the major task was to consolidate Yeltsin's power; a system of checks and balances of powers was of less concern.

According to the 1993 constitution, Russia's chief executive is its president, who is directly elected by the people. He has greater powers than the head of any other ostensibly democratic country. He nominates a prime minister (in Russian, literally the "chairman of the government"), who is to be confirmed by the Duma. However, if the Duma rejects the president's nominee three times in a row, then the president has the right to dissolve the Duma and call new parliamentary elections. Ministers of the government are responsible to the president, and he can dismiss them at any time. In other words, executive powers are concentrated in the hands of the president. If he chooses, he can even rule by decree and circumvent the legislative rights of the Duma. Thus, the office of Russia's president has an exceedingly strong position structurally, whatever the personality of the person occupying this office (Lijphardt 1984).

The Russian parliament is comprised of two houses: the Duma (lower house) and the Federation Council (the upper house). As in many other countries, the lower house is the primary holder of legislative powers. The Federation Council reviews the legislation passed by the Duma.

The Duma has 450 members who have four-year terms, and all of whom are chosen in elections. Half are directly elected by specific constituencies. The other half are elected according to the votes for various political parties. If a political party does not receive at least 5 percent of the votes, its nominees are not allowed to sit in the Duma. The 225 seats in the Duma for the nominees of political parties are allocated among the political parties with at least 5 percent of the votes; each such party is given a fraction of these 225 seats in proportion to the number of votes that the party received in the election.

The Duma's collective legislative powers do not even approach the president's executive powers. President Yeltsin vetoed many of the laws passed by the Duma. Only once has the Duma, together with the Federation Council, managed to overcome a presidential veto. The president's substantial powers have de facto made the Duma a forum for discussing (and complaining) rather than for passing legislation. The main exception has been the confirmation of the annual state budget by the Duma, which it has managed to do.

The upper house, the Federation Council, was initially chosen by a very complicated system; this system has changed somewhat over time and is still rather complex. In the late 1990s, most of its members are the locally elected heads of the 89 second-tier political-administrative units of the Russian Federation: the republics, krais, oblasts, and the two federal cities (Moscow and St. Petersburg). Its basic function is to vote on legislation passed by the Duma and to serve as the official representative of local areas. The Federation Council meets periodically and not on a day-to-day basis. Since its members are elected primarily to govern locally, the sessions of the Federation Council are brief, just long enough to perform their basic functions.

In Russia, the law is still very much a declaration that can be "improved" at any moment if it does not suit those having real power (in particular, the president). There is a Constitutional Court whose function is to adjudicate issues involving conflicts involving constitutional issues. However, law and law enforcement institutions in the new Russian state are heavily politicized and do not serve as a third power that counterbalances the executive and legislative branches of the Russian state (see also Chapter 8).

Figure 4.1 gives a pictorial description of the main features of the new Russian state. For comparative purposes, consider the analogous pictorial description of the Soviet state in the 1980s given previously in Figure 2.1.

FIGURE 4.1

Russian State: Institutions and Power Relations

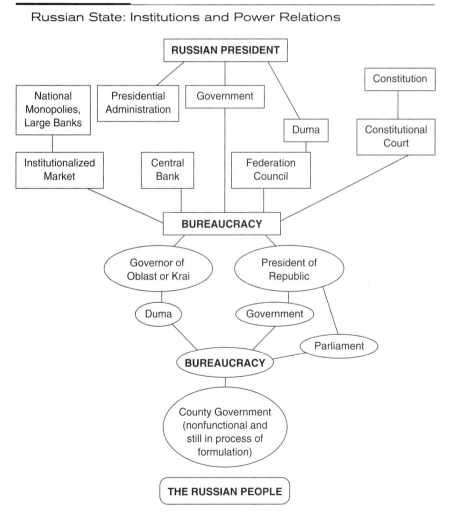

☐ —indicates national level
◯ —indicates local level

4.3 POLITICAL PARTIES AND OTHER POLITICAL INSTITUTIONS

Every stable modern society has not only a formal political structure but also political institutions and norms that shape political behavior and the course of political events. These institutions include elections, political parties and movements, the mass media, and a state apparatus (i.e., a civil service or state bureaucracy). Members of a society almost always work to achieve their political aims within the confines of existing political institutions, except when they believe this is impossible.[3]

The establishment of **elections** as the foundation of democracy is perhaps the key political institution in the new Russian state. The 1993 Russian Constitution holds supreme the right of citizens to elect their own political representatives.

To date, the percentage of official positions filled by election is smaller in Russia than in the United States. Elections are mainly used to fill the top positions at the federal and second-tier levels of the government (i.e., republic, krai, etc.). At lower administrative levels, elections are still rare, and appointments are the norm, as is also the case in many West European countries. The Russian state is too weak to put more state officials through the test of voter approval. Still, Russian elections in the 1990s have been used more widely and have involved less fraud than in most of the other 14 successor states of the USSR.

Free and open elections were the culmination of Gorbachev's policy of GLASNOST (open discussion). The Russian people warmly embraced this new method of political participation when it was initially offered. Rates of voter participation were extremely high in the first free elections of the Congress of People's Deputies in 1989, of regional deputies of the Russian Federation in 1990, and of the president of the RSFSR in June 1991. Nearly 80 percent of the electorate voted in these elections.

In these early free elections, most candidates were prominent, charismatic figures, and voters mainly elected those who were best known. When many elected officials turned out to be highly self-interested and to use their position for private gain, voters became disillusioned. Voter turnout fell to levels typical of Western democracies, with roughly half of eligible voters participating in federal elections, and a fourth or fewer in local elections. Those who did vote began to pay attention to elected officials' performance in office. For example, Moscow's mayor Yuri Luzhkov has proved to be exceptionally effective, and citizens of Moscow have responded by electing him by sizable margins in two elections with large turnouts.

---

3. For example, a movement of REFUSNIKS who operated outside of Soviet political institutions was sparked by the fact that the Soviet regime provided no legal basis for noncommunist political forces to participate in the political process (Sakharov 1975.)

It is not surprising that voters picked well-known public figures in the early Russian elections. For the first few years, there were no political parties, except the Communist Party, as we mentioned earlier. Further, the Soviet party-state had, to say the least, discouraged the formation of any organized political movements. Personality politics often occurs early in the development of democracy and electoral politics. After the first few elections, personal alignments among both the winners and the losers led to the formation of infant political parties. Remarkably, however, only once did Yeltsin directly align himself with a political movement or political party in his extended struggle to gain and retain power.

Party Politics

The 1993 elections of the Federal Assembly revealed a clear change in how support for various candidates was organized. Some new political parties and election blocs were established and became serious contenders for power throughout the country. There were also many so-called phone booth parties—parties so small that their members are jokingly said to be able to meet in a telephone booth. Some of the parties organized in 1993 continued to be active in the 1996 elections, but others nearly vanished from the Russian political scene. The picture changed again, and radically, in the December 1999 elections of the Duma. It is not unusual for the names and platforms of the leading political parties to change rapidly in newly emerging democracies, as well as for new parties to emerge and existing ones to wither away.

Political scientists generally distinguish political parties by their party platforms, placing them and their supporters on some political spectrum, either to the left, right, or center. In a society with over 70 years of totalitarian rule, in which only one party and one ideology were allowed, new political parties developed out of pressure groups and spent some time trying to find their bedrock supporters. Table 4.1 summarizes some basic facts about political movements and political parties in Russia in the 1990s, which are discussed in more detail below.

Although some former Soviet republics outlawed the Communist Party after the USSR ceased to exist, the leaders of the new Russian state allowed the **Communist Party of the Russian Federation (CPRF)** to survive. This act of seemingly tolerant benevolence was actually a calculated political tactic to let the new government handle challenges from the left by threatening to outlaw the CPRF. This tactic made all leftist and left-center parties vulnerable to public opinion and placed Yeltsin's government in the political center in Russia.

In spite of its negative legacy, the CPRF has had inherent advantages over all other political parties in Russia. From the beginning, the CPRF had infrastructure, organization, and party workers, even in the most remote provinces. It also owned a great deal of property (buildings and so on) and controlled numerous bank accounts. These organizational

CHAPTER 4

TABLE 4.1

Russian Political Parties and Blocs in the 1990s

Name of Party or Bloc	Leading Figures	Platform/Voter Appeal	Percentage of Votes in Parliamentary Elections		
			Dec. 1993	Dec. 1995	Dec. 1999
Communist Party (CPRF)	Gennady Zyuganov	Left of center; socialist-Communist; strives to rouse voter discontent	12.4	22.3	24.3
Russia's Democratic Choice	Yegor Gaidar	Proreform; pro-Western; antimilitary	15.5	—	—
Liberal Democratic Party	Vladimir Zhirinovsky	Far right; extreme nationalism; chauvinism	22.9	11.2	6.0
Our Home Russia	Viktor Chernomyrdin	Right of center; Yeltsin's supporters		10.1	—
Yabloko (Apple)	Grigory Yavlinsky	Strongly advocates market reforms at a faster pace than Yeltsin's government	7.9	6.9	5.9
Fatherland— All Russia	Yuri Luzhkov, Yevgeny Primakov	Anti-Kremlin stand; moderate democratization and marketization			13.3
Unity	Vladimir Putin	None; backs Putin			23.3
Union of Right Forces	Anatoli Chubais, Yegor Gaidar	So-called democrats			8.5
Women of Russia	No key figure	Advocates moderate economic reforms and more social programs; prowomen	8.1	4.6	—

Note: A blank denotes the party or bloc did not exist at the time of the election; a dash (—) indicates the party or bloc did not achieve the 5 percent threshold.

advantages made it the only party with any kind of strength in the early years of the new Russian state. Consequently, the CPRF was highly successful in the first three parliamentary elections (1993, 1995, and 1999), despite its awful legacy from the past. Not only did loyalists to the old Soviet regime turn out to vote for its candidates, but the CPRF captured a significant fraction of the protest vote against Yeltsin's government.

The CPRF received 12 percent of the votes in 1993, 22 percent in December 1995, and 24 percent in December 1999 (see Table 4.1). The gain in voter support for the CPRF occurred within the context of the economic failures of Yeltsin's policies. In the long run, voter support for the CPRF will almost surely shrink for three reasons. First, its constituency and elected representatives are comprised mostly of older people. Unless it can recruit younger people, its supporters will slowly decline in numbers as time passes. Second, as more people in Russia start to achieve an adequate standard of living and advance beyond the struggle for survival, the vote for the left will almost surely diminish. Lastly, the development of other parties has given the CPRF competitors, weakened its claim to a privileged political position, and cost it some voter support. Still, the CPRF continues to dominate the left of the political spectrum in Russia. As yet, no social-democratic party similar to those in most West European countries has emerged to rival the CPRF's appeal to voters with leftist orientations.

The early Yeltsin administration experimented with party associations. In the 1993 elections to the Federal Assembly, Prime Minister Yegor Gaidar organized a movement known as **Russia's Choice** (later, Russia's Democratic Choice). Although Gaidar's movement was able to draw on numerous resources, it failed in elections because his reforms were extremely unpopular among ordinary people, who had lost a great deal economically. In the elections to the Duma in December 1995, the movement did not win 5 percent of the seats, the fraction necessary for a party to be represented in the lower house. Many individuals who were elected as individuals and who had previously pledged their loyalty to the Russia's Choice party dropped out after the party's poor showing in the December 1995 election. In the 1999 parliamentary elections, the bloc representing market reformers managed to have 8 percent of the vote. This result is not bad considering the numerous failures of the reforms they had supported in the past. The price paid by this bloc for this election result was open support of war in Chechnya in 1999.

Shortly before the December 1995 elections, Prime Minister Viktor Chernomyrdin led another attempt at organizing a political party called **Our Home Russia** (**NDR,** its initials in Russian). This new election alliance was very well financed and backed by hundreds of national and local politicians. But it also did not perform as well in the elections as had been expected, garnering 10 percent of the vote. Altogether it got 72 of the 450 seats in the Duma. In the 1999 elections of the Duma, this party failed to pass the threshold of 5 percent of the votes and is likely to vanish from the political scene.

A few prominent figures outside the government and legislature have been able to establish parties. First, and surprisingly successful, was Vladimir Zhirinovsky, a very controversial figure. Just before the 1993 elections of the Federal Assembly, he capitalized on extremely strong feelings of Russian nationalism to organize the **Liberal Democratic Party**

(LDP) of Russia with a chauvinistic platform. In the 1993 election, the LDP got 23 percent of the votes, more than any other party. It was supported by protesters against Yeltsin's regime as well as by nationalists. It did reasonably well in the elections of the Duma in December 1995, amassing 11 percent of the vote. It has established itself as a viable force in most regions of Russia, getting votes in lower-level elections, too. However, as other parties have begun to strengthen their appeals to nationalists, support for the LDP has begun to wither. Zhirinovsky has begun to work with Yeltsin's government and to make normal political deals. Thus, while continuing to present himself to the public as a nationalistic leader of protest, he has actually become a regular member of the political establishment. Although the LDP was disqualified from the 1999 parliamentary elections, Zhirinovsky gave the election bloc a new name to get around this impediment and garnered 6 percent of the vote allowing the party to be represented in the Duma.

Grigory Yavlinsky, an economist who first served under Gorbachev, surprised many by helping to organize the reformist **Yabloko (Apple)** movement before the 1993 election of the Federal Assembly. This movement got 8 percent of the vote in this election, and 7 percent in the 1995 election of the Duma. By 1998, this party had begun to be competitive with the CPRF in public opinion polls. Yabloko poses a distinct alternative to Yeltsin's inner circle that also supports democracy and market reforms. Yavlinsky's avoidance of any association with Yeltsin won support for his party from reform-minded voters who disagreed with the current policies of Yeltsin's government. Yabloko is patiently waiting for an opportunity to salvage some of the original market reforms from total disaster. Yavlinsky made a significant political mistake in the context of the very dirty campaign for the 1999 parliamentary elections: He openly opposed the war in Chechnya. So-called market reformers immediately branded him a traitor. Tarred with this label, Yabloko managed to gain only 6 percent of the votes.

All of these political movements have established themselves as parties throughout Russia's regions. But except for the CPRF, they are significantly less influential outside Moscow. Local elections are influenced mainly by local elites. There are ongoing efforts to forge local elites into a single, powerful force operating at the federal level. Many regional leaders elected to the Duma in December 1995 have formed a political bloc (not a party) known as the **Regions of Russia.** Although regional elites have repeatedly tried to develop a truly effective countrywide political movement or party, they have not yet been successful.

In 1998, Moscow's mayor Yuri Luzhkov succeeded in forming an election bloc called **Fatherland—All Russia** encompassing the elites in major Russian regions. This bloc has two key attractions: Luzhkov's effective rule as Moscow's mayor and his opposition to Yeltsin and Russia's powerful economic oligarchs (see Chapter 5). In 1999, this electoral bloc was joined by Yevgeny Primakov, a recent and relatively successful prime minister as well as a leading political figure in the former Soviet Union. Under the leadership of these two prominent politicians, both known for their effectiveness, this electoral bloc had some promise to become the winner of the 1999 elections to the Duma. But in late 1999, Kremlin insiders used government-controlled media to slander this bloc. In the context of the success of Russian troops in Chechnya in fall of 1999, support for this bloc withered. This bloc got 12 percent of the votes in the 1999 elections of the Duma; it gained additional representation in the Duma through the successes of its candidates in individual elections.

The long-run future of Fatherland—All Russia is more uncertain. It seems more likely to be a onetime convenient alliance between two strong political personalities: Luzhkov and Primakov. But this in itself tells a story: Most political parties in Russia are still led by one charismatic leader, or occasionally two, and lack party organizations and stable constituencies. The exceptions to this rule are the CPRF, Yabloko, and the LDP, which have strong party organizations and well-defined constituencies.

Many important political processes in Russia occur outside of regular party politics. Access to the government has been crucial for newly rich Russians, especially bankers. Leading businesspeople were, and still are, involved in many political decisions to an extent beyond imagination in the United States. In Russia, a leading banker has served as Russia's vice prime minister and another as the deputy head of the National Council of Security. Without the support of Russia's new oligarchs, Yeltsin would not have been reelected as president in 1996.

The outcome of the presidential election in 2000 is fairly certain as this text is written. Though Kremlin insiders have isolated themselves from all other political forces, they have retained a powerful grip on the country. In late 1999, they seized the opportunity provided by Chechen warlords, who had caused a public outcry by their practices of taking hostages for ransom, raiding neighboring parts of Russia, and organizing terrorist activities against civilians in Moscow and other Russian cities. **Vladimir Putin,** Yeltsin's prime minister in late 1999, cleverly and carefully executed a military takeover of Chechnya, which de facto had been independent since 1996. Russia's military success in Chechnya caused Putin's ratings in opinion polls to skyrocket and gave the **Unity** bloc formed by Kremlin insiders considerable success in the December 1999 parliamentary elections. In this political climate, which was more favorable to Yeltsin than could have been imagined a half year earlier, Yeltsin resigned as president on December 31, 1999, and Putin became acting president. Yeltsin's resignation pushed forward to March 2000 the presidential election, which Putin won.

A powerful force in political processes is the **mass media,** especially television. During Gorbachev's policy of glasnost, journalists could objectively report on all events in the nation, and in the process, reveal secrets long kept from the people. Every day people could enjoy opening the newspaper and reading about actual events, unfiltered through party propaganda.

A Russian tradition remaining from Soviet times is that the end justifies the means, as long as the cause is right. This tradition was clearly manifested in the 1999 election campaign for the Duma, when the government-controlled media drummed away daily on the faults of the Fatherland—All Russia and Yabloko blocs. This blatantly overdrawn negative campaigning succeeded because there was only one major TV station not directly controlled by the Kremlin.

Russian television follows the European tradition in which news is mixed with newspeople's opinions, in contrast to the American tradition in which opinions are separated from descriptions of events. Some Russian newspapers still give full and accurate reports, but they no longer greatly influence national politics. In contrast, Russian television has a powerful influence on Russian politics, especially on the formation of public opinion. It has the potential to make or break even a leading politician.

For all practical purposes, control of nongovernmental television stations is in the hands of two media moguls, Boris Berezovsky and Vladimir Gusinsky. Berezovsky owns the main television station covering the entire country, another TV station, and three of the leading newspapers. He is a leading oligarch and a Kremlin insider. Berezovsky used every possible means to block alternatives to the Kremlin insiders' candidate for president because his leading position would be threatened if an anti-Kremlin candidate were elected.

Gusinsky, the other media mogul, supports anti-Kremlin forces. He owns a highly popular TV station, but it does not cover the entire country. This TV station is the only one not controlled by Kremlin insiders. Thus, Kremlin insiders control not only the state apparatus directly but indirectly almost all important media of communication. Their control of the media has been heightened by the establishment in 1998 of a state agency to oversee the media.

The Russian state itself is still being formed, and political institutions still evolving. Russia's political processes are also not yet fully institutionalized or democratized. The power of political parties is not yet firmly established. For democracy to be established, reforms of the civil service must occur and the careers of civil servants must be protected so that their own interests coincide with long-term welfare of the general public. Civil servants would then have incentives to act as guardians of the public interest. In the political situation in the late 1990s, the majority of the Russian people feel that they have no effective avenues for influencing government policy. If Russia is to be a real democracy, there need to be ways to counter people's feelings that the public is politically impotent.

According to Linz and Stepan (1996), democracy is possible only when the state is strong. Unfortunately, as Russia starts the new millennium, its state is very weak. Its weakness is a major hindrance to the development of democracy and effective political institutions in Russia.

4.4 SUMMARY

Although Russia has a long history, it is a very new state. Much more has changed than its name: A new state has truly been created. A Russian state emerged within the Soviet Union in 1991 when it was still formally called the Russian Soviet Federated Socialist Republic. The Russian state began to compete for power with Soviet state institutions. Indeed, after the collapse of the Soviet Union, some Soviet state institutions were incorporated into the Russian state, but most of these institutions were paralyzed by the loss of their previous power. Moreover, there were radical changes in the personnel of the formerly Soviet state institutions after they were incorporated into the new Russian state.

The development of a state is invariably a political process. As the first elected president in Russian history, Yeltsin initially had almost complete support from Russian society. He used it to start the controversial economic shock therapy recommended by Western economists and their Russian advocates. Liberalization of prices accompanied by high inflation and greatly slackened demand for the products of Russia's factories impoverished the Russian population and created sharp divisions among its politicians. This disastrous economic situation and the political conflicts it created led to an armed confrontation between Russia's Supreme Soviet and its president. Yeltsin solved this problem in a typically Russian way: He ordered troops to storm the White House where the Supreme Soviet sat. After this event, much of Russia's political elite opposed him. This confrontation hastened the referendum on the new Russian Constitution (ratified in December 1993) and the formation of a special Federal Assembly elected for a single two-year term. According to the new Russian Constitution, the president has sweeping powers that are not balanced by the parliament. Consequently, the principle of checks and balances has not been put into effect at the top of the Russian state. One must keep in mind, however, that a new state always needs time to start functioning well. In contrast, from this perspective the United States is an old state: Its major institutions have had 200 years of practice at checking and balancing one another's powers.

Russia's parliament consists of two houses: the Duma (the lower house) and the Federation Council (the upper house). As in Britain, the lower house has a broader range of legislative powers than the upper house. The Duma is elected directly by the citizens of Russia, partly as individual officeholders and partly by means of lists of candidates proposed by each political party. The Federation Council has seats for each of the 89 "subjects of the Russian Federation"—its 21 republics, six krais, 49 oblasts, two federal cities, 10 okrugs, and one autonomous oblast.

The 1993 constitution gave great power to the office of the president. As the constitution gives the president the right to nominate the prime minister and form a government, and as the Duma has the right only to confirm or reject the president's nominee for prime minister, Yeltsin managed to govern for the last seven years of his presidency without having the support of the majority of the deputies in the Duma or, according to public opinion polls, the majority of the population. Russia's political processes are still governed by weak rules and often proceed outside of the formal political institutions established by the constitution. Under Yeltsin, the Kremlin inner circle de facto governed the country through the presidential administration.

Democratization of Russian politics has proceeded through the emergence of its regions as major independent political actors. It represents a break with the centuries-old Russian tradition in which power is concentrated in the capital. Leaders of republics, oblasts, and krais have been elected by local populations and have begun to act on the bases of local interests. This decentralization of power has significantly changed political processes in Russia. For the first time in Russian history, local leaders are responsible to local constituencies.

Democracy requires fair elections. As the year 2000 starts, the new Russia has had six major elections: the 1993 referendum on the new constitution, three parliamentary elections, and two presidential elections. In the December 1993 referendum on the new constitution, there was substantial fraud, and questions were raised about the true number who voted. Major irregularities also occurred in the 1996 presidential election. But the old saying "it matters how you count the votes" seems largely to be part of the past. Another condition for democratic elections—exclusion of public funds from political campaigns for elections—has been neglected so far. Incumbent officials, following Yeltsin's example, have used their positions and public funds to gain reelection.

In a democracy, political parties are usually major actors in elections and in political processes more generally. As shown by the success of the Unity bloc in the December 1999 elections of the Duma, Russia's electorate can be manipulated rather easily to ignore established political parties and blocs and to shift direction and vote for an unknown political movement. It means that political parties in Russia still lack stable constituencies. Only the Communist Party has deep roots and the legs necessary to carry its message to voters. Also well organized are Yabloko, led by the reformer Yavlinsky, and the notorious (and chauvinistic) Liberal Democrats, led by Zhirinovsky. Other political movements and parties rely primarily on popular figures, the mass media, and public rallies to try to garner support. The presidential election in 2000, which Putin won, starts a new era in Russia, but whether it will bring a better way of life for ordinary Russians is not yet clear.

The Russian state is still in the process of being formed, and it is still run by state bureaucrats. The conversion of state bureaucrats to civil servants who are loyal to the state and to the public welfare is still a distant prospect. As the millennium closes, a majority of the Russian people believe that they have no effective way to influence state policies. Sadly, their perception is still largely correct, but the people do have choices in presidential and parliamentary elections. This is a significant step on the road to democracy for a country with totalitarian rule until a few years ago.

CHAPTER 5

The Economy
and Market Reforms

Throughout history, Russia's economy has failed to realize the great potential stemming from its vast natural resources. During the Soviet period, Russia developed enormous military-industrial power that rivaled that of the United States. The collapse of this gigantic military machine, which consumed at least a quarter of the USSR's GROSS NATIONAL PRODUCT (GNP), left fragments of a countrywide economy unable to meet the needs of Russia's population, at least in the short run. Its weak infrastructure, underdeveloped service industry, and substandard level of living were not an adequate basis on which to develop an economy with a unified market.

The analyses of the Russian economy in this chapter focus on the basic problems faced by this gigantic country. It seems to be on the road to a market economy, even if the precise endpoint is still uncertain. Russia's economic road depends on the choices of its leaders and people, as well as on its human and natural resources and its previous economic history.

The foremost problem for every country is to understand that there are **choices.** Becoming wealthy almost always requires hard work, but many people are willing to work hard. The result of hard work depends on choices of how to use available opportunities. These choices are not always made consciously, let alone wisely. Intelligent choices, especially of a country's leaders, have been crucial in the development of highly productive economies in many countries. Past choices help to explain why countries differ in their living standards, life expectancy, culture, and history. For example, despite a lack of natural resources, Singapore emerged from misery and became wealthy in a few decades because its political and business elites made wise choices.

Tsar Peter the Great, who modernized Russia in the eighteenth century after having been introduced to Western culture and values in the

Netherlands, made smart choices for Russia. His emulation of European technology and culture transformed Russia into a great power.

In contrast, the Communists who came to power in Russia in 1917 constructed a party-state that became a short-run world superpower (bought at a heavy human price), but they lost the long-run competition with Western market societies (Davies 1990). The Soviet elite under Gorbachev realized that change was needed but failed to make wise economic decisions. Their choices stemmed from ignorance of economic principles more than a lack of good intentions.

After the Soviet Union collapsed, the Russian elite could choose how to build a new country. After decades of living under a command economy, which gave no real understanding of a market economy, Boris Yeltsin's team decided to model the new Russia on Western market economies. The Western model seemed to be the only option because Russia's elite had no original plan for changing the economy to become more productive and more efficient.

But the really critical choices concerned which policies to adopt so that Russia could imitate the successes of Western market economies. Yeltsin's government chose policies based on MACROECONOMIC MARKETIZATION of the Russian economy.[1] In this basic approach, economic reforms start at the top—at the level of the central state. Two of the first acts were to create a replica of Wall Street in Moscow and to privatize the industrial assets of the Soviet state. This top-down approach gave the public very few ways to participate in the development of a market economy because land and small businesses were not transferred to the people.

In 1992, under the direction of Prime Minister Yegor Gaidar, the government removed controls on prices of most products but not on prices of Russian oil, gas, electricity, and other key primary resources. Russia's GNP as well as its industrial output declined sharply, overall by more than a half.[2] To see this more concretely, consider Table 5.1, which reports various areas of Russia's production in 1991 and 1996. The last column gives the 1996 level as a percentage of the 1991 level. Output of potatoes is higher in 1996 than in 1991, but production in all other areas fell. Where Russian products are of great international interest, such as natural gas, the decline was small. It was also small in areas, such as automobiles, where consumer demand was high due to former shortages and where foreign goods were too costly for most Russian buyers. On the other hand, in areas where cheap foreign goods could drive out Russian-made products (e.g., textiles, washing machines), production levels plummeted.

---

1. For an account of one of the advisors of Yeltsin's team, see Åslund (1995).
2. Here and below, *Goskomstat Rossii* (1992–1999) and Interstate Statistical Committee of CIS (1998–1999) are the sources for numerical estimates pertaining to the economy.

TABLE 5.1

Changes in Production in Russia in the 1990s

Product	1991 Level*	1996 Level*	1996 Level as a % of 1991 Level
Potatoes	34,330	38,529	112%
Natural gas	643	601	93
Automobiles	1,030	868	84
Electricity	1,068	847	79
Grain	89,094	69,310	78
Vegetable oils	1,165	880	76
Coal	353	255	72
Metals	55	39	70
Oil	462	301	65
Fertilizer	15	9	60
Fish	6,966	3,806	55
Paper	4,765	2,293	48
Concrete	78	28	36
Meat	5,815	1,887	32
Refrigerators	3,710	1,060	29
Milk	18,561	5,250	28
Plastics	529	135	26
Trucks	616	136	22
Textiles	7,619	1,401	18
Washing machines	5,541	760	14
Tractors	178	14	8
Television sets	4,439	310	7

* In millions. Quantities are measured in a variety of units but usually in tons.

Source: *Goskomstat Rossii*, 1998.

In less than a decade, the Russian economy lost much of its potential, and it was still deeply troubled as the twenty-first century began. As a result, Russia does not manage to be among the top 20 industrial countries in the world, even though it is sixth in population size. The top-down, macroeconomic approach created economic chaos and led to the impoverishment of most people. Economic survival, rather than development, has become the way of life for most people in Russia.

If Russian leaders had followed the historical examples of other nations, the transformation from socialism to capitalism could almost surely have been accomplished with much less pain and hardship. Throughout history, market economies have been built from the bottom up, engaging the majority of the people in the process. Through such an evolutionary process, Wall Street emerged as the most prominent institution integrating the American economy. Under the leadership of Deng Xiaoping, bottom-up economic developments also transformed China from a command economy to the fastest-growing market economy in the twentieth century. Chinese reforms began with a million rural communes that were given the right to control their own production and to sell their products. The transformation of China's urban areas and major areas of industrial production began later and occurred gradually.

The long-run results of Russia's approach to economic reforms are not yet clear. So far it is clear only that the top-down approach taken by Russia's leaders has benefited a few people enormously but has brought misery to the majority of Russia's population.

5.1 ORIGINS: THE SOVIET COMMAND ECONOMY[3]

To gain a greater understanding of the Russian reformers' options, one must consider the economy that Russia inherited from the Soviet regime: a **command economy.** This type of economy is an integral aspect of the Communist system. It is based on the principles of the elimination of individual freedoms grounded in private property and the absolute power of the state. These principles lead to the concentration of all natural, technological, monetary, and productive resources in the hands of the state.

In a command economy, resources are distributed through a state command structure of ministries, divisions, and work organizations (e.g., factories, retail stores, schools). In the Soviets' heyday, there were nearly a hundred ministries (or their equivalent), which covered all activity in a designated branch of the economy (i.e., an industry). For example, a single ministry was in charge of all factories in light industry (e.g., shoemaking, clothing manufacturing), from the Atlantic to the Pacific Ocean. This ministry planned production in its area and gave each plant detailed annual production goals.

For short-term breakthroughs, this system of economic organization was usually effective, especially when a lot of labor and other resources were readily available. It resulted in the rapid industrialization of the country and allowed the Soviet Union to create a defense industry that roughly equaled that of the United States by the end of World War II. It helped to concentrate resources on certain economic activities where breakthroughs were needed, such as the Soviet Union's nuclear weapons and space programs. It was especially effective in the defense industry, where Soviet successes were very impressive.

The command system allocated raw materials, labor, and technology that were needed for various targets of production. Even though fear

---

3. One of the best analyses of the Soviet economy is given by Nove (1986).

of punishment and some degree of patriotism motivated people's efforts during the first 40 years of the Soviet Union, this economic system managed to produce the first satellite in space (Sputnik) and a sophisticated hydrogen bomb before the United States. Money had a secondary role because a command economy operates without the need for enterprises to be profitable or efficient in order to survive. As long as fear and ideology succeeded in motivating people to work, money and salaries were also secondary sources of motivation for people to work.

Lacking profitability and efficiency as primary motivations, a command economy first estimates needs and then fixes supplies by state decree. There is a constant shortage of labor, products, and machinery because no human minds can accurately estimate all needs, let alone fully control what is produced and supplied. Hence, after the first extensive stages of development, when all underutilized workers and other resources have mostly been exhausted, a command economy becomes a **shortage economy,** so named by the Hungarian economist Janos Kornai (1980, 1992). A shortage economy is one in which virtually all basic raw materials, labor, and goods are in short supply relative to demand. In contrast, a free market economy works under the law of supply and demand. If demand for a certain kind of product is greater than the existing supply, the market reallocates resources so that more of the product is supplied; if demand is less than the existing supply, resources are reallocated so that less is supplied. This extremely fundamental principle was not followed in the Soviet Union or in any other Communist country with a command economy.

Under the Soviet command economy, factories and other enterprises had devised various informal ways to meet the production levels mandated by the state. They were, however, totally unprepared to compete for the demand of their products in a free market system. Marketization required a fundamental restructuring of all mechanisms of production. This statement does not refer primarily to the technological aspects of production but rather to the social arrangements by which goods are produced, distributed, and sold. In a market economy, every producer must make major efforts to sell its product (or service) and cannot assume that there is a demand for the product at any price. Every producer must try to reduce its costs of production, increase the quantity of the product produced, and adjust the price of the product so that what is produced can be sold at a profit. No Soviet manager needed to worry about these aspects of production. Soviet managers worried only about getting necessary resources and motivating workers to produce goods, despite working conditions that were often unfavorable.

The command economy created monopolies in most areas of production. Factories in each area were centrally commanded by some central state office or a ministry, which had been given the responsibility of overseeing that area and other related areas. Because there were so many

Mother, father, and child unloading the family car after returning from a weekend at their dacha *in the countryside where many urban residents grow extra food.*

shortages and bottlenecks in acquiring the raw materials needed to produce various goods, ministries tried to organize the economic activities involved in their specific area of production so that they would be nearly autonomous and independent of other ministries and local administrations. The ministries' successes in approaching autonomy resulted in the widespread proliferation of factory towns that still exist in Russia today. For all practical purposes, each ministry created its own social infrastructure with construction, services, and communication. The richer and more powerful ministries fully controlled their factory towns and supplied their labor force with everything needed for survival. Since salaries were officially equalized, the real inducements attracting more qualified workers to a particular ministry were a greater supply of apartments, plots of land, food, and other consumer goods in its enterprises and factory towns.

Under the command economy, all production units were actually **socioproduction units,** meaning that the usual divisions of work and personal life (including the freedom to choose a place to live and the quantity of goods desired) did not exist. Essentially, the lives of the hired labor force were organized by subunits of the major ministries. By all economic standards, this social infrastructure was extremely wasteful. Under market conditions, the corporation provides the above kinds of services very rarely and only in extreme conditions. Usually it happens only in mining in remote regions or in the defense industry, where such services are provided to help maintain secrecy. Consequently, marketization of the Soviet command economy led to the immediate elimination of these supply structures in most Russian factories.

An industrial society, by virtue of its mode of production, allowed a command economy to operate relatively effectively. Its command economy allowed the Soviet Union to develop heavy industry involving huge industrial giants that employed more than 200,000 people in one factory. It is worth noting that very large factories and factory towns are no longer a part of the American landscape. A POSTINDUSTRIAL, service-oriented society, however, has different kinds of consumer products and a different manner of production. A command economy is not flexible enough to face the new challenges thrown up by a postindustrial society. In a rapidly evolving postindustrial society, new products and production technologies continually appear and old ones change with amazing speed. Adapting to these changes requires flexibility. Only markets can successfully regulate the rapidly changing economy of a postindustrial society. Russia's industrial giants with huge capital investments in infrastructure are almost useless in such an economy. The Soviet command economy could not meet this new challenge, even though the Soviet labor force was highly educated and well qualified in many areas of production.

Reforming the command economy was a much more complex task in Russia than in Hungary or even Poland. The sheer size of both Russia's economy and territory was one major reason for the greater complexity of the task. In addition, the command economy, with the huge defense industry serving as its backbone, was more integrated into Russian society than anywhere else in the Soviet bloc. Finally, Russian agriculture was an unmitigated disaster as compared even to agriculture in Hungary and Poland, where agricultural production was also much lower than in West European countries. The fact that the Soviet command economy could not be reformed contributed importantly to the collapse of the Soviet Union and the breakdown of Russia's economic infrastructure. Russia has been trying to evolve into a modern, market-oriented economic power, but it has found this transformation exceedingly difficult to accomplish.

5.2 SHOCK WITHOUT THERAPY

In the late 1980s, as Communist regimes in East Europe began to fray at their edges, Western economic experts began to theorize about how a command economy could be switched to a market economy. Many experts, such as Swedish economist Anders Åslund (1995) and Harvard economist Jeffrey Sachs (1996), advocated "shock therapy," a comparatively rapid set of changes in state policies intended to lay the foundation for a market economy. They proposed the immediate introduction of market institutions and a Western-style legal framework in order to alter the character of the Russian economy rapidly and radically.

The Russian elite was prepared to deal with almost any difficulty except the transformation to a market economy. During the Soviet era, any kind of economic analysis of market systems was considered dangerous to the prevailing ideology, even as recently as the 1980s. As a result, Russia's elite lacked almost any theoretical understanding of market economies and their principles. The experiences of managers under the command economy also gave little practical guidance; they understood production but not marketing. Thus, both market experience and educated managers who could compete in a market were virtually nonexistent in Russia when the Soviet Union collapsed.

Russia's leaders largely accepted the recommendations of Western experts. The Gaidar government, which took charge early in 1992, utilized the concept of shock therapy to transform the Russian economy. There were five main aspects of this "therapy": price liberalization, establishment of a new convertible currency, PRIVATIZATION of state property, the development of a new tax system to provide the revenues that would fund the essential activities of a state (McFaul and Perlmutter 1995), and balancing of the state budget.

Price Liberalization

In a market economy, prices and supplies of goods and services rise and fall until supply and demand come into balance. If demand for a good increases relative to its supply, the price rises or producers try to produce more of the good until the demand matches the supply, or both occur. Contrarily, if demand falls relative to the supply, the price falls or producers cut back on production until supply and demand are equalized.

The best known mechanism for balancing supply and demand in a command economy is a BLACK MARKET, where market mechanisms set the prices for goods and services in short supply. Black market prices are higher than official prices, and their high level both stimulates some extra production of the good and reduces the demand for it at the black market price. Near the end of the Soviet era, many state factories participated in a gray market, exchanging goods and services with one another at prices close to the market value. Other unofficial mechanisms to balance supply and demand involve bartering (i.e., direct exchange) of goods and services and exchange of goods for favors, or for promises of future favors (Burawoy and Krotov 1992).

Naturally, the Soviet state sternly condemned all such unofficial, illegal mechanisms. Still, their surreptitious existence caused Soviet citizens to become accustomed to various illegal ways to get around laws and rules. The general population's widespread tolerance for such illegal practices in the past has consequences for modern Russia, where the potential gains from using illegal mechanisms to circumvent laws and rules greatly exceed those in the Soviet era.

Russia took its first step toward a market economy by removing state controls on prices on January 2, 1992, a week after Mikhail Gorbachev declared the dissolution of the Soviet Union. This step was designed to eliminate shortages of goods and services and simultaneously to legalize the black and gray markets that had arisen in the Soviet era. It achieved both goals, but it also had some serious, adverse side effects. As a Russian proverb says, "We wanted better, but it happened as usual: Worse!"

Prices of most goods and services rather rapidly tripled or quadrupled. Some increased tenfold. The state simultaneously doubled salaries. Simple arithmetic tells that if prices quadrupled but salaries only doubled, the real standard of living fell by half. The substantial decline in the standard of living is a very important negative consequence of price liberalization. A second harmful consequence of the economic changes was rampant inflation, which the Russian government could not bring under control.

A New Convertible Currency

The government introduced a new, devalued Russian ruble in July 1992, six months after price liberalization. Devaluation of the ruble did little to combat inflation. In the first five years, the value of the new Russian ruble relative to major Western currencies (e.g., the U.S. dollar, the German mark) fell to a thousandth of its original official value. Eventually the rate of inflation began to slow somewhat. Russia's currency was revalued again in January 1998, with the new ruble equal to a thousand of the old rubles. Initially a dollar equaled around six of the new rubles, but after further inflation, nearly 30 were needed to buy a dollar early in the year 2000. Thus, inflation was not stopped by currency devaluation, and it has steadily whittled away the buying power of ordinary Russians.

Privatization

Uncontrollable inflation resulted partly from the introduction of market rules while leaving Soviet monopolies intact. Many existing monopolistic producers arbitrarily raised prices on some key products to exorbitant levels. The government realized that something had to be done about these monopolies. Privatization was another major step taken to build a market economy. It began in August 1992. All citizens were given vouchers with which they could (in theory) participate in the privatization of the state's property. This policy did privatize much of the state's property, but it also had some detrimental results.

Importantly, this policy markedly increased the speculative purchase of state property by a few people.[4] The large majority of people raised under the Communist system did not know how to use the vouchers for personal gain. Most sold them cheaply, sometimes for a bottle of vodka. Most vouchers were bought by relatively few sharp operators, including some criminals who used them to launder money acquired in various illegal activities. The widespread, large-scale purchase of the vouchers was predictable (if unforeseen) because one person's vouchers had almost no value. After the purchasers of the vouchers had accumulated a great many of them, they used them in closed auctions to buy large amounts of state property. The illusion of the "people's privatization" did not last long, and its devastating results brought down the Gaidar government on December 14, 1992, less than a year after the Soviet Union had collapsed.

Even though the adverse consequences of this method of privatization were widely recognized, until autumn of 1997 state property continued to be sold behind closed doors, without even a veneer of public auctions. These sales of state property not only concentrated major economic assets in the hands of a few but also were ruinous for the state budget: The vouchers that the public had originally been given were used to purchase very valuable state assets at incredibly low prices. In this fashion, the state lost valuable properties but gained almost no money with which to replenish its coffers.

The darkest process in the marketization of Russia's economy also began in 1992: Ponzi schemes, which used fake banks and financial institutions to extract large sums of money from state organizations and the general population. A Ponzi scheme, which is similar to a pyramid scheme, works something like a chain letter; someone is promised a big return on an essentially worthless asset, which is purchased for a comparatively small sum of money that goes to those starting the scheme and other early "investors." Eventually the scheme collapses because the asset purchased is actually of little if any value. These schemes are, however, lucrative for the few people who initiate them or who join them early. After some time, when the Ponzi schemes in Russia ceased to be profitable to the few at the top of the chain, the false banks and financial institutions closed their doors and vanished, leaving the few much richer and the majority even poorer than before. The Ponzi schemes in Russia led to a huge public outcry. The Russian government dodged consideration of this issue, which led to questions about possible corruption at the highest levels of the government. The government's silence led the general public to be cynical (at best) about their new "democratic" government.

---

4. For a good analysis of this stage of development of transitional economies, see Burawoy (1997).

In 1998, Western financial leaders learned that even the Russian Central Bank had used a Ponzi scheme to extract money from them. To raise revenues, the Russian government had sold a series of short-term government bonds for about 40 billion dollars at steadily escalating interest rates that were clearly not sustainable. On August 17, 1998, the Russian government defaulted on these bonds, causing sharp declines in Western stock and bond markets, especially in the stocks of the large international banks that had bought these bonds.

Meanwhile, real commercial banks in Russia multiplied their assets in a way that is typical in a transitional economy. Money deposited in these banks was loaned at some interest rate, which was naturally very high due to the runaway inflation. Since ordinary people had few savings, deposits in commercial banks came mainly from state budgets of both the central government and various regional and local governments. Most borrowers were also governmental agencies and state organizations because few private individuals were in a position to borrow money from a bank.

When lending money to various governments and state organizations, the commercial banks required that state assets be used as collateral for the loans. State organizations had difficulty repaying their loans on time because government revenues were falling (e.g., because privatization did not generate much revenue and because taxes were being avoided). Demands on the state budget continued to be as high or even higher than in the past. Sometimes this situation led to more borrowing at even higher interest rates; at other times, the commercial banks foreclosed on the loans and took ownership of the valuable state assets that had been given as collateral. The most notorious bank to acquire state assets in this way was Onexim Bank, whose president was Russia's first vice prime minister for a brief period in 1996.

The state budget was transferred from Russia's private commercial banks to the state-controlled Sberbank only in 1998. For seven years, the state budget was the main source of growth for private commercial banks. The growth of these banks helped to drain state resources.

Taxation

In Soviet times, small, essentially symbolic taxes were deducted from all official salaries. Although all enterprises and organizations were owned by the state, they also paid the state an easily calculated tax. Consequently, the Soviet state developed no major procedures and institutions for establishing and collecting taxes. This meant that a new system of taxation had to be built from scratch in the new Russia. It took time to develop tax laws, and it took state resources and still more time to build the organizational infrastructure needed to collect taxes. A major new tax code was passed in 1993, but it took nearly five years to develop the concrete mechanisms needed to collect taxes in the new way. By 1997, only the shadow of an organization comparable to the U.S. Internal Revenue Service had begun to function.

While building the infrastructure for collecting taxes, the Russian government issued more decrees and passed additional tax laws. These actions were not surprising because the state had lost a great many revenue sources from privatization while it still owed huge sums for salaries of state officials and members of the military, for pensions for the elderly, for various other state-provided services, and lastly, but not least, for the interest on the loans that it had borrowed.

Although the continual passing of new tax laws is unsurprising, it too had adverse consequences. Since the tax code was seen as unstable, foreign investors were understandably wary of pouring capital into the Russian economy. Businesspeople are inherently risk takers, but not when the rules are constantly shifting. For many businesses, the easiest way to survive with a profit, especially under uncertain conditions, is to avoid taxes or at least to minimize them. To do this, many businesses in Russia have bribed various state bureaucrats so that they could get away with underreporting their income and thereby pay a smaller tax than they really owed. In 1997, fewer than five million individuals in Russia declared their income.

Avoidance of taxes helps private businesses and individuals to survive, but it keeps the state from having the revenues that it needs to function properly. Tax avoidance contributes to a truly vicious cycle of counterproductive economic actions. It is very hard to break this cycle.

Balancing the State Budget

Balancing the state budget may appear to require only parliamentary decisions and the determination of the government to keep revenues and expenses in balance. In reality, the task is much trickier. First a state must have revenues: It must collect taxes, duties on imports, and so on. As described above, development of a system of tax collection that is even remotely as effective as that in the United States will take a long time. In the meantime, Russian citizens and firms are better at avoiding taxes than at paying them, so this source of state revenues is comparatively small. Privatization and the sale of Soviet factories and properties offered the possibility of onetime augmentation of the state budget, but the way it was done also did not add much to the state budget, as explained previously. The net result is that income to Russia's state budget is tiny, roughly equal to that in Finland.

On the other side of the coin, it has also been hard for the Russian state to cut expenses. First of all, the state bureaucracy that Russia inherited from the Soviet Union is good above all at spending allocations received from the state and at exaggerating future costs. In Soviet times, fighting for a larger share of the budget was the most fundamental and important economic task for all enterprises and state offices. New, top-level people brought in by President Yeltsin's team lacked experience in managing budgets and finances. They were no match for the holdover state bureaucrats, who were highly experienced in fighting for bigger budgets. In addition, those in charge of Russia's monetary policies took care first with their own private interests and then declared about the common cause: stabilization of Russia's currency and budget. So projected expenses in all detailed budgets were grossly larger than state revenues, and the actual budgetary deficits at the end of each fiscal year were even larger than projected. The Russian state has tried to balance its budget by borrowing. But its delays and difficulties in debt repayment limit its ability to borrow more in the future in order to balance the state budget.

5.3 CREATION OF A PRIVATE SECTOR

The advice of Western economic experts concerning how to switch from a command economy to a market economy was centered on **what the state should do** to shed itself of its property and its direct control over the economy. But to have a successful market economy requires much more than that the state refrains from organizing the economy. There needs to be an effective private sector. Actors other than the state must take responsibility for producing, marketing, and transporting goods and services. The Gaidar government seems to have given little thought to this problem, perhaps assuming a private sector would arise naturally, like mushrooms popping up after a spring rain, or fall from the sky like manna from heaven.

To succeed with some economic activity, even in a country with a fairly stable economic environment like that of the United States, a person, group, or existing organization needs some capital, knowledge of the tasks involved in performing the particular economic activity, preferably some experience doing it, and some willingness and capacity to work hard. The last has not been in short supply in Russia. One would be basically correct in asserting that most working-age Russians are equally willing to work hard. In contrast, capital, knowledge, and experience have been in short supply and unequally distributed. Moreover, the need for capital, knowledge, and experience depends on the nature of the economic activity: its technological requirements, its social organization, and the location of its resources and markets.

When the Soviet Union collapsed, individual Russians had few savings or other real assets that could be considered economic capital, other than their own HUMAN CAPITAL—their minds and their muscles. Using world standards, Soviet citizens were poor in monetary terms and were relatively equal in other forms of capital. They typically rented a place to live (often from their employing organization) and owned some clothing, some furniture, and a few assorted personal goods (e.g., a TV, books). This kind of private capital is not a good basis for starting a business. The vouchers each person got in the state privatization scheme did not appreciably augment anyone's initial financial capital.

In theory, groups of individuals can pool their very limited individual resources to have sufficient capital to engage in some economic activities. Coordinated economic activity by a large group of individuals rarely happens, however, especially in an period of great uncertainty. It occurs mainly in families (leading to family businesses) and in situations where a few people have already worked together successfully and can agree to continue doing their old economic activity as a new private organization. In Russia, the latter happened to some degree, for example, when restaurants and small retail shops were taken over by their former employees. Privatization by former employees is unimaginable in many other contexts, such as mining operations and former Soviet factories with tens of thousands of workers.

The principal groups with the means to buy or to start a business in the new Russia were foreign businesses, managers of state-owned enterprises, and Russian criminals. That foreign businesses and Russia's underworld have become major economic actors in Russia should not surprise anyone because both had the necessary capital.

Individual Russians were less equal in their knowledge and experience with producing various goods and services than they were in their lack of money and property. Those with the most knowledge and experience relevant to profit-making economic activity were almost always the **former managers of Soviet enterprises.** Former managers had the advantage of knowing the Russian economic landscape and the people in key positions in the Soviet command economy, as well as the various technological and organizational facets of producing certain goods or services. They did not know much at all about marketing and finding customers for their products (which was never a problem in a shortage economy) or about adjusting prices and output to make a profit (which had been a heretical idea in the Soviet system) when faced with competitors. Moreover, their advantages were somewhat diminished because many of the new economic actors in Russia are different than those in the Soviet system. Still, former Soviet managers had many more opportunities than other Russians to either start new businesses or remain as managers in the new Russian economy.

Not surprisingly, quite a few former managers of Soviet enterprises not only retained managerial positions in their enterprises but were able to become their owners. A person could sometimes raise the necessary capital to acquire the enterprise that he or she had formerly managed, though not always by entirely legitimate means. There are numerous reports of how former managers, as well as some former state officials, used enterprise funds to turn the organization that they had headed or supervised in the Soviet system into a new market-oriented business. The most prominent example occurred when the former Soviet ministry controlling a substantial portion of the world's known gas reserves became the private company Gazprom. Privatization of these assets was done in a closed auction with the participation of the former head of the Soviet Gas Ministry, Viktor Chernomyrdin, who was also Russia's prime minister at the time of this auction. After Chernomyrdin ceased to be prime minister, he became head of Gazprom's board of directors.

Foreign businesses knew a lot about both production and marketing of the goods and services in which they specialized. Naturally, almost all of them lacked knowledge of the unique Russian context, and initially they did not have good local contacts. Still, foreign businesses were well positioned to take over many economic activities in Russia because they had both financial capital and the requisite knowledge to run various businesses successfully. The issue for foreign companies was whether, and how quickly, they could turn a profit in Russia.

In sum, there are two main points. First, the leading economic actors in marketization have tended to be former Soviet managers, foreign businesses, and the Russian underworld because they were the main initial groups with the financial capital, knowledge, or experience to develop profitable economic activities in many different areas. Second, the nature of the economic activity itself (its scale of operations, its potential market, its technological complexity, and so on) affects the way that the transition to a market economy has occurred.

For a more detailed consideration of Russia's economic transition, it is useful to distinguish the following **areas of economic activity:** retail trade and the provision of consumer services; light industry (production of consumer goods); extraction of primary resources (oil, metals); agriculture; heavy industry (e.g., production of steel; manufacturing of machinery); and defense. These six industries were in completely different situations when the Soviet Union collapsed, and their transition to a market economy has proceeded very differently.

A. Retail trade and consumer services (e.g., restaurants, retail stores, repair shops) were most easily converted to a market system. In the first place, these areas of economic activity were not organized as large monopolies in the Soviet period. Second, relatively little capital was needed to acquire and operate enterprises in this industry in a market economy. Finally, practice in simple exchanges and with basic services could provide the necessary expertise to engage in this economic activity. Hence, ordinary Russians had their best chance to be entrepreneurial in this economic area. Although the state was surprisingly slow to privatize shops engaged in retail trade and services, millions of Russians be-

The Old Arbat street in Moscow. A good place to walk, look, and shop.

came traders who buy and then resell various consumer goods. It has been the main entrepreneurial activity open to ordinary people.

The only serious problem in this industry has been criminal racketeering. Some people realized that it is even easier to extract protection money from real businesspeople than to operate a business directly. The protection money can be regarded as a kind of tax or insurance payment. Virtually all small entrepreneurs in Russia initially had to pay protection money to the criminal organizations that control their markets. Eventually local police (militia) units also began to collect protection money and either compete or collaborate with the criminals selling protection. The situation varies substantially across Russia's regions, but it makes operating a small business extremely difficult everywhere.

Some businesses have, however, restructured their organizations and been able to operate with a profit. Car dealerships offer a good example. Automobiles were in short supply in the Soviet era. With the opening of Russia's borders in 1991 came a flood of automobiles imported from the West. Individuals engaged in such importing were quickly pushed aside by larger dealers, who established import policies that fixed routes of import and prices for consumers. Conflicts soon arose among the official importers, local producers, and all unregulated dealers. As a result, import fees and rules were introduced, as well as other legal protection for official dealers. The automobile market began to be regulated by those who operated within it.

B. Light industry (e.g., manufacturing of wearing apparel; food processing) was also switched to the market economy fairly easily. Relatively little capital was needed for this transfer, and most markets were local (often due to their inaccessibility), furnishing local industries with some degree of protection from outside competition.

Initially numerous medium-sized factories were privatized with the intention of stopping production and using the factory buildings for other purposes. For example, banks acquired some medium-sized factories to have office space for the newly developing commercial sector. Soon, however, factories in light industry began to be acquired in order to produce for consumers in Russia. The main obstacle to success was a flood of cheap, low-quality imported consumer goods. Nonetheless, many local producers managed to outsell their foreign competitors because they produced for local markets and had a better idea what local consumers wanted.

One of the earliest and most successful was Russian designer Tom Kleim, whose pseudonym plays on the names of world-famous designers Calvin Klein and Tommy Hilfiger. Tom Kleim not only managed to become the best known designer in Russia, but also was successful in establishing specialty shops in many countries in West Europe.

Success was hard to achieve in some areas of light industry, especially those making products where a small number of firms usually dominate a single market spanning an entire country. Examples include producers of clothing, shoes, and hardware for homes. Ivanovo, a famous textile city of nearly a million people in Russia's Central region, had great difficulty in maintaining its dominant position in manufacturing textiles and clothing after large quantities of these goods began to be imported from China and other developing countries in Southeast Asia. Not many factories facing stiff foreign competition managed to survive.

The main problem for light industry in the near future is acquiring equipment, as well as the development of countrywide chains of distributors and retail stores. But products of light industries have become widely available in Russia's major cities, and many are locally made. There has even been some progress in the quality and quantity of food products grown and processed in Russia. Only Russia's retail trade and service industry has been more successful in the transition to a market economy.

C. Mining operations in Russia offer the potential for great profit in a market economy because Russia has the world's richest deposits of metals, minerals, and petroleum resources.[5] In the 1990s, however, most mining operations have not been profitable. (Some exceptions include

---

5. Russia provides the world market with nearly half of all diamonds and platinum, as well as several other rare minerals and metals. It also has nearly half of the world's known gas reserve.

Gazprom, the owner of the world's largest known reserves of natural gas, and Lukoil, the biggest oil producer.)

Because mining was concentrated in a few large monopolies in the Soviet period, it has not been easily converted into a private Russian business, let alone been purchased by the people working in this industry. Foreign investors have naturally been very interested in gaining access to Russia's buried treasures, and they have offered to provide capital for incorporating advanced technology in mining, as well as to buy the mines or shares in the mines.

For several reasons, Russia's large reserves of primary resources have not yet been tapped appreciably. First, the Russian government has been unwilling to give majority ownership of its valuable natural resources to foreign companies. Second, in the absence of an established and effective legal and judicial system, foreign investors regard large investments in Russia as very risky, especially in business deals in which they are minority partners. Not surprisingly, therefore, foreign investors' offers to incorporate advanced technology into mining have not yet noticeably improved mining operations. Finally, lacking good legal advice, the Russian government has usually come up short in mining deals with foreign investors, which has increased its skepticism about making new mining deals. Consequently, many known reserves of minerals, metals, and petroleum products (e.g., Russia's many oil fields and its diamond fields near Arkhangelsk) remain undeveloped.

The Russian state has preferred to privatize working mines and ore-processing factories by selling them to Russian companies. As mentioned earlier, such sales occurred through the voucher privatization schemes and transferred highly valuable state assets at cheap prices to a few leading commercial banks and tycoons. These few newly wealthy and economically powerful individuals have come to be known as Russia's oligarchs. The former Soviet managers of mines were unable to accumulate enough vouchers to buy these major assets.

For example, the world's richest platinum, copper, and nickel mine in Norilsk, the world's largest city situated on permafrost, was sold at a fraction of its real value to Onexim Bank on the condition that mining profits would partly be used to support the city and its 200,000 citizens. Onexim Bank reneged on this agreement, however. It started to lay off workers in the mines to increase its profits and left the city in dire straits to be supported by Russia's central government. Thus, the Russian central government acquired significant new problems but very little money from the sale of this major economic asset. After a series of similar experiences, the Russian government became leery about selling its valuable assets in the earth to private businesses.

D. Agriculture could have been privatized with some success. In actuality, there have been few changes in this area of economic activity, and most of them have been for the worse.

In the late 1970s, China had an organization of state and collective farms similar to that in the Soviet Union, but China's Communist leadership helped agriculture and rural areas to become highly productive and profitable. They did this by allowing the "responsibility system" of farming (Zhou 1996). This system left decisions about agricultural production and marketing in the hands of Chinese peasants, who had formerly lived in agricultural communes. The new system allowed economic liberalization to follow its own path of development in the Chinese countryside. Not only did agricultural output rise dramatically, but rural residents began to manufacture a variety of goods to be sold elsewhere—first in neighboring cities, then in more distant cities in China, and eventually around the world.

In 1992 Yeltsin had a similar opportunity in Russia. Roughly three-fourths of Soviet state and collective farms were unprofitable and required large subsidies from the state to keep them going. Since Russia had been Europe's breadbasket in the nineteenth century, the potential for good agricultural yields in Russia exists. First and foremost, the organization of agriculture needs to be changed radically. If Yeltsin had responded like China's Deng Xiaoping, he could have greatly furthered agricultural development in Russia. He could have permitted Russia's rural population (roughly a fourth of the whole population) to participate in the new market economy by letting them acquire land and then assume responsibility for their own futures. But the Gaidar government chose to leave the system of agricultural production virtually unchanged from Soviet times. As a result, agricultural output in Russia in the 1990s was considerably lower than before the Soviet Union collapsed. Output of potatoes, a basic foodstuff easily grown on family plots, is one of the few that has risen (see Table 5.1). The standard of living of peasants in Russia can most accurately be described as miserable.

Legal steps to allow Russian peasants to own and work their own land began only in 1998. Because some opportunities to earn a living had arisen in the cities in the interim, the most energetic and entrepreneurial peasants left the countryside before 1998. It is unclear whether even great sums of money, which only the state could provide, could make agricultural production profitable on the basis of the remaining agricultural labor force.

E. Heavy industry was a sizable part of Soviet economic activity. This industry managed to meet the Soviet Union's internal needs and had substantial export capacity. During the Soviet era, a large factory usually hired at least 10,000 people and was built in a small town, or created a small town around it. A typical example is Magnitogorsk, a well-known industrial center born in the rapid industrialization of the 1930s, which eventually grew into the largest factory town in the Ural region. In its heyday, its factories employed nearly 200,000 workers. In the 1990s,

Magnitogorsk still existed as a town, but its factories could support only a far smaller labor force.

When the Soviet Union collapsed, factories that had previously been directed and supported by the state system of mandated supply and demand were left to founder on their own. Industrial managers were unprepared for a market economy. They knew how to organize workers and raw materials to make products, but they had no idea how to market and sell these products and how to react to competition. The old Soviet system of supply also broke down, and managers had to devise and learn new ways to acquire the raw materials needed to make products.

The breakup of the Soviet Union into 15 new countries also contributed to the collapse of heavy industry. Russia's own need for the outputs of heavy industry is much smaller than the USSR's had been. Moreover, without Soviet threats of military reprisal, opportunities for export were greatly reduced because potential buyers in East Europe and the CIS (COMMONWEALTH OF INDEPENDENT STATES)—those that had purchased the output of these factories during the Soviet period—lacked the funds to buy the output of Russian heavy industry.

The pressure on factories in heavy industry has been heightened by inflation and by the state apparatus, which no longer oversees industry and helps managers to acquire raw materials but instead pursues individual interests within the market. Very few factories have been able to handle these pressures and to compete successfully in a market economy. Small, local factories have tended to be more successful. Output and employment for large factories have shrunk dramatically. Many factories in heavy industry have closed or ceased production.

For most workers in this industry, moving elsewhere to find work is an impossible dream because their factory-supplied apartment is their main asset. If a factory closes, retail trade and consumer services are usually the only other local employment, and these economic activities are unable to furnish a livelihood to the majority of unemployed factory workers.

F. The defense industry, comprising a third of Russia's industrial potential (in terms of output and employment), presents an especially thorny problem for the Russian government. Since Russia is no longer a world superpower, a very large military force is an expensive waste of state revenues. It does not need so many factories engaged in military production, even if they are highly competitive with the United States technologically. Nevertheless, factories in the defense industry have been closed very slowly because everyone in the Russian government has sought to dodge decisions about reducing the size of the military.

The defense factories that have been closed have put millions of highly skilled workers out of work. Since most defense factories were located in remote places, the development of profitable nonmilitary enterprises in these sites requires not only capital but also entrepreneurial activity, which is rarely found in such areas. Moreover, because housing is in short supply in most Russian cities, even the most qualified workers have problems getting new jobs outside the area where the defense factory is located. Unemployment among former workers in the defense industry is a tremendous problem for the new Russia.

Even the necessary defense factories are undercapitalized. The defense industry is solely the state's responsibility, but the Russian state is so poor that it cannot afford to pay even its defense workers. This poverty has resulted in widespread corruption and bribery. Most military secrets and advanced weaponry are available for a price. Some of the most qualified defense workers have quit to work for foreign companies—an embarrassing situation in a country with a long tradition of extreme military secrecy.

Russian defense factories have tried to compete in the international market for arms, but success in this arena is significantly harder for Russia than for the former Soviet Union. The Soviet Union could provide integrated weapons systems and sophisticated military training in this weaponry. Russia cannot do this: It is too expensive, and Russia's army cannot offer such training. Defense factories can sell only individual weapons in competition with other providers on the world's arms market. The new economic system has dramatically reduced Russia's real income from weapons sales.

Russia's inability to handle the transition to a market economy in the defense industry has jeopardized its best scientific and industrial potential. The well-publicized difficulties that Russia has had in maintaining (let alone expanding) its space program, such as the Mir space station, are just the tip of the iceberg.

This discussion of Russia's economic transition undoubtedly sounds very gloomy, and the prospects are indeed not bright. Production of goods and services has plummeted. Unemployment (hidden as well as open) has been high. Inflation has been rampant. The standard of living has declined sharply. The state and many ordinary people have been impoverished. Tax avoidance among those who are making money has been massive. Major economic assets have ended up in the hands of relatively few: oligarchs, former Soviet managers, the Russian underworld, and foreign businesses. One may well ask, as Russians often do: Has anything positive come from this?

Moscow offers a success story of marketization in Russia. The mayor of Moscow, Yuri Luzhkov, prevented shock therapy from becoming the marketization policy in Russia's capital. He has successfully run the city like a large corporation. Privatization has been gradual and has always resulted in a profit for the Moscow government. In sharp contrast to the central government, the Moscow government has had a steady supply of funds and has generated very impressive results over a short period of time. Moscow has a viable job market, and its residents enjoy a standard of living roughly four times higher than the country as a whole. Even heavy industry in Moscow has survived and has found a strong demand for many of its products.

To a considerable extent, Moscow's success derives from its old position as receiver and exploiter of many of the country's resources. But its positive results have come mainly from the practical management of its resources and its restrained, gradual development of markets. These policies have allowed marketization to proceed on a pragmatic rather than an ideological basis.

Several examples illustrate its success. In Moscow, the privatization of apartments has occurred slowly. Prices for utilities have been raised gradually in tandem with increases in personal incomes so that apartment owners have been able to cope with this new burden. In Moscow, unlike the rest of the country, retired people receive their pensions on time. A similar practical approach to marketization has been implemented with some success in a few other places, such as the oblasts of Novgorod and Nizhniy Novgorod.

In sum, localities with responsible, pragmatic elites have succeeded in managing the transition from a command economy to a market economy much more smoothly than the country as a whole. But such localities are the exceptions. It is unclear whether these exceptional successes can serve as models for economic development in the rest of Russia.

5.4 THE LABOR FORCE

In terms of sheer numbers of people, Russia has an impressive workforce, 73 million working-age citizens in 1998, of whom 34 million (46 percent) were women. In 1997, 2.4 million young people entered the labor force. A decade later, that number will decrease to roughly 1.5 million due to declines in the sizes of birth COHORTS during the 1980s. Russia's high mortality rate is also helping to reduce the size of its workforce. A shrinking labor force is not a new phenomenon in West European countries, but it is for Russia.

In 1997, the private sector employed 40 percent of the labor force. Another 36 percent worked in the state-owned sector, and the remaining 24 percent worked in the public, state-budgeted sector (e.g., in government agencies, schools). The year 1996 was the first time that the private sector provided more jobs than the state-owned sector.

Official 1998 statistics reported that 90 percent of the working-age population was currently employed. Thus, at least officially, unemployment in Russia is fairly low, only 10 percent. But many factories have put workers on leave without pay. Formally these individuals are still

TABLE 5.2

Distribution of Employment among Different Industries

Economic Sector	Employed in 1991 N[a]	%	Employed in 1996 N[a]	%	1996 Work force as % of 1991 Work force (except as noted)
All sectors	73,848	100.0%	66,000	100.0%	89.3%
Heavy, light, and defense industries	22,407	30.3	16,300	24.7	72.7
Agriculture, fishing, forestry	9,970	13.5	9,800	14.9	98.3
Construction	8,488	11.5	6,300	9.6	74.2
Transportation, communications	5,750	7.8	5,240	7.9	91.1
Retail trade, services	5,626	7.6	6,840	10.4	121.6
Computers, information technology	134	0.2	77[c]	0.1[c]	57.5[d]
Real estate	70[b]	1.0[b]	19[c]	0.1[c]	27.1[e]
Other material production	1,698[b]	2.7[b]	1,759[c]	2.7[c]	103.6[e]
Utilities, public services	3,159	4.3	3,300	5.0	104.5
Health, social security	4,305	5.8	4,600	7.0	106.9
Education, culture, arts	7,273	9.9	7,420	11.2	102.0
Science	3,075	4.2	1,600	2.4	52.0
Financial institutions	440	0.6	900	1.4	204.5
Government	1,722	2.3	1,900	2.9	110.3

[a] In thousands.
[b] In 1992 (no information for 1991).
[c] In 1995 (no information for 1996).
[d] 1995 workforce as percent of 1991 workforce.
[e] 1995 workforce as percent of 1992 workforce.
Source: Interstate Statistical Committee of CIS, 1998, pp. 379–426.

employed by the factory; however, they do not do any work, and they do not get any salary. The 10 percent figure for official unemployment does not take into account the "hidden unemployed" who find themselves in such situations.

Since the fate of individuals depends on the industry in which they work, the composition of the workforce by industry (Table 5.2) tells something about the labor force's prospects for economic improvement. In 1997, 24 percent worked in the light, heavy, or defense industries; 21 percent in education, health care, social welfare, and cultural fields; and

15 percent in agriculture. The percentage working in industry will almost surely decline rapidly if the state ceases to subsidize nonoperational factories that formally still have workers. The large percentage of people still hired in the heavy, defense, and light industries demonstrates that Russia is only gradually transforming into a postindustrial, service economy. Inexplicably, the number working in education, culture, the arts, health care, and social security has begun to increase. The percentage working in agriculture is much higher than in the United States and has been relatively stable for some time.

These figures tell only the most basic facts about Russia's labor force because the **quality of the labor force** is crucial in a modern economy. By world standards, Russia's labor force is well educated, with 70 percent having achieved some kind of secondary education and 13 percent having graduated from a university.

After the fall of the Soviet Union, people were forced to switch rapidly from a well-established and relatively stable work environment in which personal responsibility was the exception to a continually shifting and unstable labor market in which willingness and ability to take personal responsibility were major assets. This sharp shift was unprecedented in Russian history. Russia's past experience offered no lessons on how to manage this transition.

The idea of **free labor**—working for one's own benefit—had never been introduced or implemented in the general Russian population until this new Russian state. Although this idea had been incorporated into the culture of the settlers moving into the newly conquered lands of the tsarist empire, it had remained localized and never reached the Russian heartland. Merchants, a numerically small group, were historically the main segment of Russian society with the mentality of free labor. But this idea vanished in the 70 years of Soviet rule, as every foreigner meeting Russians (even those in Moscow) quickly notices.

Capitalism entered Russia rather oddly. Factories were originally staffed by serfs, not free citizens. Only after the tsar's decree freed the serfs in 1861 were peasants able to move to factory towns and to begin to have individual work careers with a sense of personal achievement and meaning. Most people in Russia spent their entire lives just trying to earn enough money to survive. A true market society, with opportunities for ordinary people to have personal goals at work beyond satisfying their immediate needs, never emerged before the Bolshevik Revolution, even in St. Petersburg, the tsarist capital. Stalin's repressions made forced labor a common feature of life in the Soviet Union. With some liberalization after Stalin's death, work became primarily an official duty rather than the result of coercion. However, in most occupations, hard work did not produce rewards such as a higher income, more consumer goods, or a better career. In this situation, there was little motivation for individuals to work hard.

The situation was rather different for intellectuals. Most had an opportunity to develop a solid professional career. But usually hard work did not pay off in either the short or long run because promotions brought little improvement in income and, in any case, were based on many factors other than achievements. Not surprisingly, the belief and the principle that hard work can lead to a better life have not yet been fully incorporated into the Russian work ethic.

The **entrepreneurial** characteristics of people are formed as part of their work culture (Millar 1987). Rural, especially peasant, life does not require much entrepreneurial skill. Until the beginning of this century, Russians had very little experience with private business, which was concentrated in only a few cities. The command economy gave some entrepreneurial-like opportunities only to the few managers who were responsible enough to organize production, services, or labor. The state-oriented structure strived to suppress the kind of entrepreneurship needed for success in a market economy. The result was that the Soviet economy had efficient and skilled managers, but it had very few who could become entrepreneurs.

"Business" is a new word for Russians, since this kind of activity rarely existed previously. Profit making is an entirely new concept for most Russians, one that cannot be taught easily in a school or university. In the Soviet system, profit was an ideological evil, synonymous with capitalism. It was taboo even among Soviet managers and the party-state bureaucracy. In the 1990s, schools and courses teaching business were profitable enterprises because many people in Russia want to learn how to make money but had no idea how to start. Ordinary people's knowledge was limited to whether a product was "a good buy." Most Russians never even had a family budget. Most had the habit of using whatever money was available until it ran out and then to wait for the next paycheck to arrive.

The emerging **job market** is also a new phenomenon in Russia. In the Soviet era, education largely determined a person's work career (see Chapter 6). Graduation from a vocational school, college, or university led automatically to a person being assigned to a specific occupation and job. Though this system did not work flawlessly, job openings occurred only in the jobs with the lowest salaries. Higher-level jobs were open only to people with the necessary qualifications and experience relevant to the particular kind of work.

A change in occupation was extremely unlikely for the majority of the population. Career changers were looked down upon, and their nickname, "flyers" (*letuny*), had a clear negative connotation. Titma, Silver, and Anderson (1996) found that people in their early 40s had averaged slightly over two jobs in their career. Only a very few people were oriented toward a work career and actively tried on their own initiative to advance at work. Many more people were promoted at work, but promotion was the result of external evaluation by higher authorities; internal motivation and personal effort were strictly secondary.

The labor market in the new Russia has developed very rapidly. It has had both positive and negative consequences. The negative effects have been more visible. Many previous enterprises have died slowly, with people still officially listed as employed but in reality without any real work or salary. The practice of refusing to close an enterprise and fire its employees has persevered for a long time.

On the positive side, marketization has created new opportunities, and the most entrepreneurial people have begun to organize some segments of the labor force in private businesses. After five years, Russia's private sector employed more people than the state-owned sector. Open competition for jobs and for labor began. In this new situation, two clear strategies of work behavior have emerged.[6]

Most people chose a **survival strategy;** often they had no other option. That is, they simply tried to keep their existing job and did not search for a better job. Their aim was simply to have enough income to meet their basic needs. For example, the vast majority of people living in rural areas are not actively working because the collective and state farms on which they worked are deteriorating. Attempts to start individual, private-property farms were thwarted by the agricultural bureaucracy and by most of the rural population, who were accustomed to living poor but egalitarian lives. In industry, very few new jobs have appeared, and most people have remained nominally employed at the dying factories where they had always worked because their only other option was to move to another place with a totally uncertain future. Many people have remained in their current places of work fearful of entering new careers in which their previous qualifications are irrelevant.

The second strategy was an **active search for a new career.** The emerging job market forced everyone from 17-year-old youths to adults in their 50s to compete for newly emerging job opportunities. Past work experience was evaluated only in terms of present skills and abilities. Many people pursued multiple opportunities. Many began to be traders, trying to sell some kind of merchandise, which they bought and later sold at a higher price. Few of these people eventually became merchants or owners of shops. In the emerging labor market, a middleman who brokers work opportunities is a typical but largely transitional figure. Naturally, the new, wild, unregulated economic environment has created many failures. New businesses have even lower survival rates than in stable market economies.

---

6. See Róna-Tas (1994) or Silverman and Yanowitch (1997) on winners and losers in the new economy.

5.5 SUMMARY

Since the economy had never been a dominant institution in Russia, marketization was an especially difficult process. To achieve a successful economic transformation, Russia's huge economic space required entrepreneurs and entrepreneurial activity. Starting with a command economy, Russia did not have enough of either. In a small country, such as Estonia, a few hundred entrepreneurs could jump-start the transition from a command economy to a market economy. But Russia needed tens of thousands of entrepreneurs widely dispersed over its vast territory. The dearth of entrepreneurs in Russia made its leaders' choices on the road to a market economy extremely important. The available resources, including its few potential entrepreneurs, limited the choices that could be made in developing a market economy.

With its huge territory, Russia had every opportunity to develop a large domestic market using its existing economic assets: its highly educated workforce, its strong industrial and technological bases, and last but not least, the demands of its own consumers. Each major industry needed a distinctive approach to developing its market. One way that might have worked was the bottom-up approach adopted by China's leaders, who first allowed peasants to acquire land and then to choose when, how, and what was best to produce and sell.

Instead, Russia's leaders chose a macroeconomic approach. They freed most prices, created a new currency, privatized key state properties, developed a new system of taxation, and tried (though unsuccessfully) to balance the state budget. They aimed to develop a financial market. This top-down approach to marketization bypassed the vast majority of people in Russia. The circle of people who have actively participated in developing a market economy in Russia has been very small. The voucher scheme of privatization was doomed to fail because a single individual's vouchers were of almost no value. Moreover, vouchers hid the darkest side of privatization: the transfer of state assets to a few insiders behind closed doors. This whole approach paralyzed the sectors of the economy engaged in production (industry and agriculture).

Russia's leaders failed to create the environment needed for marketization to succeed. First, Russia needed a stable currency and a trustworthy banking system. Ponzi schemes not only impoverished people but left them feeling cheated by the new economic system. In a situation in which the only viable monetary instrument was the American dollar, long-term investments in industry made no sense. Survival and, when possible, short-term profit making have been the pervasive goals. The flight of capital abroad has been a major goal of successful entrepreneurs. To solve the problem of competition, entrepreneurs in some regions have found it easier to kill their competitors than to outsmart them, be more productive, or make better deals—the normal ways that entre-preneurs in market economies overcome their competitors.

It is no wonder that the Russian economy is still a mess and that its real economic output may not yet have bottomed out. Not surprisingly, most people in Russia have become rather cynical about the promises of a better life that a market economy was supposed to bring them.

CHAPTER 6

Education

During the Soviet period, Russia enjoyed many impressive gains (e.g., in space travel, military hardware, and sports), and most of these gains were linked with advances in the education and training of its population. At the beginning of the twentieth century, 80 percent of the Russian population was illiterate, and a university education was a rarity. By the start of World War II, literacy was nearly universal. Starting in the 1970s, a secondary education became obligatory. From the 1960s to the 1980s, the percentage of university graduates in Russia was second only to that in the United States. Russia was the first country in which the average educational attainment of women surpassed that of men. All in all, Russia's educational achievements under the Soviet regime were substantial.

It is not surprising, therefore, that the new Russia's main legacy from the Soviet period is its educated workforce. According to the 1994 microcensus on the Russian population (*Goskomstat Rossii* 1995), 13 percent of the adult population had completed a university education. For example, among those 30–34 years old, 19 percent had completed a university education, and 52 percent a secondary education. In terms of secondary school completion, those 25–29 years old were reported to be the most highly educated, with 75 percent having completed a secondary education, and another 18 percent a university education. These figures imply that 93 percent of the 25–29 year-old age cohort had completed at least a secondary education. This percentage is so high that one must view it with some skepticism; however, the reported percentage with a university education seems plausible.[1]

---

1. Here and below, official statistics for Russia should be taken as rough indicators. Russian statistics were unreliable in Soviet times. (Clem 1986). They have not yet improved and may even be worse now.

6.1 THE FORMAL EDUCATIONAL SYSTEM[2]

Comprehensive versus Differentiated Schools

The system of formal education in the United States differs in a fundamental way from that in most European countries, including Russia. The United States has adopted a comprehensive system of education. That is, elementary and secondary schools (and even colleges and universities) are not significantly differentiated, even though students within a particular school are often in different tracks (e.g., fast or slow) or programs (e.g., academic or vocational). A comprehensive school system allows students to move from one track to another if their interests or competencies change. Moreover, students in different tracks or studying different subjects interact routinely with students in other tracks because they are in the same school.

Both the Soviet Union and the new Russia utilize the German system of differentiated schools. At the secondary level, the different types of schools have different curricula. Even at the elementary level, different types of schools offer pupils different educational experiences and future prospects. A differentiated system of schools makes it hard for students to move from one educational path to another because it requires them to change schools. Moreover, since students in different schools do not interact much with each other, Russian students in one type of school have little awareness of the educational experiences and family backgrounds of students in other types of schools.

Observers often point out that residential segregation on the basis of race, ethnicity, and social class keeps Americans of different races, ethnic groups, and social classes from interacting with each other, except in very impersonal ways (on the streets and in shops). America's schools and universities are often one of the few places where racial, ethnic, and CLASS DIVISIONS can be bridged. In Russia, residential segregation within a given town or city is minor. A manager of an enterprise might live in the same housing complex as workers in the same enterprise. But, in contrast with America, Russia's differentiated system of schools means that young people with different family backgrounds and future prospects mainly attend school with others whose family backgrounds and prospects are similar to their own.

Elementary Education

In Russia, both now and during the Soviet era, the channeling of youths into different kinds of schools starts at very young ages. Indeed, the first fork in the road occurs in the first grade when children are six or seven

---

2. Unless indicated otherwise, numerical estimates are based on *Goskomstat Rossii* (1998).

The future of Russia with smiles on their faces and one Oakland Raiders cap.

years old. Two main types of schools offer elementary education: One type has eight grades; the other offers both schooling in grades 1–8 and a general secondary education (grades 9 through 11 or 12). Elementary schools with eight grades are very common in rural areas and small towns but are also found in some urban suburbs. The elementary curriculum in the two types of schools is basically the same, but elementary schools with only eight grades usually provide a poorer quality of education. The allocation of a child to one or the other type of elementary school depends primarily on where the child lives.

There are also a few elite general secondary schools offering an elementary education to a very small percentage of all children. Usually children enter the elite educational path around age seven or eight, and almost none leave it before secondary school graduation. The elite schools were located almost exclusively in regional capitals during the Soviet period but have now spread to almost all major cities. Since the abilities of young children are hard to judge, admission to elite schools is popularly described as the "competition of parents."

Secondary Schools

For most children in Russia, the first crucial branch occurs after completion of the eighth grade when a youth is 13–14 years old and ready to begin secondary education. Russia, like the Soviet Union, has four main types of secondary schools:

1. *PTU* (vocational secondary schools), which are designed to prepare youths for jobs as workers.

2. *Tekhnikum* (specialized, technically oriented secondary schools), which are intended to prepare youths for jobs as skilled workers (e.g., foremen, some semiprofessionals).

3. General secondary schools, which offer a general academic curriculum.

4. Elite general secondary schools (e.g., *gymnasia, lyceums*), which give advanced training in science, mathematics, foreign languages, and so on.

Depending on the type of school, secondary school typically ends after grade 11 when a youth is usually 16 or 17 years old.

During the Soviet period, Russia had the same types of secondary schools in every region, but the proportion of each type varied dramatically across regions and localities (Titma and Saar 1995). For example, elite schools were (and are) widespread in Moscow and St. Petersburg (formerly Leningrad). In contrast, industrial cities like Samara, Ufa, Omsk, and Kazan had (and have) few elite schools, and more than half of their eighth-grade graduates enter vocational secondary schools. In areas with large populations of minority nationalities (e.g., Dagestan, Bashkortostan, Chechnya), 90 percent of secondary school students were (and are) in general secondary schools.

All types of secondary schools are undergoing substantial change in the new Russia, but the changes are especially marked in the PTU (vocational secondary schools). In the Soviet period, most vocational schools were linked with and financed by a particular ministry of the economy because these schools were intended to provide trained workers for the enterprises and organizations overseen by that specific ministry. In the new Russia, vocational education is being downsized substantially because most of the industrial ministries and factories that once financed the PTU are shrinking and have too few resources to support schools. Vocational schools are also declining because they can no longer provide jobs for most of their graduates and therefore have great difficulty attracting new students.

There is somewhat greater demand for education in a tekhnikum, especially if it provides training for secretarial-clerical work, for work in accounting and bookkeeping, or for other occupations in the service industry. The reported number of tekhnikum in Russia in 1998 was 1,657, a little larger than it was in Soviet times; however, they have 10 percent fewer students than in the past, two million. There have been major changes in the fields of study. The number of tekhnikum providing preparation for work in manufacturing and agriculture (the core of the Soviet command economy) has declined considerably. The biggest decrease in enrollments has occurred in the tekhnikum in education and medicine; they had only three-fourths as many students in 1998 as they had in 1992. Enrollments in agricultural tekhnikum have also shrunk a lot; they had 20 percent fewer students in 1998 than in 1992.

The new Russia has added new types of schools to the Soviet system of formal education. In particular, two types of schools with roots in the tsarist period, gymnasia and lyceums, have been reestablished. Both provide a general education, but a gymnasium emphasizes the natural sciences, whereas a lyceum has an enlarged curriculum in the humanities. In 1998, Russia had 1,121 gymnasia with a total of 848,000 students and 723 lyceums with 452,000 students. Since 22 million students were in elementary or secondary schools in 1998, these two new types have fewer than 1 percent of the student population in Russia (Interstate Statistical Committee of CIS 1999). Still, these two types of schools are the most rapidly expanding and better-off part of the educational system in the new Russia. Students in these schools receive a better quality of education and can make real choices within schools, as is typical in American schools.

Postsecondary Schools

After secondary school graduation, youths can begin postsecondary education or enter the workforce (including military service). There were (and are) two main types of postsecondary schools: (1) lower-level colleges, which prepare students to work in semiprofessions, such as engineering, teaching, and nursing; and (2) universities. There also were (and are) a few postsecondary vocational schools that offer more advanced training than secondary vocational schools.

A university education is in demand in the new Russia, despite overproduction of university graduates during Soviet times. New private universities have sprung up, causing the number of universities to increase from 514 in 1991 to 880 in 1998. The number of university students has increased more modestly, from 2.8 million to 3.2 million. The increase in the number of students results largely from changes in the demand for graduates in various fields. According to official statistics, the number of university students has increased by a third in the arts and by 20 percent in pedagogical universities, but it has decreased by a quarter in medical schools.

In Soviet times, 25 percent of all university openings were in Moscow. In many parts of Russia, the opportunity to obtain a university education was very remote. Educational institutes (somewhat like America's ubiquitous community colleges) were common in Soviet times, but they offered only very narrow training for specific occupations, such as teaching and engineering. Many of these institutes have upgraded their status to universities in the decade since the Soviet Union collapsed. These upgraded institutes account for much of the growth in the number of universities in Russia.

There are also some genuinely new universities, especially ones offering training in business (including marketing), law, economics, and finances, due to the new and high demand for study in these fields. Other especially popular fields of study are foreign languages, computers, and journalism. Declining fields of study include agriculture, transportation, and communication. As a rule, new universities as well as some state universities offer education and training aimed at one sphere of the economy. Very few offer students the comprehensive range of options found in almost all American colleges and universities.

Recent statistics on the number of university applicants give the misleading impression that a great many more students than in the past are applying to study at a university. In Soviet times, secondary school graduates were permitted to apply to only one university; now they are allowed to apply to multiple universities, as in the United States. Consequently, much of the post-Soviet growth in the number of applicants results partly from students starting to apply to several universities.

One reason for growth in the numbers of university applicants and university students is that many general secondary school graduates prefer to attend a university than to be unemployed. In the Soviet period, a student was sent to a particular workplace after graduation. Now a youth must find his or her own job and must face the reality that there are few job vacancies. Hence, the decision to attend a university rather than to enter the labor force is often rational from the viewpoint of an individual, especially because the cost of a university education is still low. It is not so rational in the aggregate because Russia still has more people working in white-collar jobs than the economy really needs.

6.2 EDUCATION AND THE ECONOMY

In every modern society, there is a certain relationship between the system of formal education and the way the economy is organized and functions. Some relationship is inevitable because formal education concentrates most of its attention on children and youths, whereas participation in the economy is the main public activity of adults. Since in every modern society education is typically deemed as "preparation for life," schools are expected to prepare students for working, a major part of a person's life. Societies vary, however, in the extent to which "preparation for work" is seen as the primary task of formal education, in the dominant views of what preparation for work requires, and in the linkages between the educational system and the economy. Russia has differed from the United States in all three respects. Importantly, the linkages between education and the economy were strikingly different in the Soviet period than they are in the new Russia.

The Soviet Period

Industries' need for labor was the driving force behind educational tracking during the Soviet period. The rationale behind school tracking was the same as for production of goods in the rest of the command economy: Planners decided the economy needed X million units of some product, which in turn required production and allocation of Y million raw materials. The graduates of the various types of schools were just another one of the necessary raw materials. Consequently, the command economy led to a concrete plan for allocating various numbers of youths among different types of schools. The number of students allocated was intended to produce the number of graduates from each type that planners estimated would be needed to fulfill other production targets a few years later. Educational authorities knew that their task was to assign enough incoming students to each type of school to fulfill these targets.

Graduates of vocational schools were always in greater demand in the Soviet Union than the natural supply based on the preferences of youths and their parents. For most manual jobs, supervisors and managers preferred men over women. School authorities largely complied with this preference for male workers by assigning disproportionate numbers of boys to vocational schools. It was easier for school authorities to assign youths who had poorer grades and were troublemakers to vocational schools. Since these characteristics are more common among young males than among young females, school authorities could justify sending more boys to vocational schools on the basis of these individual differences. As a result of the processes that funneled males disproportionately into vocational schools, girls comprised roughly two-thirds of students in general secondary schools (the academic track).

School authorities also found it easier to assign children of less-educated parents to vocational schools. Just as in America, Soviet parents who were more educated or who had jobs higher on the occupational ladder resisted efforts of school authorities to put their children in educational tracks leading to blue-collar work. Not surprisingly, then, there was an excess of students in vocational schools with parents who were less educated.

For whatever reason, the actual qualifications and skills of the graduates of various types of schools were not a special focus of concern in the Soviet period. Consequently, the practice of sending to vocational schools those who had poor grades, caused trouble at school, and had parents with low education and low-status occupations was not seen as problematic because economic planners focused on quantities of workers, not their qualities and qualifications.

The New Russia

The relationship between education and the economy is markedly different in the new Russia. The command economy has vanished, and with it the direct connection between the economy's needs for workers and the allocation of students to various types of schools. The end of this connection has had important effects.

First, it has stopped the tracking of students into different types of secondary schools to produce certain quantities of workers with different qualifications. For school authorities, especially those dealing with secondary education, it has also meant the freedom to develop educational programs without pressure from party-state agencies. Correspondingly, it has made students and their parents the primary decision makers in choices involving students' education.

Second, general education is now confronted with a large number of school dropouts. As in impoverished areas of the United States where job opportunities are scarce, many parents in Russia (e.g., those in the countryside and members of national minorities) do not put much value on education. As a result, the educational attainment of younger age cohorts is likely to be lower than in the late Soviet period until parents and youths believe that education pays.

The new situation is harder for vocational education than for general education because employers in the new Russia often demand a certain quality of education rather than simply a particular quantity of graduates as in the Soviet period. Because students are no longer assigned directly to vocational schools, authorities in such schools need to learn how to attract students and to rely on parents' and students' assessments of what to study.

Naturally, vocational schools try to survive by any possible means. One of the easiest is to relabel vocational schools and their educational programs. But students and their parents are not easily fooled by name changes. The basic problem of Russia's vocational schools is that most of them offer a kind of education that is just not in high demand.

The problems of vocational schools are aggravated by the fact that they recruit eighth-graders from outside their immediate area. Consequently, in contrast to general secondary schools, they house most of their students in dormitories, an extra expense. Nowadays, parents of potential vocational school students cannot afford to support their children to study in vocational schools, and very few factories are willing to do this either. As a result, vocational schools are definitely the most troubled part of Russia's school system.

Many former tekhnikum are now being upgraded and transformed into local colleges. Their survival depends on local authorities and local communities more than on educational authorities in Moscow. As compared to vocational schools, they have more prestige and offer their students somewhat better job prospects, which keep the inflow of students at a reasonable level. But many of them also drew students from afar in the Soviet past and then housed these teenagers in dormitories. As with vocational schools, the added expense of dormitory living reduces the ability of tekhnikum to attract students, especially ones living outside a school's immediate area.

Universities are faring the best. With the collapse of the command economy, universities have more independence, and the demand for certain types of university education is high. There is great competition for entrance to universities that can supply graduates in business, economics, marketing, law, and other areas in short supply in the new market economy. But universities offering traditional forms of education are struggling to survive in difficult conditions.

Students flock to universities for two main reasons. First, there is a widespread belief that a university education improves job opportunities. Support for this belief comes from vigorous recruitment of university graduates in selected fields by private businesses. Second, few nonmanual jobs are open to recent graduates of secondary schools, and the children of well-educated parents are not keen to compete for manual jobs. For them, any kind of university education is more appealing than manual work. So they enter a university. In reality, most are simply postponing the search for a job.

It will take some time before parents and youth comprehend the cruel reality that Russian economic production in the late 1990s is approximately a third of its size a decade ago. Correspondingly, the overall demand for employees with a university education has shrunk by at least half, and even more in some regions and in certain professions.

For example, engineers, who were a third of all professionals in 1990, have seen the industrial bases for their jobs shrink by at least threefold. The situation is similar for teachers and physicians, both of whom were oversupplied by Western criteria. The number of physicians per capita was twice as large in the Soviet Union as in the United States. Teachers were a fourth of Russian professionals. Because the age cohorts born in the 1990s are half the size of those a decade ago, the demand for teachers, and therefore for teacher education, has declined. Since school authorities are reluctant to dismiss experienced teachers, openings for new teachers are few, except for those who can teach the new areas of high demand, such as business.

When new graduates in the professions cannot find jobs in fields requiring years of study, there develops a reverse bandwagon effect, otherwise known as the phenomenon of "rats leaving a sinking ship." Most youngsters rationally decide that it does not make much sense to get a university degree in a field that does not lead to a professional job. Some choose to get a university education in a more promising field, and others to abandon a university education.

6.3 THE VALUE OF EDUCATION

In modern Western societies, most people believe that an education is valuable. They mean various things by this. Some think that an education is **intrinsically valuable** because it gives people factual and theoretical knowledge about the world; helps them learn to solve problems, both alone and in cooperation with other people; offers understanding of how the world works; and generally enhances a wide variety of human abilities. Others think that an education is **extrinsically valuable** because it improves a person's work opportunities: It not only makes a person more employable but also increases the chances for obtaining jobs that are better paid, have better working conditions, and have more authority in the workplace. Naturally, some people think education is both intrinsically and extrinsically valuable, but most people stress one aspect more than the other.

The extrinsic value of being highly educated was not large during the Soviet era. Almost all able-bodied adults had jobs, and salary differences were fairly small. Manual workers, who did not need to be highly educated to perform their jobs, were paid comparatively well. In contrast, physicians, whose work demands many years of schooling, were not paid very well—considerably less than miners and truck drivers. The main extrinsic value of higher education during the Soviet era was access to a white-collar job. Consequently, people mainly chose to be more or less educated on the basis of their perception of its intrinsic value, the degree to which they liked school, and the kind of work to which a given level and type of education led.

As Russia has moved toward a market economy, the extrinsic value of an education has changed significantly; for the most part, it has grown. The private sector has already begun to reward people on the basis of their education because profits have begun to depend on the quality of services and products, which in turn tends to be higher when employees have more skills and are better educated. (Naturally, motivation and effort also tend to improve quality and profits.)

Moreover, a job is no longer guaranteed, and the direct linkage between educational track and a person's work career has been broken, as noted in Section 6.2. The change from the Soviet Union's command economy has forced people of all ages to reenter the labor market. Privately owned businesses have not automatically accepted diplomas from the Soviet past, and employers have reevaluated people's skills and abilities.

At first, new private businesses offered huge opportunities for economic gain as compared with state-owned enterprises and public organizations supported by the state budget. Because a university education had very little to do with understanding markets and business, people with various kinds and levels of education could start a small business. Success depended on entrepreneurial skills and risk-taking behaviors. For example, millions of Russians began to travel abroad to bring back various goods that could be sold in Russia. These small-scale individual efforts could be profitable (sometimes very profitable) because many goods were underproduced by the old Soviet economy. This widespread individual-level economic activity gave the biggest initial boost to entrepreneurship in Russia.

The next part of the private sector to develop were businesses providing every imaginable kind of service and consumer product, from banking and credit, to small restaurants, to selling clothing and shoes on the street. As private business developed still further, many of the early entrepreneurs were driven out by larger and more efficient business organizations. By the late 1990s, regular shops had driven out most of the early individual entrepreneurs, and street businesses had largely vanished from Moscow.

Initially the new private entrepreneurs could hire the best workers. At first, employees were needed to perform all kind of service jobs, not many of which required a university education. In general, the private labor market initially valued and rewarded entrepreneurial skills and the ability to provide services, leaving more educated people with reduced incomes because their particular skills were not in great demand.

As Russia's private sector has expanded and developed, education has gradually begun to be valued as in other developed countries. Although many university graduates employed by the Russian state continue to be poorly paid, those in the private sector have begun to receive a high return on their education, especially when their education has given them competencies needed in the new market economy.

With the direct connection between education and a work career broken in the new Russia, each new generation evaluates education under different circumstances. In Russia in the late 1990s, the economic returns for a secondary education are low. They are uncertain for a university education because not only teachers, but also physicians, engineers, and even top scientists are often not paid for months. As long as white-collars workers paid by the state budget have incomes lower than workers in the construction and service industries in the private sector, incentives to build a career through many years of study are weak. Eventually, the disparity between educational level and the level of economic rewards from work is likely to become smaller, however.

Real life is also changing the educational careers of young people. In the first stage of market reforms, employers greatly preferred to hire younger people to older ones. Eventually a stage was reached where most jobs in the new private sector were filled. Then young people entering the labor market found few job vacancies and faced tough competition for these few jobs from people already holding jobs.

This situation influences the behavior of students. First of all, many jobs, especially in Russia's periphery, do not require much education. It encourages students to drop out of school early, as even Russia's notoriously inaccurate statistics reveal. The actual numbers dropping out are probably much larger than reported by official statistics. Illiteracy could again become a problem, especially in remote parts of Russia. In a situation in which many people barely manage to exist on a poverty level and education does not provide clear economic returns or even a job at the end of their studies, many youngsters lack the motivation to study and stay in school. The loss of a direct linkage between education and work has decreased the motivation for an education. This devaluation of an education is likely to be a temporary phenomenon, part of Russia's transition to a market economy. It is likely to persist for some time, however, if the economic returns to an education continue to be low and uncertain.

6.4 FACTORS INFLUENCING EDUCATIONAL ATTAINMENT

In every modern society, a person's ultimate educational attainment is determined by a variety of factors. Educators decide whether to advance a student to the next level of school or to put him or her into a certain educational track. Students and their parents also make choices. After a certain age, a student may decide to drop out of school or to try to obtain more education. A student may try to continue his or her studies but not be admitted to the school of choice. A student may enter the next level of school but then not pass the school's exams and fail to get a diploma. The possibilities are manifold; consequently, many different factors turn out to influence a person's completed educational level.[3]

According to our own research, by far the most potent predictor of eventual educational attainment in the Soviet era was the **educational track** on which a child was placed. Those in a track designed to lead to higher educational attainment were indeed much more likely to obtain more schooling. This is true in every country that has educational tracks. What was unusual about the Soviet educational system were the factors that affected placement in a particular track.

As noted in Section 6.1, the first major point at which youths were allocated among different school tracks occurred after graduation from the eighth grade, when children were about 13–14 years old. Although a student's family background and school performance influenced track placement, the two most important factors were **location** and **gender.** Location was critical because schools leading to a university diploma were not located in remote or rural areas; hence, a youth's own intelligence and preferences were almost irrelevant.

Gender was important because factories and farms preferred male workers. Consequently, around age 13–14, a large percentage of boys were shunted into vocational schools while most girls were kept in the academic track. Vocational schools were not designed to lead to higher education, so on average boys suffered an educational disadvantage. Not

---

3. The results described in this section are based on our own analyses of survey data collected in the "Paths of a Generation" project; see Tuma and Titma (1998). See also Gerber and Hout (1995).

surprisingly, then, a much higher percentage of women than men achieved a university education. According to the 1994 microcensus (*Goskomstat Rossii* 1995), 21 percent of young women 25–29 years old obtained a university degree, but only 15 percent of young men did.

In a market economy, the most important factor predicting educational attainment is the **availability and desirability of various types of work careers.** Students and their parents look at the demand for labor in a general way. They consider what types of careers are available, what different careers offer in terms of pay and working conditions, and then choose the educational path corresponding to their abilities, values, and perceived opportunities.

It was similar in the former Soviet Union, except that youths and their parents had less freedom of choice. Although government propaganda trumpeted the value of being a worker or collective farmer, youths and their parents (especially educated ones) mainly preferred white-collar jobs. The pay was not better (and sometimes worse) than in blue-collar jobs, but the work itself was physically easier and was performed in a better work environment. Vigorous governmental attempts to recruit youths to enter engineering and agricultural universities were not very successful, and vacancies in these types of universities were only partially filled in the 1980s. However, there was stiff competition for prestigious universities (such as Moscow State University and the Moscow Diplomatic Academy) and ones offering degrees in the humanities.

Soviet society did not foster a strong work orientation in individuals. In general, ordinary people in the Soviet Union in its final years did not work very hard at their jobs. Since hard work was not greatly rewarded, people rationally chose to focus on other aspects of life, such as family, friends, and hobbies. Moreover, there was an extensive social safety net (e.g., free health care, guaranteed housing, cheap food) in place to support almost everyone (except political dissidents) on a low level of existence if they were disabled and could not work. The safety net acted to devalue hard work even further. As a result, how much education a person attained depended not only on educational track and location but also on **internal motivation** and **individual values.**

In Soviet schools, competition among students for good academic grades was very low, and the few who excelled tended to be negatively evaluated by their peers. An environment that promoted individual efforts to be academically successful existed only in elite schools and at the university level. In elementary and secondary schools, physical prowess and interpersonal relations dominated student life, just as they do in most American schools.

Soviet youths' **life plans** just before they graduated from secondary school also affected their eventual educational attainment. Their plans turned out to be powerful predictors of their efforts to enter a postsecondary school and of actually entering one. Plans to enter a lower-level college also helped to predict successful completion of postsecondary study. These results mean that even in the relatively uncompetitive environment of Soviet society, young people with clear goals were more likely to attain a high level of education.

There are no good empirical studies of Russian schools in the 1990s, but it is highly likely that the predominant approach of youths and their parents to education is the same as in the last years of the Soviet Union. The values of younger Russians are, however, being influenced by the newly emerging market society. In contrast to middle-aged and older adults, they still hope to achieve a better life and actively seek ways to be materially successful. Most are ready to work hard to achieve a higher economic status and a better way of life. Consequently, an orientation toward work seems to be spreading among youth and young adults in Russia. A prime example is furnished by young adults in business, who often have a strong work orientation and view competition as normal. This kind of orientation toward life is eroding the former collectivistic orientation that was very widespread in Russia. The change is especially visible in the high level of competition for a university education in business, law, and so on.

Encouragement of significant others (e.g., mothers, fathers, friends, teachers) was another factor determining youths' educational attainment. Encouragement by significant others to get a postsecondary education had a strong impact on Soviet youths' plans to continue in school and to try to enter a postsecondary school. Parents' encouragement even affected the likelihood of entering a postsecondary school, perhaps because youths whose parents encouraged them were more likely to keep trying to get admitted to a postsecondary school until they eventually succeeded. It is important to know that parents' encouragement matters, even when children's abilities are controlled.

The traditional pattern around the world has been for boys to receive more encouragement to continue studying. However, Soviet parents encouraged girls more than boys to continue their education. In a society in which work was required of every adult (even women with young children), and women were responsible for caring for children and the home, it was generally accepted that women should have jobs that were less physically demanding, namely, white-collar jobs. Since differences in the material rewards from work were comparatively small in the Soviet Union, it was a priority for urban parents to help their daughters get white-collar jobs, which meant attaining relatively high levels of education. Consequently, parents were especially likely to encourage daughters to get more education.

Both **past academic success** and **good behavior at school** tended to lead to more education in Soviet times. More youths who were academically able and well behaved planned to continue their education and actually tried to do so. Such youths were only slightly more likely to enter a postsecondary school and to get a university diploma. However, by setting their sights on higher education and actually attempting to get more education, they took steps that eventually led to more education.

Interestingly, a youth's **self-assessment as a top student** had larger effects in advancing a Soviet youth toward a higher education than the youth's grade point average in secondary school. It is unclear to what extent a youth's self-assessment reflected better knowledge of his or her real abilities and to what extent it reflected self-confidence and willingness to work hard. Undoubtedly, willingness to work hard and self-confidence, as well as pure abilities, are positive factors in getting a higher education.

Findings about the effects of **family background** (e.g., parents' education, occupation, and economic well-being) reveal a picture roughly similar to that in the United States and other developed countries. The usual finding is that children whose parents are more educated, in more prestigious occupations, and economically better off tend to go further in school. This was true in the Soviet Union, and there is no reason to expect it not to be in the new Russia. If anything, the effects of parental background on educational attainment are likely to be stronger in the new Russia than in the Soviet period, but empirical evidence on this issue is not yet available.

6.5 WHAT SCHOOLS TEACH

Soviet education was modeled on the European tradition in which the aim of education is to provide enlightenment: A school should impart **knowledge.** Soviet education was indeed strong in imparting knowledge of the humanities, mathematics, and the natural sciences. Soviet education was also designed to train skilled workers, and so some parts of the Soviet educational system trained large numbers of people to perform very specific tasks related to certain occupations, such as welding or nursing.

Russian and American education differ most strikingly in the extent to which they teach **know-how.** The aim of American education has long been to prepare students for real life—to provide the skills needed to live and thrive in American society. American schools and universities try to teach students not only basic, practical skills but also how to use their knowledge to do various sophisticated tasks. Neither Soviet nor Russian educators have thought of education in these terms.

It will take time to turn education in Russia from one that has provided much knowledge irrelevant to personal life to one that promotes skills helping people to succeed in daily life, the job market, and most of all in their personal life. Most Russians have difficulty coping with their new society, in which everyone must take responsibility for his or her

Russia's State Library still bears the name of Vladimir Lenin, founder of the Soviet state, but a statue of Fyodor Dostoevsky, one of the world's most famous writers, greets visitors to the library first.

own life and must accumulate assets in order to be secure. People in Russia understand in principle that they need to do this, but actually doing it is another story. Educators have not figured out how to give people the skills that they need to handle their lives.

An example illustrates the problem. Most Russian university students have more formal knowledge about the world than their American counterparts and can recite many facts about some small country in Europe or Africa. Many American students will not recognize the names of the same countries, let alone be able to find them on the map of the world. But say an American student should happen to visit a small European country with a friend from Russia. The Russian is likely to have real trouble. He or she might not have thought to get a map of the city where the friends are arriving. Worse, once there the Russian might not know how to read the map, find a hotel, use a telephone book, change money at a bank, rent a car, drive the car around to see the sites, or figure out when various tourist attractions are open for visitors. The American will almost surely succeed with all of these practical tasks.

The development of a more pragmatic orientation of education in Russia is likely to evolve only slowly, mainly as a result of the demands of mastering everyday life. Before market reforms were introduced in Russia, most university graduates had difficulty counting their personal income and expenses, let alone figuring out how to stay within their budget. Indeed, the idea of having a family budget was uncommon. It is no wonder that Russia's shift to a market economy has been unsuccessful and that shock therapy has been a disaster for Russia.

From having attended schools stressing knowledge and living in a command economy, most adults in Russia entered the post-Soviet period knowing next to nothing (either in theory or in practice) about money, budgeting, accounting, and business. They certainly lacked the practical skills for dealing with these aspects of life. Even law schools provided little knowledge about the actual practice of law, or even about the meaning and importance of law in society.

As Russia moves to a market economy and starts to develop and elaborate its legal system, a huge demand for legal and business education has been generated. Often this booming demand (which exceeds that for any other type of education) is being met by private schools, which cannot always give their students much useful information. As a result, many students have left the country to study business and law abroad. It will not be surprising if many of them do not return to Russia, contributing to the "brain drain" problem—the massive exodus of the most educated and able members of society. Western textbooks on business and law are being translated into Russian. More generally, American and Western European know-how is being transferred to Russia in almost every imaginable way. This is a valuable contribution to Russian society, whose troubles are highly associated with people's lack of expertise with all aspects of a market economy.

In sum, the average education of people in Russia is high in terms of years of formal schooling, but their level of useful knowledge and of practical skills in dealing with their own lives is very limited. For Russia's transition to a market economy to become successful, its schools will need to teach more of the practical skills that its people need.

6.6 SUMMARY

For the Russian people, the main achievement during the Soviet era was the expansion and development of education. As a result, the new Russian state began with a well-developed system of education and a highly educated population according to world standards. But the educational system that Russia inherited from the Soviet Union was organized on different principles than America's comprehensive system of education. Like most Western European countries, Russia has a differentiated educational system in which tracking of students into different schools with different curricula is a basic principle. Although there is a limited degree of tracking at the level of elementary schools, the most extensive and important tracking occurs after completion of the eighth grade. Secondary school students are allocated among three main types of schools: general secondary schools (an academic track); vocational secondary schools (PTU, which prepares students for manual work), and specialized, technically oriented secondary schools (tekhnikum, which prepares students for lower-level white-collar jobs). A fourth type, elite general secondary schools, which existed to a limited extent in Soviet times, has rapidly spread in the new Russia.

In Soviet times, the educational system had strong and direct linkages to the workforce. Indeed, most vocational schools were operated by ministries other than the ministry of education. For example, the ministry of agriculture ran many vocational schools to train youths to do various jobs on state and collective farms. Large factories often had their own vocational schools. Most students were sent to specific jobs after they graduated from secondary school. Naturally some applied to a university or other schools offering advanced training. After graduating from a university or other higher-level school, most students were also assigned to jobs.

The Soviet system in which schools and employers were directly linked no longer exists in Russia. This represents a huge change for young people. Nowadays, graduating students in Russia must find jobs for themselves, just as in the United States. Moreover, schools are starting to compete with each other and some have changed the educational curriculum radically. In Soviet times, education was based on the philosophy of enlightenment in the academic track and on very concrete skills needed in jobs in the vocational track. As everyday life and private entrepreneurs in the new Russia require practical know-how, educators in Russia are starting to develop curricula that are more oriented to helping students succeed in their lives. Like American education, schools increasingly try to help students learn how to function effectively in daily life, in the new job market, and in their personal life. Practical know-how is especially in demand in business and in the professions. In universities, legal and business know-how (especially that related to being an entrepreneur) is in great demand.

Social Stratification

Every society has some identifiable pattern of SOCIAL STRATIFICATION—some durable ordering of its members in terms of power, wealth, prestige, and other scarce social values. Stratification structures and processes vary to a greater and lesser extent across societies, as well as over time within a given society.

A common view is that social stratification stems from the structural foundations of a particular society. Russian history offers many examples that bolster this view. In 1917, peasants and workers comprised 90 percent of Russia's population. Though greatly outnumbering the tsarist elite, this 90 percent was being crushed by the misery of World War I, in which the tsarist elite was enmeshed. In this situation, a tiny group of Communist intellectuals was able to bring down the existing tsarist state almost solely through their effective usage of attractive slogans for the masses of workers and peasants. These few intellectuals not only introduced a new political regime and changed the basic organization of Russian society, they also fundamentally altered its system of social stratification.

To understand the SOCIAL STRUCTURE emerging after the collapse of the Soviet regime, we must examine history closely. More than any other social phenomenon considered in this book, the present-day realities of societal divisions and hierarchies in Russia are best understood through a historical approach.

7.1 HISTORICAL ROOTS

The historical roots of social stratification in Russia are uniquely distinct from those in the rest of Europe in several ways.

Every European society began as an agricultural society, and Russia is no exception. As an agricultural society, Russia had three unusual features, however. First, peasants have comprised an unusually large fraction of Russia's population long after most European countries. At the turn of the nineteenth century, peasants still constituted roughly four-fifths of the population in the Russian heartland, and even larger fractions in its borderlands. Second, most peasants in Russia lived in tiny village communities and traveled to work the fields. They did not live on separate family farms in the middle of their own fields as in the American West. Third, until 1861, most of Russia's peasants were serfs. While serfs were not slaves (they could not be bought and sold), they had very limited rights and many obligations to the nobleman on whose lands they lived. Even after they were freed from serfdom, most continued to live and work as they had before. The huge fraction of Russia's population who were serfs (and their descendants) were near the bottom of the social pyramid of traditional Russian society. They had almost no power, wealth, or prestige.

In the late nineteenth century, Russia began to inch toward **industrialization.** Although some individual industrialists and merchants became influential members of tsarist society, their numbers were tiny, and collectively they were not an important social force. Concurrently, urban workers started to increase in number. But, at the turn of the nineteenth century, workers still comprised only about 5 percent of Russia's population, much fewer than in core European countries, such as Britain, France, and Germany. Only the western areas of Russia had sufficient signs of industry and of an emerging market economy that could have spurred further economic and political development in pre-Soviet Russia (Braudel 1979).

Until 1917, the nobility (in conjunction with state bureaucrats) ruled Russia, whereas other core countries in Europe had experienced the growing power of parliamentary rule. This fact is the basic reason why Russia's status declined relative to other countries in the rapidly modernizing world of Europe in that period. This feudal-age political organization and social structure provided few opportunities for people to change their lives, and it postponed political and economic modernization in Russia.

Since the middle of the nineteenth century, the most progressive social force in Russian society has been the **intelligentsia.** At that time, only Italy and France had a corresponding social entity. The intelligentsia was composed entirely of educated citizens—those with a university or a secondary education. They were united as a STRATUM that was socially distinct from both the ruling nobility and the uneducated masses. This social stratum had great influence in the nineteenth century and later provided the Communists with both the intellectual power and recruits to rule the Soviet state. Much of the intelligentsia worked within the state bureaucracy of tsarist Russia, which helped to make it the second-most powerful elite group after the nobility.

The power of the tsarist political elite declined as World War I dragged on. This war resulted in a horrifying number of casualties and further impoverished the masses in Russia. Having eschewed gradual change, Russia was ripe for revolution. Employing surprisingly little force in 1917, the Bolsheviks overthrew the tsar in the name of the working class and put Russia in the hands of the Communists.

The Communist system is based on a view of society as composed of SOCIAL CLASSES. This view was developed by French historians around the end of the eighteenth century. The class-based depiction of a society's hierarchy became entrenched as the classical view of social stratification in Europe. According to this view, industrialization had divided European societies into two major, antagonistic classes: the BOURGEOISIE (capitalists) and the PROLETARIAT (workers). All leading European nations (England, France, Germany) took this twofold division to be a natural phenomenon and developed political-party systems based on these two classes in the nineteenth and first half of the twentieth centuries.

After years of studying the capitalist system in the nineteenth century, Karl Marx concluded that persistent exploitation of workers by capitalists would inevitably lead to the seizure of power by the working class, thereby creating the conditions for a Communist society. Ironically, when Marx's conclusion was first put into action in Russia in 1917, Russia had few workers or capitalists. The peasants and nobility were the dominant social groups when a Communist government was proclaimed in Russia.

Since the Communist system was ideologically and manifestly based on the principle of two major antagonistic social classes, stratification was a major political issue. Communism was intended to create a classless society in which social distinctions among people would recede. In theory, this process was to occur in two phases. In the first, the bourgeoisie would be eliminated; in the second, a wealthy society providing an equal standard of living for all citizens would be developed.

In Russia, the first phase was quickly accomplished through the abolition of private property, which removed the material support of the elite, and through mass killings and deportations of millions of the nobility and the bourgeoisie. In addition, faced with the extreme hostility of the new Soviet regime, roughly two million members of the former tsarist elite migrated to other countries.

The second phase—economic development to create equal conditions for all—was much harder to achieve. The Soviets were successful in the second phase, but not in the intended way. Most Soviet citizens enjoyed relative equality, but it was equality with a low standard of living. Even the Communist ruling elite had a modest standard of living as compared to elites in Western countries with market economies.

After the nobility and bourgeoisie were eliminated, the Soviet Union still had social inequality. It was based on two main structural features (Titma and Tuma 1993): SPATIAL DIVISIONS, and the economic branches (industries) where people worked.

It is hard for Americans to imagine the extent of **spatial inequalities** in the Soviet system. The Soviet command economy provided relatively equal salaries, housing, and material goods within a city, town, or village, but there were huge disparities between highly developed urban areas and the far-off hinterlands of industrial towns and rural areas. These disparities were evidenced in the priorities for the allocation of food and other consumer goods to various places according to roughly 10 ranks of settlements. Moscow had the highest priority; it had the first rank. Most regional capitals were next in line, and so on down a hierarchy that depended on a place's administrative functions and to a lesser extent on its population size. There were a few exceptions for places of importance to the defense industry that were unusually favored given their size. The countryside was not even included within this system of ranks and had to fend for itself to acquire resources. It was a common saying in the Soviet Union that Moscow and the rest of the country were as far apart as earth and sky. This saying did not refer primarily to physical distance but to social distance and, in particular, to differences in the quality of life.

The second major element of stratification in the Soviet Union reflected the structure of the command economy. Each branch of the economy (**industry**) was governed by a certain economic ministry. Each ministry controlled the main resources of production, consumption, and infrastructure within its own sphere. The ministries differed greatly in their resources and influence. Some had enormous resources and power; others were quite deprived. As a result, people's standard of living depended greatly on the industry where they or their spouse worked. This was especially true because many workplaces provided housing, meals, and some consumer goods to their workers.

Above we have described the main features of Soviet stratification in actuality. The official ideological view differentiated people into three main social groups on the basis of their **occupation** (type of work): peasants, workers, and the intelligentsia (all white-collar workers). Clerks and other lower white-collar workers (*slushchashchie*) were occasionally mentioned as a fourth, distinct social group, but usually they were regarded as part of the intelligentsia.

At the bottom in terms of their standard of living were the peasants, who lived and worked in substandard conditions on poorly managed collective or state farms. Due to industrialization and urbanization, their numbers steadily shrunk during the Soviet era. The ideology referred to peasants as a friendly class to the working class.

Workers "doing a job" on a stairway in basically the same way as in the Soviet past.

Officially the working class was at the top of the social hierarchy. Throughout the Soviet era, state statistics showed that most people were members of the working class. One must keep in mind, however, that statistics can be easily manipulated, especially in a highly centralized state like the Soviet Union. The party-state apparatus found it harder to maintain the target that at least half of the members of the Communist Party would be workers or peasants. During most of the Soviet Union's history, the majority of the Party's members belonged to the intelligentsia.

The Soviet state used these official labels of workers, peasants, and intelligentsia only for propaganda. Actual state policies were designed to avoid the development of any real social groups with a sense of class consciousness. It was feared that some group might challenge the state's power if it ever became a cohesive force.

When perestroika began in the mid-1980s, Russia's rural population stood at 27 percent and its urban population at 73 percent. Peasants comprised only a fifth of the total population, signifying a dramatic shift in the social composition of society since the last years of tsarist rule. Urban residents included industrial workers and the intelligentsia. Industrial workers were 25 percent of the workforce; another 25 percent were employed in a service industry. With its disregard for economic efficiency, the Soviet state had vastly enlarged the number of white-collar workers. Consequently, after the demise of the USSR, Russia inherited a large and lopsided percentage of white-collar workers, about a third of the total workforce, far more than the economy actually needed. The social distinctions between the intelligentsia and the working class in the urban population became increasingly pronounced during perestroika as the prominence and influence of the intelligentsia grew.

7.2 RUSSIA'S SOCIAL STRUCTURE

Two political-economic processes have reshaped the social structure of the new Russia in the first years after the fall of communism: privatization and industrial restructuring.

Although the newly emerging Russian state was weak, it did take major steps to reform the command economy. From 1991 onward, the government began large-scale privatization of state enterprises, the sale of state property to private individuals or groups. As in many other post-Communist countries, the only broad-based privatization of state assets occurred with apartments, which was done relatively equally on a mass scale. Privatization of major state properties benefited only a few. Nevertheless, increasing private ownership successfully promoted the market economy, which rather quickly became the healthiest sector of the Russian economy. People working in the private sector have begun to identify themselves with the market economy and form the social foundation for a democratic market society. Indeed, those working in the private sector have become a distinct social group.

No post-Communist country has been able to make the transition to a market economy without considerable industrial restructuring. The industries favored most in the Soviet era, especially defense and heavy manufacturing, suffered serious losses in production due to a sharp decline in the demand for their products. Changes in the patterns of economic demand led to widespread industrial downsizing, which precipitated a massive loss of jobs for both manual and white-collar workers in industry.

The collapse of industry had a major impact on the formation of social actors in the new Russia. Under Soviet rule, the working class was central to the ideology, but in actuality workers had no strong identity or organization. Workers' strikes and open demonstrations against the Soviet state rarely occurred due to the party-state's careful control to prevent such incidents. (A 1957 workers' strike in Novocherkassk was one of the few exceptions.) The new Russia has seen more worker organization, starting with miners and workers in the defense industry. A countrywide workers' movement has begun to emerge. Independent labor unions have arisen to provide organizational support for effective labor action. When miners blocked the railroads in 1998, the government was deterred from using force, not by the number of miners actually on strike, but by the knowledge that the entire working class could turn against the state at any moment. The working class is the best organized and most formidable popular force in Russia in the 1990s. It has an anti-market stance due to major decreases in living standards of the working class since reforms began. Only when the market economy begins to improve workers' lives is their stance likely to change. Until then, the danger of class cleavage remains a threat.

In the late 1980s, the intelligentsia almost unanimously supported Gorbachev's policy of perestroika. In the new Russia, market reforms have divided this social group into two camps. One part has moved into the private sector, either as employers or employees, and strongly supports market reforms. The second and larger part of the intelligentsia feels rejected by the new market economy and opposes reform. The majority of the previous intelligentsia have suffered heavy losses in both jobs and salaries because the new market economy does not need the many unproductive white-collar workers that the Soviet Union had created and supported.

To illustrate this point, consider the intelligentsia on collective farms, who constituted about a third of the workforce on these farms in the Soviet era. They are not linked with primary agricultural production but instead have various white-collar jobs—as managers, teachers, nurses, bookkeepers, clerks, agronomists, and so on. Efficient, profitable, private farms need few people in these kinds of positions. Not surprisingly, therefore, rural white-collar workers are resisting privatization of agricultural land because it threatens their entire way of life.

An excess of white-collar workers was found in nooks and crannies throughout the Soviet economy. They were (and still are) especially common in the state apparatus. Even though the new Russian state is nearly bankrupt, the percentage of white-collar workers in the public sector (e.g., teachers, health care personnel) is the largest in Russian history. Since most white-collar workers in the public sector are not being paid by the state, they are starting to organize to fight against government reforms that threaten their positions. Labor unions are gaining strength among white-collar workers, and their actions have begun to be more effective. Strikes by white-collar workers, the closing of schools by teachers, and other such protest actions have become routine events. This group's support for market reforms, which had initially been very high, is slowly declining.

The formation of Russian society remains an ongoing process. Old social classes, strata, and social groups not only continue to exist but are gaining a greater voice in public affairs as they seek to organize themselves to support or oppose the actions of the government.

7.3 SOCIAL MOBILITY

SOCIAL MOBILITY refers to movements along a society's dimensions of scarce and socially desirable rewards (e.g., wealth, power, prestige). One basic distinction is between INTERGENERATIONAL MOBILITY, which compares a person's position to those of his or her parents, and INTRAGENERATIONAL MOBILITY, which refers to the mobility that is made over the course of a person's life, from entry into adulthood until old age.

A society's openness depends on both kinds of mobility. **Intergenerational mobility** is, however, an especially important indicator of openness because it tells the extent to which socioeconomic advantages and disadvantages are transmitted from one generation to another. Historically, most stable societies have been characterized by high inheritance of social positions. Thus, in tsarist Russia, the sons and daughters of the nobility also belonged to the nobility, and the children of serfs were also serfs. The development of societies with market economies has generally increased mobility and societal openness. That is, it has increased the likelihood that the social positions of adult children and their parents differ.

Social scientists further distinguish between STRUCTURAL MOBILITY and EXCHANGE MOBILITY. The former refers to mobility resulting from shifts in the composition of positions in society or of the population. For example, the decline of agriculture in both Soviet Russia and the United States was a major source of structural mobility because it propelled farmers and their children into the industrial workforce. In contrast, exchange mobility refers to mobility occurring for other reasons. For example, society may begin to reward people differentially on the basis of skills they have acquired rather than on attributes that they have inherited.

By many criteria Soviet society generated much **structural mobility.** Three main factors caused this mobility. First, both during and after the Civil War following the 1917 Revolution, there occurred the elimination of the old tsarist elite, including the nobility, industrialists, merchants, and part of the intelligentsia. The removal of the tsarist elite created a pressing need for a new elite to perform many functions of the old elite, such as administering and managing.

This need was amplified by the second and third main reasons for much social mobility in the Soviet period: industrialization and urbanization. Industrialization produced many enormous factories, which led to the founding and rapid growth of industrial towns and cities, such as Yekaterinburg, Novosibirsk, Nizhniy Novgorod, and Samara. The swift development of industry spawned a great deal of mobility, especially for peasants. Peasants accounted for about 80 percent of the population of Russia proper in 1920 but only about 20 percent in 1990. This huge shift in the composition of the population points to both the massive migration from villages to cities in the Soviet era and the high level of mobility of peasants, mainly into the working class. The command economy stripped rural areas of the most productive and hard-working farmers, who saw greater opportunities in urban areas. Even in the 1980s, most cities and towns in Russia, with the exception of its million-cities, had large populations who had been born in the countryside.

Urbanization induced another wave of structural mobility because cities required the development of a sizable urban infrastructure, which in turn created positions for white-collar workers at all levels (e.g., managers, clerks, professionals, sales personnel) to operate this infrastructure. By the 1970s, the Soviet Union had begun to shift toward a postindustrial, service-centered economy, creating even more opportunities for mobility to white-collar work.

To an overwhelming degree, structural mobility in the Soviet era generated upward mobility (cf. Yanowitch and Fischer 1973). That is, state-mandated changes in the economy led to the development of more skilled and prestigious jobs and the shrinking of simpler (often manual) jobs. Structural changes in every modern society have increased the numbers of jobs for white-collar workers and professionals and reduced the numbers of farmers and workers.

To date, much structural mobility in the new Russia has generated downward mobility. It comes in the form of forced early retirement for older adults and high unemployment (often permanent unemployment) among middle-aged and some younger adults. In Soviet times, a job was guaranteed, as was housing, health care, and a pension for the elderly and disabled. The dismantling of the social safety network in Russia has heightened the economic hardships and psychological distress resulting from its seemingly endless unemployment. Official statistics say that the unemployment rate in Russia is only about 10 percent of the labor force. Unofficial surveys suggest, however, that actual unemployment is three to four times higher than this.

Unemployment is not randomly or equally distributed. In some regions (e.g., the North Caucasus) and some towns (e.g., those with a single large factory whose products are not in demand), it is estimated that more than two-thirds of the working-age adults are jobless. In contrast, unemployment is fairly low in Moscow. Unemployment is also linked to industry. Enterprises in heavy manufacturing and in much of the defense industry have enormous difficulties in finding products that they can produce and sell. Layoffs from idling and closed factories affect not only workers but the intelligentsia. Russia cannot sustain the huge scientific and engineering workforce that was required to feed the Soviet military machine. The Russian government is faced with the challenge of how to handle the huge downward structural mobility induced by industrial downsizing and the resulting dearth of employment opportunities for those who formerly worked in the affected industries and factories in Soviet times.

The picture is not totally bleak, however, as we have noted earlier. With the blossoming of the private sector, the rise of entrepreneurship, and the expansion of the service sector, some upward structural mobility has been induced by Russia's transition. Still, as we write this book in the late 1990s, more Russians have experienced downward mobility than upward mobility to date. For most people, economic improvement and upward movement on the social ladder continue to be a distant hope, not the present reality.

Mobility that is not linked to structural changes in the economy is called **exchange mobility.** It means that some people move up or down in the social hierarchy, even when the structure of employment and population composition are constant. No good data exist to give a clear picture of exchange mobility in either the Soviet Union or the new Russia because large-scale, random, countrywide surveys of the population were never done. The following discussion is based on several empirical studies of regions of Russia with uncertain generalizability to the whole country as a whole (Ilin 1996; Titma 1997; Gerber and Hout 1998).

With regard to intergenerational mobility, about 20 percent of adult children had a position higher or lower than their parents (Titma 1997). It can largely be explained by other types of mobility. A typical example of downward mobility occurred when the children of agricultural professionals living in a rural area became lower white-collar or agricultural workers. Another common pattern was that parents moved to the ranks of professionals and migrated to a larger city, where their children ended up as workers. Many youths in major cities did not work hard to be admitted to a university because higher education did not seem to offer any significant material benefits in Soviet society.

During the 1970s, Soviet society was fairly noncompetitive from the viewpoint of individuals, partly due to the comparatively high degree of equality in income and standard of living. Even admittance to a university was not especially competitive. Most colleges and universities had acceptance rates of around 50 percent. The exceptions where competition was stiff included the top universities, such as Moscow State University and the Mathematical-Physics Institute. Entrance into the Diplomatic Academy and the Foreign Trade Institute was also very competitive, though somewhat less so than at the few top universities.

Entrance into the Russian elite, on the other hand, was highly competitive. As with elites everywhere, having parents in an elite position was a big asset in this competition. Among the Soviet elite broadly defined, there was the least competition for three major professions: agricultural specialists, engineers, and teachers. Most university graduates who filled these positions had parents who were workers, lower white-collar workers, or peasants. Competition in law, medicine, and the humanities was much tougher, and the university graduates who gained these positions generally came from professional families. Entrance into the top elite in cultural arenas was influenced even more by parents' high social status.

Upward mobility was manifested in three main ways in the Soviet Union. First, since a person's social status was primarily defined by occupation, upward social mobility included moving from professions with lower prestige to ones with higher prestige, or from lower-status occupations to professions (which typically have high status). Second, migration from a particular city or region to a more developed one was another form of upward mobility. Finally, moving from one industry, enterprise, or organization to one with more prestige or resources also moved someone up the social ladder and could improve his or her quality of life, even if the person kept the same occupation.

In Western countries, a person's social position stems largely from the parents' education and occupation, especially the father's. In analyses of survey data collected in regions of Russia during the Soviet era (Titma 1997), the mother's status often had a greater influence than the father's in determining a person's social position. Further, the mother's education rather than her occupation was the more important factor. It appears that the mother had more influence on major decisions about children's future and that the father's views mattered less.

Another factor promoting social mobility was the expansion of education during the Soviet period (see Chapter 6). In the 1920s, roughly a quarter of Russia's population was literate. By 1990, four out of five Russians had at least a secondary education according to official statistics. A secondary or higher education was not needed to be a peasant or do manual work, so the rising educational levels of the population applied a subtle pressure to expand the intelligentsia. Because of the command economy's neglect of the market forces of supply and demand, a third of the Russian labor force was employed as a member of the intelligentsia by 1990. As the Soviet era ended, it was the fastest-growing social group. There was high upward mobility into the ranks of the intelligentsia from both the working class and the peasantry.

A third source of social mobility in Soviet Russia was migration, which generally began when youths moved to cities to receive secondary and higher education, and then continued to reside in the same city after graduation. A better quality of life in an urban area, rather than education per se, seemed to be the primary motivation for migration.

Yet another way to be upwardly mobile was to change jobs and move to a more rewarding industry, enterprise, or organization. As explained in Chapter 5, each industry was under the control of a particular ministry, and industries varied enormously in working and living conditions, as well as in the benefits that they provided to their employees. The defense industry received not only an abundance of resources for production and research but also various social benefits, such as housing and a comfortable supply of goods and services. Such benefits outweighed most salary differentials. For example, it was usually materially more advantageous to be a locksmith in a defense plant than to be a university professor. Since almost all positions in industry were assigned by the state, a youth's parents needed to make careful social arrangements with the appropriate agents in the state apparatus in order for the youth to be assigned work in the wealthier and more beneficial industries.

Social mobility during a person's own life is called **intragenerational mobility.** It starts with a person's educational history and lasts through his or her entire working life. Generally, a young person considering a specific job or occupation weighs the future prospects of that position. The possibility for upward intragenerational mobility is a very important motivation for work. In the United States, it is not uncommon for students to transfer to different universities, and for adults to change their workplaces and even their occupations, especially in early adulthood. The situation under the Soviet economy was very different because careers were planned for labor in specific plants or institutional organizations. In highly selected areas, such as science, sports, and the arts, talented individuals could experience upward mobility on the basis of their achievements. But positions as managers or in the upper levels of the party-state were not filled on the basis of talent and high achievement.

Students were assigned to different educational tracks, sometimes from the first grade, and more commonly around the eighth grade. At a later point, university graduates were assigned to a specific factory or organization. Gradual promotion within an organization or industry was standard, and any career change not initiated by the state greatly diminished future opportunities for advancement. A predictable career with slow advancement was the rule.

Given this societal background, people's difficulty in making the transition to the fast-paced, constantly shifting market economy is not very surprising. To take responsibility for, plan, and execute one's own career is an entirely new concept for Russians. Younger generations of Russians are clearly and willingly taking advantage of labor market opportunities when they arise, and their intragenerational mobility can soon be as diversified as in Western countries.

7.4 THE ELITE

Under the tsars and in the Stalinist era, the military (including those in state security) and state bureaucrats were the predominant members of Russia's elite. Because Russia has had the largest standing army in the world since the first half of the eighteenth century, its military elite has accordingly been large and complex. And, as the tsar and the nobility lived lives of leisure, a large state bureaucracy was needed to run the Russian Empire. The Soviet state reduced the size of the military elite, but it accomplished this feat by swelling the state bureaucracy.

In the Soviet era, for the first time in Russian history, the elite included a third important group, industrialists and managers. Indeed, shortly before the demise of the Soviet Union, industrialists had begun to outnumber state bureaucrats within the elite, even filling top positions in the party-state apparatus. A fourth component of the Soviet elite con-

sisted of the humanities-oriented intelligentsia, including writers, journalists, and artists.

Of the four groups in the Soviet elite, the intelligentsia had the
broadest base.[1] It was also the most influential group in facilitating the
collapse of the Soviet Union. Under glasnost, a plurality of opinions and
open intellectual competition were established in the mass media. Representatives of all titular nations within the borders of the USSR could be
found in the elite in the arts and humanities, and they continually be-
rated the Soviet government for its imperial mentality. They began to
protest openly against the Communist system and to accuse Soviet leaders of failing to achieve the promise of a better life through communism.

Other groups in the Soviet elite had, for the most part, also lost
their strong ideological commitment to communism. Members of these
elites were increasingly motivated primarily by their individual interests
and were unable to act collectively to promote their survival under the
Soviet system. Without clear goals and plans for reform emanating from
the top Soviet leadership, the Soviet Empire collapsed from within. Importantly, in the sudden and nonviolent shift to a new political system,
members of the old Soviet political elite were not immediately pushed
out of their privileged positions. They therefore had time to adapt to the
changes. More significantly yet, they held positions that allowed them to
act as midwives to the new system, which insofar as possible meant trying to find and create ways to maintain their elite status.

Not surprisingly, therefore, the **new elite** in Russia generally re-
flects its counterpart in the Soviet era, but with some important differences. The greatest similarity lies in simple overlap, with the overwhelming majority of the new elite comprised of former members of the CPSU
(cf. Róna-Tas 1994). This incongruity is actually essential because former
members of the CPSU usually had the most administrative experience
and were among the most educated. In the Soviet Union, membership in
the Communist Party generally reached 50 percent among university-
educated people, where it was required to obtain a good job and was not
usually chosen on the basis of personal belief. Another reason for high
persistence within the elite is that Russia endured four generations of
Communist rule. To a large extent, initial recruitment into the new elite
was possible only on the basis of the previous Soviet elite. The situation
contrasts with that in the East European countries that became Communist after World War II. More of the pre-Communist elites were still
available to fill positions in the new post-Communist elite in these other
East European countries.

---

1. For influential discussions of the elite in Communist countries, see Djilas (1957) and
   Konrad and Szelényi (1979).

The most visible part of the new Russian elite that is formed on the basis of the previous Soviet party-state apparatus is the **political elite.** Former members and staff of the Soviet Union's Politburo and Central Committee serve in the Duma, the Federation Council, the Council of Ministers, and the president's staff. On the national level, the second echelon of the Soviet party-state apparatus form the majority of Russia's new political elite. It also has many recruits from former leaders of the KOMSOMOL, the Communist Youth League.

During the Soviet era, only a few people in the provinces, such as local party bosses and their entourages, were regarded as members of the country's political elite. In the new Russia, democratic elections of both local legislative bodies and administration heads in the provinces have widened the base of the local political elite, which is accountable to local constituents. Local elites also have a voice on a countrywide level through Russia's upper house, the Federation Council. The increasing importance of local political elites translates into greater influence over countrywide elections, and fresh blood is entering the national political scene directly from success in the provinces. For example, 29-year-old Alexandr Ryzhkov from the remote Altay Republic became the deputy speaker of the Duma in 1999. He rocketed onto the national scene five years after graduating from Altay University, a not very prestigious university. After decentralization of power to lower regional levels and competitive elections, the Russian political elite is likely to be increasingly geographically dispersed like its counterpart in the United States.

The former managers of the command economy were not well equipped to manage their old enterprises in the new economy and have had difficulty surviving in the new **business elite.** Only managers in natural monopolies (like Gazprom) and unusually competent individuals from the former state managers (such as former premier Viktor Chernomyrdin) have managed to retain their positions within the new elite. For the most part, the composition of the new business elite is dramatically different than the economic elite in Soviet times. Hardworking, highly skilled young people are advancing rapidly in the new system, and business leadership has fallen into the hands of a younger generation who are well versed in the laws of supply and demand, many through earlier experience in the black market. Many former officials in the Komsomol also quickly figured out that making money is better than a political career, and some of them have been quite successful in private business. More than a few of these new businesspeople will not be able to survive the tough competition that they face. Nevertheless, in its first decade, the new Russia has developed a powerful business elite whose members have exerted and will continue to exert great influence in Russian political life. In view of the influence that the business elite has acquired, it is all the more striking that this new elite has been penetrated by many individuals who were not in the former Soviet elite.

Russia's **state bureaucrats** not only continue to endure but have become the most influential force in society. No other modern European country has a larger proportion of state bureaucrats. The number of state bureaucrats is actually even greater in the new Russia than in Soviet times, and the percentage of the state budget that supports the bureaucracy is also much greater than in the Soviet era. These bureaucrats are the most entrenched and persistent segment of Russia's elite. They easily made the transition to a market society because their actual activities and functions are not very different from what they were in Soviet times. The bureaucracy had (and to a great extent still has) control of all state assets. It is also in charge of the privatization of state enterprises. With their control of all state institutions, state bureaucrats are able to skim personal benefits from the public goods and services that they are supposed to allocate to the public. Though the overwhelming majority of bribes in the new Russia end up in their hands, they are rarely punished for corrupt behavior. The state bureaucracy lobbies extensively for its institutional interests in the political arena, and its enormous power ensures its survival.

A large part of the new elite in Russia are members of the **law enforcement establishment.** Judges, prosecutors, police officers, and other security officers are generally the same people who held these positions during the Soviet era. This is not very surprising because they knew how to perform tasks associated with this kind of work and other people did not have this knowledge. Corruption runs rampant throughout law enforcement personnel because their salaries are low and not even paid on a regular basis (see Chapter 8). This huge group of mostly underqualified state employees has been relegated to the margins of the national elite. However, the importance of their official duties still make them immensely powerful, and they are steadily learning how to wield that power. Changes in the law enforcement system are happening very slowly.

The **cultural elite** has changed significantly since the fall of communism. The intelligentsia in the creative arts, who had worked so hard to bring down the Soviet regime, expected art and culture to flourish in the new Russia. In reality, state subsidies of cultural activities have been drastically reduced. At the same time, the national cultural elite has begun to be selected in open competition where outcomes are determined by supply and demand. Security of an elite position and an adequate income has come first to those working in the popular media. Television anchorpersons, talk-show hosts, movie actors, and pop singers have acquired substantial incomes and prestige. In contrast, writers, theater actors, classical musicians, dancers, and artists, who had been very prominent under the restrictive Soviet atmosphere, have lost their influential positions, and their number has been radically reduced.

The income and social status of doctors, scientists, university professors, and educators are low compared to their counterparts in the

United States, and also much lower than during Soviet times. It is likely to take a long time for even the cream of these highly educated professionals to become reincorporated into Russia's national elite.

After 70 years of near nonexistence, the Russian Orthodox Church reestablished itself quickly as a powerful force in the national arena. Church leaders have become an obligatory part of national and local ceremonies. As the most significant spiritual force in Russia, the Church is providing careers for hundreds of thousands of new clergymen. These new clergymen have some prestige in local communities, but very few could be said to belong to the national elite.

7.5 EMERGING STRATIFICATION

Social stratification in the new Russia is being reshaped. Two different themes stand out in the new system: the basic grounds of stratification and the distinct social groups being formed. Below we try to discern the basic trends in stratification that will characterize the new Russia. One must keep in mind, however, that Russia at the end of the twentieth century is very much a transitional society. Some phenomena seemingly significant now may be transitory.

As indicated in Section 7.1, the official ideology of the Soviet Union differentiated among workers, peasants, and the intelligentsia. However, the three were essentially social categories and were not actual, organized groups or collective actors in society. Because salaries were relatively equal and a secondary source of economic well-being, actual divisions in Soviet society were based primarily on locality and the branch of the economy in which people worked. Occupation was not entirely irrelevant (e.g., it affected working conditions), but it was of secondary importance. Other individual attributes of lesser significance included education, gender, nationality, and membership in the CPSU.

Social hierarchies in the new Russia are still evolving but seem to be organized on different lines. Most strikingly, **earned income,** which was fairly unimportant during the Soviet era, has become a major dimension of social inequality. After decades of Soviet rule, in which the extremes of wealth and poverty had been eliminated, income inequality has quickly emerged in Russia, even though it is not yet a fully capitalist society. Because official statistics are unreliable, we give only rough estimates based on incomplete data. Still, preliminary evidence suggests that the top fifth enjoys an average income 25 times greater than the bottom fifth, a much larger ratio than in established market-based societies in Europe. Worse, there are no signs yet that a sizable middle-income group is emerging. At least two-thirds of all Russians are struggling in poverty. All post-Communist countries have experienced heightened income differentiation, but it has rarely been as great as in Russia (Silverman and Yanowitch 1997).

The division of property and economic assets is also much less equal. To some extent, this change was inevitable since the Soviet system forbade ownership of private property, excluding personal belongings like clothing and furnishings. Through privatization, most private property and financial capital in Russia has become concentrated in the hands of a very few.

Ownership of private property is still a socially distinguishing characteristic in Russia because the majority of farms, factories, and other production units are still in the hands of the state. This situation is clearly a transitional phenomenon. Private, communal, and other non-state forms of ownership seem to be gradually acquiring most enterprises. Income differences between the private sector and the sector financed by the state budget are now sizable, as mentioned previously, and are unlikely to be abolished soon. The private sector provides jobs with higher incomes, but the state sector, despite the irregularity of salary payments, still offers more security.

In the Soviet era, **locality** was extremely important to material well-being. This line of SOCIAL DIFFERENTIATION still exists but for different reasons than in the Soviet past where localities were allocated resources by the state according to a system of ranked categories. Ironically, the market allocates resources to places in ways that resemble those of the old category system of allocation.

Moscow continues to be a magnet for money and power. Almost all of the new Russia's finances (around 90 percent) are located there. The city has grown rapidly in almost every imaginable respect. Its physical appearance has changed even more quickly than Berlin's, which has undergone a building boom since German reunification. The labor market in Moscow, unlike that anywhere else in Russia, has job vacancies and even provides work for people living outside the city's boundaries. Its residents enjoy a much higher standard of living than the rest of the country, and the median income is much higher than in the country as a whole. Moscow even has a sizable and flourishing middle class, which is becoming politically active.

At the other extreme is the countryside, which is generally even more destitute than under communism. The dire straits of rural areas largely result from restructuring of industry, the other major line of differentiation in the Soviet era. On the whole, the impact of industry on inequalities in Russia is losing its significance. The only clear exception is agriculture, which has a unique position in every industrialized country. Russian peasants live in extreme poverty and are not experiencing a smooth transition to a market economy. The enormous unproductive state farms left from the Soviet era remain in place in the 1990s. Except in a few isolated places, peasants still have no property rights to the land that they farm. The fourth of Russians who live in villages are a distinct group having a survival strategy; they make up the most conservative constituency in Russia. Village leaders typically come from this group of people, and their conservative mentality and lack of preparedness for market conditions dominate the countryside. Russia's rural elite might organize a grassroots movement and start to play a larger role in Russian politics. The main factors working against such a movement are their physical dispersion over Russia's huge landmass and its hopelessly inadequate transportation and communication systems—the same factors that Marx argued made French peasants hard to mobilize in the eighteenth century.

In industrial and postindustrial countries around the world, occupation is usually the most important basis of societal stratification schemes. As we pointed out earlier, the impact of occupation on social inequality was secondary in the Soviet Union. Russia's transformation to a market economy heightens the importance of the OCCUPATIONAL STRUCTURE. Eventually its importance is likely to resemble that in the United States.

Historically, Russia has differed radically from the United States in one particular respect. Namely, professions have never been distinct social actors in Russia. The Soviet system effectively prevented attempts to organize professionals independently from the party-state apparatus. This situation has changed. Leading professionals in business, law, and other core fields of a market economy are likely to organize as distinct social actors in Russia. When this happens, the intelligentsia will cease to be the large cohesive (if unorganized) social group that it was in the Soviet era. Fission of the intelligentsia into distinctive professions, semiprofessions, and other occupational groups would diminish the likelihood of class-based division of Russia.

The most significant result of marketization may be the fate of the working class, the social basis for the October Revolution of 1917. It was actually miners and factory workers who brought Yeltsin to power. But their numbers have fallen sharply in the 1990s, and the Russian working class may eventually cease to be a major, unified political force. Instead it may disperse into smaller, more differentiated social groups as workers in different occupations and industries begin to have markedly different pay, living conditions, and chances to better their lives.

There are no signs yet that Russia's political leadership understands the dangers of these new societal divisions. If the working class does not differentiate into smaller groups, this formidable and sometimes volatile social class could prevent Russia from achieving stability. Emerging class divisions could intensify hostility and make the new Russia resemble tsarist Russia in its major social cleavages. Russian society could become divided into large, powerful, oppositional social actors. As the development in Europe in the last two centuries shows, such social cleavages can be dangerous. To follow the American path—one that avoids such divisions and includes numerous social actors in the national arena—would facilitate Russia's political and economic development and help it become a reasonable member of the world polity.

7.6 SUMMARY

Until the end of World War I, the tsar and a feudal-style nobility ruled Russia. In the second half of the nineteenth century, Russia's social structure was dreadful from the viewpoint of modern America. Ninety percent of the Russian population were either peasants tied to the estates of the nobility or members of various conquered nations (e.g., Poles, Ukrainians, Uzbeks). The world's first socialist state began in 1917 when the Communists were able to gain the support of suppressed people—soldiers, peasants, workers, and conquered nations—using simple slogans with a broad popular appeal and an effective organization.

In accord with Communist ideology, the Soviet Union officially had two social classes, workers and peasants. Workers were the ruling class, and the "friendly" peasant class cooperated with them. Eventually the intelligentsia, an expanding segment of the Soviet population, were recognized as a cooperating stratum. Thus, the Soviet Union officially had a class system lacking a capitalist bourgeoisie or a nobility because members of these classes had been eliminated or had emigrated.

To achieve the "equality" that was one of the basic Communist slogans, the Soviet state restricted people's salaries and income to a fairly narrow range. As a result, hard work and achievements at work were not rewarded because salaries were fixed and depended very little on talent or effort.

Social inequality exists in every society, and Soviet society was no exception. Real inequalities occurred within two main institutions. One was locality: the regions and types of settlements where people lived. A common saying was that a place a 100 kilometers from Moscow was as far from Moscow as the moon is from the sun. This was because the quality of life was so much better in Moscow than outside it. In the 1980s, on average two million people visited Moscow each nonwork day in order to buy food and consumer goods that were unobtainable in the places where they lived. The source of these differences was the allocation of the state budget. There were roughly 10 ranks of localities, with Moscow occupying the top rank and other places having lower ranks, largely based on their function within the state.[2] Rural areas had no rank at all, and consequently received no state subsidies. In a society in which everything was state controlled and regulated, this system of allocating the state budget generated enormous social inequalities.

---

2. Thus, the capital of a small oblast had a higher rank and received more resources than a larger city that was not a political center.

Inside GUM, formerly the leading Soviet department store, now the outpost of well-known western retailers.

Another dimension of inequality was based on the economic sector in which a person worked. The Soviet Union's resources were divided at the highest level among different economic ministries, and these resources were then further allocated among workplaces by each ministry. The ministries receiving the most resources (in particular, the defense ministry) were able to furnish their workers with ample stocks of food and consumer goods, as well as housing. They were also able to build and operate their own resorts for workers to use for vacations and other communal facilities (e.g., medical clinics, child care centers, athletic facilities). For employees of ministries receiving the least resources, such as the ministry of education, life offered a lifetime of long queues and years of waiting for a small apartment or a washing machine. All in all, the variation in benefits due to a person's workplace was vastly greater than the differences in official salaries.

For the Soviet elite, their main privilege was the complete power that they had over resources and the people under their command. Thus, stratification among individuals in Soviet society was based primarily on power rather than on money and material well-being.

Because the Soviet Union rapidly developed from a backward and mainly rural country to a predominantly urbanized and industrialized country, its people experienced considerable mobility from generation to generation. Mobility within a person's lifetime was fairly low because the Soviet command economy allocated people to certain jobs and expected people in most occupations to remain where they were put for their entire lives. More than a third of adults stayed in their first job until they retired.

It is not yet possible to describe the system of social stratification in the new Russia, which is slowly emerging with some legacies from its tsarist and Soviet pasts. Some patterns are apparent. According to some estimates, two-thirds of the Russian population can be categorized as poor. As a group, those in the most desperate situation are older adults, those ages 50 and above. Most of them have lost their jobs, and inflation has eaten up their life savings. They try to eke out a living on pensions of under 10 dollars a month (when the state does manage to pay their pensions). Another clear line of inequality is between people working in the private sector and those working in state-owned enterprises; the former are much better off than the latter. As in the past, those living in Moscow tend to be much better off than people living in other parts of Russia, with incomes in Moscow averaging four times those elsewhere.

As usual, the elite in the new Russia is better off than the rest of the population. The majority of the new elite come from the previous Soviet elite. However, many younger people have managed to enter the new business elite.

Last but not least, collective action by workers has emerged. Workers are the most numerous social class in the new Russia and may become a major actor in the future. Russia may not be on the road to an American-style system of stratification in which multiple strata pursue their interests and make compromises to achieve their goals. Instead, polarization of society between the working class and a ruling political and business elite may reemerge. It would be ironic if the world's first Communist society ends up with two opposing classes, workers and capitalists, as Marx had predicted would be the endpoint of capitalist societies.

CHAPTER 8

Law and Crime

8.1 LAW VERSUS ORDERS AND FEAR

Like many other aspects of the new Russian state, the role of law and the structure of its legal system have roots in the past. Traces of the tsarist period are evident; but having endured for over 70 years, the Soviet system especially influences the present. Persistent effects of two main features of the Soviet system are particularly noteworthy. One concerns the centrality of **law** as contrasted with **orders from above.** The second involves the basic means used to maintain people's compliance with laws and decrees: **fear.**

Although the USSR had a great many laws, law was not actually held to be supreme in the Soviet system. The 1936 constitution was full of democratic pronouncements, but the Soviet state never treated it as the actual legal bedrock for the USSR. Rather, the state regarded it as a declaration of good intentions, with no inalienable legal consequences. For all practical purposes, the Soviet state, courts, and law enforcement agencies ignored the constitution. Some laws were passed that even contradicted the constitution directly.

Early versions of Soviet law were called REVOLUTIONARY JUSTICE and were declarations by the leaders of the October Revolution of 1917. Following the subsequent development of a sophisticated party-state apparatus, law in the Soviet Union evolved into what was commonly termed PHONE-CALL LAW, in which orders were passed downward from the top, usually through a series of telephone calls. Soviet officials treated orders from their superiors as taking precedent over laws, and this mentality still exists in the new Russia.

In the Soviet Union's final years, law acquired more importance, but it never outweighed the decisions of top officials in the CPSU. In practice, laws were nuisances to be bypassed. This was especially true when the basic interests of the CPSU or the Soviet state were at issue. Law had much greater relevance to and real consequences for criminal behavior (criminal law) and relations between citizens and corporate actors (civil law). But even in these domains, party-state officials regularly (though not especially frequently) used phone-call law.

The primary means used to obtain the compliance of people in the Soviet Union was fear of punishment (cf. Conquest 1991). This fear was firmly instilled in people's minds after Stalin developed the world's largest and most extensive system of forced labor camps, the GULAG (Solzhenitsyn 1973). Fear remained a major motivator of people's behaviors throughout Stalin's rule and was the main incentive for the loyalty of members of the party-state apparatus. As long as people remained within the NOMENKLATURA, the list of categories of people eligible for certain party-state jobs, party APPARATCHIKS were usually given a reasonably comfortable standard of living. But they could be punished, or at least dropped from the nomenklatura, if they did not "behave properly." For a party bureaucrat, loss of a job meant the end of a career and eliminated the source of a livelihood.

The new Russia has largely succeeded in eliminating the top elite's fear of violent or extreme reprisals. For the first time in Russian history, the preceding political elite (the Soviet elite) was incorporated into the new Russian state, instead of being ousted from power. Yeltsin took major steps toward eradicating the long-held Russian tradition of revenge against one's enemies. He not only refused to take punitive actions against the orchestrators of both the August 1991 PUTSCH against Gorbachev and the October 1993 rebellion against him in the Supreme Soviet, but he allowed these individuals to retain their positions within the elite. Moreover, he refrained from extreme forms of revenge despite many calls for their blood from some of his advisors. Restrained reactions like these have changed the entire climate within the Russian political elite.

These developments have also helped to eliminate the pervasive fear surrounding the state and its law enforcement agencies among the general public. With this fear largely gone, the quality and actions of law enforcement agencies can be questioned.

Declaring that law reigns supreme, and actually **behaving** as if law is supreme are two entirely different things. Creating a social and political system founded on the rule of law is arguably the most difficult task confronting the new Russia.

All Soviet bureaucrats were ingrained with the doctrine of following the orders of their superior or boss, NACHALNIK. To get bureaucrats to obey written laws is a completely different and much harder task. In a time of rapid transition, many people perceive laws as irrelevant abstractions unless directly applied to themselves. The mentality of "just following orders" can seem the safest way to survive in an unstable environment. This mentality still permeates Russia's entire state apparatus.

For ordinary people, laws remain tools of the state that are mainly used against them for the benefit of the state or state bureaucrats. Confusion and disillusionment reign in the new Russia because there is no longer a local office of the CPSU or a trade union to listen to people's complaints and to dispense some type of rough-and-ready justice. Turning to the courts for adjudicating possible violations of laws and rules is still considered abnormal. In Russia, courts have been associated with meting out severe punishments to criminals from the days of the tsars.

A well-known Russian joke illustrates this point: "Someone said that either Ivanov's bicycle was stolen or he stole someone's bicycle. Something suspicious happened to him." It really was not important to his neighbors whether Ivanov was the victim or the perpetrator of an offense: Ivanov was involved in something suspicious! The same was and still is true with regard to Russian courts. An ordinary person would not go to a court if it could possibly be avoided because he or she would be tainted afterward. In this sort of social and political climate, it could take generations for law to assume a central role in Russian society, as it does in the United States.

There are new issues about how law enforcement itself is acting within the framework of law. Adherence to law, if it is to be internalized by the population at large, needs to begin with a country's top leaders, who serve as role models for the rest of the country. Americans know this well from Nixon's need to resign the presidency because of the Watergate break-in and cover-up and more recently from President Clinton's impeachment.

In 1990–1991, repressive actions against movements toward independence in the Baltic, Georgian, Azerbaidjan and Tajik republics were initiated by Gorbachev's team (usually when Gorbachev was said to be "traveling") and carried out by Soviet military commanders, who usually were given the blame for these actions later on. Interestingly, in the new Russia, top military commanders have been the first to start caring about obeying laws. In October 1993, when Yeltsin arrived at army headquarters to order troops to storm the White House where the rebellious members of the Supreme Soviet were sitting, the minister of defense, Pavel Grachev, demanded that Yeltsin give his orders to the troops in writing. Surprised at being asked to give written orders, Yeltsin answered that he would send them by his adjutant. This incident illustrates how even loyal people in the government (for this description certainly applied to Grachev) have begun to demand obedience to the law in crises and to try to force the president to comply with the law. Such incidents are hopeful signs that law may begin to be more central in Russia.

There is considerable evidence, however, that President Yeltsin broke laws. When unhappy with the way things were going, he sometimes reverted to the old Russian style of personal command, firing his prime ministers and ruling the country through orders from above rather than through law. Understandable excuses for his aberrant behavior, such as his poor health, do not negate the fact that orders from above can still dominate law in the new Russia.

Legislation per se has a lengthy history in Russia. Rulers were always concerned about the "proper" behavior of their subjects and introduced numerous and broad-ranging prescriptions to make sure that their wishes were followed. To give one example, in the late 1980s, the SOVIET COUNCIL OF MINISTERS issued a decree regulating the construction of summer *dachas* (small vacation homes) throughout the country. The decree specified that bathrooms would have the same dimensions and the same location (outside the main building) from the Arctic Circle to the Black Sea. Not surprisingly, much of such highly detailed and often irrelevant legislation was ignored by everyone, who understood that its real purpose had little to do with the actual content of the law. Extensive and detailed legislation was created mainly in case someone needed to be punished. One could be certain that everyone had violated some law. If officials wanted to punish someone, they only needed to figure out which law had been violated.

Russia's constitution gives the power to initiate legislation to the Duma, the lower house of parliament. To go into effect, however, all laws must also be approved by a majority of the Federation Council (the upper house) and signed by the president. This procedure is close to the American system. The main difference between the two systems is the Russian president's constitutional right to govern by decree without the consent of the Duma under exceptional circumstances. Since its introduction, President Yeltsin used this right fairly often, far more often than "exceptional circumstances" suggests, with far-reaching and adverse effects on the development of the rule of law and the balance of power among branches of the government.

Another major problem concerns the legislative rights of the Duma and the rights of the various subjects of the Russian Federation (e.g., Russia's republics). Foreign companies would like to invest in Russia (e.g., in mining) but have been understandably reluctant to do so because laws regulating contracts and other economic activities, especially those involving property relations, have been unclear. Many contracts signed with Western investors were later declared invalid because some law or right (or the interpretation thereof) was subsequently changed through the actions of the central or regional governments.

Legal processes are not defined as clearly or as explicitly in Russia as in the United States, mainly due to the newness of the Russian regime. New legislation has, however, been introduced to create a new legal code.

In particular, civil laws—laws governing interactions and behaviors of individuals and private corporate actors—are rapidly being developed. The introduction of a private sphere has created new opportunities for individuals and groups to damage others in nonviolent ways. This change has created a need for entirely new kinds of civil laws, especially ones pertaining to property rights and business activities. Civil law was scarcely needed and highly underdeveloped under the Soviet state, which controlled all individual behavior and forbade the existence of private corporate actors.

The INSTITUTIONALIZATION of the supremacy of law in Russia started in 1993, when the new constitution was approved in a referendum. In the long run, one of the most important features of this constitution is likely to be its built-in resistance to being amended. No other developed country has a constitution that is harder to amend. In the long run, the extreme difficulty of amending the 1993 constitution, which is flawed in many important ways, is a serious hindrance to Russia's ability to evolve a legal system that meets the needs of its people.

8.2 ENFORCEMENT BY THE STATE

According to standard definitions and assumptions of social science, the legitimate use of force and law enforcement are the exclusive monopoly of the state. Though the Soviet state did not respect law, as a TOTALITARIAN state it had a very strong enforcement system and certainly monopolized the use of force very effectively. During Stalin's era, enforcement agencies, especially the NKVD (the precursor of the KGB), acted above the law. By the 1980s, however, Soviet enforcement agencies had come under the basic control of the party-state apparatus. Although they still ignored most actual laws, these agencies did obey orders from above in the party-state apparatus. Abuse of power by enforcement agencies toward the end of the Soviet era was the result of the supremacy of orders from above.

As the new Russian state began to function, former Soviet traditions and state enforcement agencies were taken over. It is premature to announce the independence of Russia's enforcement agencies and their allegiance to law. One clear example of the dominance of orders over law occurred in the 1994–1996 war in Chechnya when President Yeltsin ordered Internal Ministry troops to go to Chechnya without the benefit of the proper legal procedure for this action: a declaration of a state of emergency in Chechnya. The result was that Russia's enforcement agencies became mired in a tragic war that ended in 1996 with the de facto defeat of Russia's central authorities as well as large losses of human life and devastation in Chechnya.

In Russia, enforcement agencies include: the MILITIA (police); the Internal Ministry; the FEDERAL SECURITY BUREAU (FSB), the KGB's successor; and the Office of the Chief Prosecutor, which is analogous to the Office of the Attorney General in the United States. All of these enforcement agencies existed in Soviet times, though with some differences in names, and their basic foundations were inherited from the Soviet era. Russia's president has replaced the general secretary of the Communist Party as the chief order-giver. The head of each enforcement agency is directly responsible to the president of Russia, not the prime minister.

Officially the **militia** is part of the Internal Ministry, but in actuality it exists as a separate agency charged with maintaining order in public and private domains. Similar to the police in the United States, the militia primarily attempts to prevent crime and to investigate criminal activities when they occur.

There are major problems with the militia. Its officials, most of whom were trained in the Soviet system, are still more loyal to their superiors than to the law itself. In addition, their salaries are low and not paid promptly; this does not increase their loyalty to the state. Not surprisingly, corruption is rampant among the militia and will surely continue to be so until the government actually pays them to do their jobs.

This point is illustrated by an incident witnessed by one author of this book, which occurred in front of what was then the Soviet Central Committee Building in Moscow on November 7, 1991 (a major holiday—the anniversary of the October Revolution of 1917). People were waiting in line to exchange money when a traffic militiaman walked up and pushed ahead of everyone standing in the line. Though it was not yet noon, he had already collected enough bribes of rubles from drivers wanting to avoid traffic tickets that he could exchange the rubles for $100, a very large sum at that time. Moreover, he did not hesitate to convert these rubles into dollars, openly and without fear, even in front of this building where Gorbachev had his office. His casual attitude toward a public demonstration of his bribe taking points to the widespread corruption of the militia.

Another problem is linked with habits learned in the Soviet period. Soviet law enforcement was rough and ready, and the militia never needed to deal with the finer points of law and legal behavior. Careful gathering of evidence was not part of police practice in the Soviet Union. Members of the militia and other enforcement agencies were accustomed to thinking that they could decide who was a criminal. The later judgment of a court was secondary.

Such behavior is vividly illustrated in the "The Meeting Place Cannot Be Changed," a popular TV serial still shown in Russia. This TV program details the crime-stopping efforts of a police investigator battling a major criminal gang in Moscow in 1945. The investigator brings the gangsters to justice, but he breaks countless laws in the process. The program's message resonates with the militia in the new Russia: Use any means necessary, even break the law, in order to catch criminals.

The **Internal Ministry** and the **FSB** have substantially greater authority than the militia. These two agencies have roles similar to the FBI in the United States, except that they jointly have troops of about a half million men, who have helicopters, tanks, and armored personnel carriers at their disposal. These troops make up the majority of armed patrolmen seen on city streets in Russia.

Violent internal conflicts, such as the rebellion in Chechnya, are generally handled by the Internal Ministry. Due to the Chechen conflict, in 1995 the budget of the Internal Ministry was actually higher than the budget of the Defense Ministry, which oversees the military. The Internal Ministry troops act as a relatively effective counterbalance to the forces of the army.

Investigation of major organized crime is another responsibility of Russia's Internal Ministry. This task is being performed very poorly in the new Russia, despite the effectiveness of criminal investigations under the Soviet regime. The main cause of this poor performance is undoubtedly corruption within the enforcement agencies. The corruption exists not only among the rank-and-file troops but surely extends to much higher levels.

An American example clarifies the reasoning behind this conclusion. United States agencies investigating international drug traffic analyze rates of arrests of members of major drug cartels in Colombia and other countries exporting drugs. If members of certain drug cartels are never arrested, agency leaders conclude that law enforcement officials are being bribed by the drug cartels. Otherwise, the law enforcement officials in those countries would arrest some members of every cartel through pure luck. Applying the same logic to Russia, one can conclude that contract killers (or the criminal organizations employing them) have paid law enforcement agents to look the other way since almost no contract killers of prominent Russians were brought to trial, let alone convicted, in the first five years of the new Russia.

Now we come to a new phenomenon in Russian society: the PRIVATIZATION OF LAW ENFORCEMENT. Private security offices have flourished because state security agencies have proven unable to protect private business. The most important consequence of this new development is the introduction of competition into law enforcement. While privatization almost surely improves law enforcement (if it were not successful, private businesses would not pay for it), it challenges the state's monopoly over the use of force. This phenomenon could have some very disturbing consequences in the long run.

Many private enforcement agencies were formed by hiring former members of the previous KGB, Alpha (a special army commando unit), the Internal Ministry, and paratroop units to work as "enforcers." Moreover, individuals currently employed primarily by state enforcement agencies are employed to work "after hours" for private enforcement agencies. This phenomenon is very different from the common practice of moonlighting by American police. In the United States, with its very stable and highly regulated system of law enforcement, after-hours jobs of police do not usually mean that private security agencies have penetrated the public system of law enforcement. In Russia, private security agencies hire state enforcement agents in order to have inside information about what the state enforcement agencies know and are doing. In Russia, the loyalty of state enforcement agents working part-time for private enforcement agencies is clearly compromised. Consequently, one can say that private enforcement agencies in Russia have penetrated state law enforcement agencies. Yet it is hard to blame employees of the state enforcement agencies for moonlighting when the state does not pay them very well or on time. This form of corruption is a systemwide problem within Russia's state enforcement agencies.

As Americans have learned from Clinton's impeachment, investigations by prosecutors and threats of legal actions can be used in political battles. In 1999, there emerged a fierce political scandal concerning Russia's **chief prosecutor,** Yuri Skuratov. President Yeltsin tried to fire Skuratov three times, but each time the Federation Council refused to confirm firing him. The official justification for Yeltsin's action was Skuratov's illicit sexual activity, which was videotaped and shown on TV. The real reason was almost surely highly sensitive criminal cases that were being diligently pursued by the Office of the Chief Prosecutor. His office was starting to prosecute not only notorious contract killers but also prominent businesspeople, such as Boris Berezovsky. Skuratov's aggressive anticrime fighting stance was a clear violation of unwritten rules. During Yeltsin's presidency, many top officials were fired from their jobs, but none was prosecuted, whatever improprieties might have been done. The latent message of Skuratov's actions was that many members of the ruling elite were at risk of prosecution. Kremlin insiders found this intolerable, not only because Skuratov violated unwritten rules, but because their future was endangered.

It is too early in Russia's political development for the Office of the Chief Prosecutor to act independently. That legal cases are intertwined with politics in Russia is not unusual in a newly emerging democracy. Overall, Russian law enforcement in 1999 showed signs of effectiveness and independence that were almost beyond imagination just a few years ago. But arrests are not the end. Those arrested must be brought to the court and tried for justice to be done. It is not yet clear if these hopeful signs will turn into something more substantial.

8.3 THE JUDICIARY

Courts and a judicial system are not new to Russia. Indeed, the overwhelming majority of Russia's judges were appointed during the Soviet era. There have, however, been major institutional changes.

Russia's December 1993 constitution established a CONSTITUTIONAL COURT, which oversees the interpretation of the constitution, and a SUPREME COURT, which oversees lower courts. The new constitution declares the judiciary to be independent of the other branches of the government. The Constitutional Court has shown some signs of independence from the government and parliament. In addition, the Supreme Court has started to back lower courts in their difficult struggle to enforce laws independently. Thus, there is some reason to hope that Russia may eventually develop a judiciary that is truly independent of the executive and legislative branches of the central government.

A very important test of the independence of the Supreme Court occurred when it ruled that an October 1993 action of the Supreme Soviet opposed by President Yeltsin was legal. In response, Yeltsin replaced the head of the Supreme Court and appointed additional new justices to make the "right" decisions in the future. His retribution for the Court's ruling against his desires in this matter led the Constitutional and Supreme Courts to be more cautious in their decisions thereafter. Nonetheless, from 1997 through 1999, Russia's higher courts achieved a remarkable measure of autonomy, with politics seeming to play a very small role in their decisions. This newfound independence has inspired the lower courts to show somewhat greater independence, too.

Most **judicial courts** in the Russian Federation are holdovers from the Soviet regime when phone-call law was dominant. In the Soviet era, prosecutors usually discussed cases with CPSU officials and got their advice on how to handle cases. To keep their jobs, most judges, whose status was lower than prosecutors', generally toed the line set by the prosecutor. This pattern persisted into the 1990s, but some judges have begun to take advantage of the greater independence granted them by the new constitution. The ramifications have been felt especially by prosecutors, who are often unqualified and ill-prepared to handle their cases.

Because Russian courts have always handled criminal cases, the criminal courts have a fairly experienced judiciary. Consequently, the transition to the new Russia has been smoother for the criminal courts than for the civil courts. The size of the criminal caseload is suggested by the roughly one million prisoners in Russia (Farmer 1999). This figure means that roughly 1 percent of Russia's adult population is in prison. In some oblasts, such as Kemerovo, the number rises to 5 percent. Very few people are imprisoned for economic crimes, such as tax evasion, embezzlement, and so on. Rather, the low value placed on human life in both tsarist and Soviet Russia continues to shape Russian society, leading to high levels of violence and commensurably high rates of imprisonment for violent crimes.

The civil courts are the weakest part of the judiciary due to the host of new legislation arising from marketization and the resulting explosion of civil cases. In the Soviet era, civil courts were few in number and handled a much narrower range of cases. The new Russian civil courts were not prepared to meet the challenge of the much broader scope of the civil law or to keep up with the much larger caseload, which increased by more than tenfold within a five-year period in the mid-1990s. It could easily increase by another tenfold in the next decade.

The overload of the civil courts creates other problems. Since joining the world economy, Russia has a much greater need for judges, prosecutors, and defense attorneys who can protect Russian assets and businesses. The need is especially great in civil law, particularly in the international arena where the financial stakes are often high. There is a critical shortage of legal specialists qualified to practice civil law, especially business law, and particularly business law involving international issues. Because civil law offers enormous career opportunities, Russia's universities have many potential law students. However, it takes time to train Russian specialists in the law. To make matters worse, there are severe shortages of law faculty, especially in civil law. Consequently, leading banks and businesspeople often hire foreigners to assist with internal as well as international cases involving other countries' laws.

In Soviet times, leading **defense attorneys** were usually better qualified than prosecutors and judges. Since the Russian government has barely enough money to pay prosecutors' salaries, and since judges have never been paid well, the most talented legal professionals in the new Russia work as defense attorneys in private firms, where they may be paid 10 times more than judges and prosecutors. During Soviet times, attorneys' fees were higher for criminal cases than for civil ones. Sometimes this is still true, but nowadays civil cases usually pay more than criminal cases. This trend is resulting in a new generation of defense attorneys specializing in civil law, who have much better qualifications than prosecutors. Such highly paid defense attorneys are not only the most qualified participants in the entire judicial process but usually win most of their cases. Of course, most defendants are too poor to be represented by their own defense attorney, so it is mainly big businesses and the rich that benefit from the greater skills and successes of defense attorneys.

During Soviet times, the most qualified **prosecutors** prepared cases concerning murder, robbery, and other high crimes. With organized crime at sky-high levels in the new Russia, personnel in criminal courts have been subjected to physical threats and offered much more money than in the Soviet era to "look the right way." In major cases, the accused (especially if a member of a major criminal gang) usually has a well-qualified defense attorney. Cases that initially seem clear-cut often disintegrate in court because the police work has been slipshod, or the prosecution's evidence is thin, or witnesses (even victims) change their stories. The relatively low competencies of the militia and prosecutors are no match for highly paid, well-qualified defense attorneys, who often succeed in gaining the acquittal of defendants who seem clearly guilty to an outside observer. The relatively mild sentences given to mafia members result not only from the hard work of talented defense attorneys but also from suborning of witnesses. However, most low-profile cases are routine and end in convictions because those accused cannot afford to use such means to defend themselves.

Since corruption and "supplemental income" in the judiciary were common in the Soviet period, their continuation in the new Russia is not too surprising, especially when salaries of state officials are both low and slow to be paid. Corruption of judges in Russia is rumored to be widespread. But since judges are in charge of the law, it is very hard to mount cases against them. Their corruption, along with their relatively poor qualifications for their jobs, ensures that judges will continue to bear the low authority and esteem inherited from the Soviet period.

The mentality of "innocent until proven guilty" was and still is a foreign idea in Russian law enforcement and courts. In most countries, detention and methods of investigation follow certain laws, and the burden of proof lies with the prosecution. Soviet law enforcers began with the assumption that the defendant was guilty and then gathered and constructed the evidence to support that assumption. This long-held mentality is difficult to overcome in the new Russia.

Though not very respectful of the rights of the accused, the Soviet law enforcement system was very effective in handling ordinary criminal behavior such as murder, rape, and larceny. Its main problem was to prevent prison overcrowding. It solved this problem by freeing everyone not deemed dangerous to society. Judges and prosecutors had special instructions to acquit all but the most violent criminals. The new Russia has a similar problem of prison overpopulation. As a result, law enforcers neglect most petty crimes and conflicts within families and among neighbors because they are overburdened by the problems of dealing with more dangerous criminal elements than the perpetrators of ordinary violent crimes against persons and property.

Prisons and other correction facilities were formerly under the control of the Internal Ministry, the primary law enforcement agency in Russia. But in 1997, these facilities were formally transferred to the Ministry of Justice, the agency with the responsibility to administer justice. This change is important because it holds the promise of eventually fairer and better treatment for those accused and for those convicted.

In Russia, prisons and prison camps (*lageriia*) have always been essentially institutions of punishment, not rehabilitation. This situation has created a huge number of recidivists because felons continue to perpetuate the criminal culture to which they become accustomed in prison. For more on this problem, see Section 8.4.

The most compelling potential dangers of the overcrowded prisons, however, are not increased criminal activities due to high recidivism, but rather matters of public health. Poor living conditions and overcrowding always cause infectious diseases to flourish. Russian prisons have produced new, highly virulent strains of tuberculosis (TB) that are incurable by known medicines. It has been estimated that more than a hundred thousand inmates of Russian prisons are currently infected with TB (Farmer 1999). Physicians worldwide are concerned that the new strains may cause mass epidemics of TB, not only in Russia but across the entire planet. AIDS is another disease spreading like wildfire among Russia's prison population. It is rumored that a tenth of Russia's prison inmates are infected with the HIV virus. This segment of the Russian population is the primary carrier of the disease. The probability is very high that a youth charged with some minor offense will be infected with TB or HIV while in prison awaiting trial.

8.4 CRIMES AND CRIMINALS

Both the number and kinds of crimes and criminals are usually very indicative of societal norms. For instance, the homicide rate helps to gauge how readily people will take another person's life. Emile Durkheim, one of the fathers of sociology, wrote in his famous book *Suicide* that the number of suicides in a country, and the characteristics of those who commit suicide, reveal the strength of societal integration—in other words, the strength of the ties that bind people together into a larger community. In the 1990s, Russia has led the world in suicides, suggesting that societal integration is low.

Russia's homicide rate has also been among the world's highest. Homicides, when not related to the criminal underworld, are often linked to alcohol. Every foreign visitor to Russia is amazed at the extent and degree of alcohol consumption by Russians. It would not be a lie to say that some people will kill for a bottle of vodka. Alcohol-based crime has surged along with economic hardship as people seek to forget their horrific present and their grim future.

Although crimes against family members have not increased very much, street and other petty crimes have risen dramatically. Hordes of unemployed and homeless people contribute the most to these particular types of crime. Homeless children are ubiquitous in Russian cities, except Moscow, where the militia continually clears them out of public places. The kinds of criminal behaviors that typically result from indigence and alcohol abuse—physical assaults and theft—make the living environment unsafe and unpleasant, but they do not substantially worsen the overall quality of life for more fortunate people.

Young amateur lawbreakers threaten society much more. Many youths have organized small groups that specialize in theft or robbery from apartments, small businesses, and public conveyances. This criminal activity has become almost a kind of business. Because of the high

Two young women stand before the barred windows of an apartment. However, bars are not always enough to protect your belongings from burglars.

rate of unemployment, it is one of the few routes to economic gain for some young people.

The Russian television station NTV provided a vivid example of this type of collective theft in a 1998 story. A Dutch farmer who had rented a lot of farmland in Russia had a very good crop of potatoes. Peasants from neighboring villages provided him with massive "help" in harvesting the potatoes. Confronted by the TV cameras, the "helpers" said, "We heard he needed help. Since we didn't have a harvest this year and since he can't collect all the potatoes himself, we decided to have a few for ourselves." The local militia did nothing to stop their theft, which comes as no surprise to a Russian TV audience. Collective theft of crops is regarded as normal.

Still more dangerous criminal activity is that controlled by the **Russian underworld,** which has a long history and a well-established organization. By tradition, it has even had governing generals (*vor v zakone*), its own budget (*obshchak*), and its own code of conduct—a kind of "thieves' law." This highly elaborated criminal culture developed in the prison camps, which were first instituted by the tsars and subsequently expanded in the Soviet era. These camps were completely isolated from the outside world. The prisoners in these camps, who had a steadfast will to survive, no hope of escape, and almost no chance of eventual release from prison, developed their own social organization and their own rules of conduct, which allowed more of them to survive in this harsh environment. Their desperate situation led to the rise of a criminal underworld within the prison camps. This underworld was able to maintain its hold on the few who managed to leave, and it thereby managed to perpetuate itself and endure outside as well as within prison camps (Frank 1999).

Not surprisingly, criminals leaders from the Soviet era provided the new Russian underworld with the first new criminal generals. The new Russia has, however, generated a new wave of professional criminals, which has rapidly supplanted the previously established criminal order and given rise to new criminal bosses. The old leaders of the underworld were just as ill-prepared as Soviet managers for the marketization of the economy, privatization, and the emergence of private businesses. New skills and new methods of organization were needed to be really successful at crime in the new Russia. The criminal underworld has been transformed into organized criminal enterprises in the new Russia.

After the fall of the USSR, the number of criminal organizations exploded. For a variety of reasons, these criminal organizations cause many more problems in the new Russia than they did in Soviet times. First, the effectiveness of law enforcement in Russia does not approach that of the Soviet regime. Second, marketization has resulted in widespread poverty and a dearth of economic opportunities throughout the country. Poor people are always prime targets of recruitment by criminal organizations. Consequently, the number of criminal gangs has swollen to levels beyond anyone's imagination when the Soviet Union collapsed. The situation is roughly comparable to that in the United States in the 1920s, when criminal gangs organized and controlled gambling, prostitution, and bootlegging in virtually every major American city.

Only part of Russia's criminal underworld is popularly called the **mafia,** organizations based on residence in certain localities or on nationality. A good example is provided by Kurgan, a typical provincial city in the Ural region of western Siberia. In 1992–1995, at least a third of the young men in Kurgan were jobless. These jobless men included ones with a university education, with previous organizational experience, and with special elite military training. Many talented young men decided that their opportunities were best in the criminal world and entered the Kurgan mafia, which has become well known for its work in contract killing. From one perspective, it is one of the more successful private businesses in Kurgan.

The homelands of national minorities, such as Chechnya, are the kinds of places where a regional mafia easily develops. In the regions of many national minorities, joblessness among men in their prime is incredibly high, on the order of 80–90 percent. In a bleak situation, organizing to earn some money outside of one's own community is necessary for survival. In the Soviet era, young men could get summer jobs in the north or the east, but such summer jobs have evaporated. Now young men can try to develop a monopoly on extortion or robbery in some other area or to specialize in a particular kind of criminal activity in one of Russia's million-cities. In such ways, a Sicilian-style mafia based on nationality or place of origin is born. A visitor to an outdoor market *(rynok)* in Moscow or St. Petersburg will notice that almost all of them are run by one or another national mafia (e.g., Azeris, Avars, Chechens). One can only guess at the real power of the various national mafias in Russian society.

Some criminal enterprises are not only profitable but well organized. With its profits, a criminal organization can not only hire skillful defense attorneys but pay corrupt police officers, prosecutors, and judges to look the other way and protect members of the criminal organization from enforcement of the laws. Killings and gang fights occur mainly in conflicts over turf between mafiosi or organized criminals; they are not normal activities of the mafia. Random killing is too disruptive of the organized means to illegal gains. For Russia, the main problem of the mafia is its extensive infiltration into both the private sector and the state. So far, few mafiosi have been brought to justice, and this suggests that their penetration of the state is pervasive and deep.

The climate of unregulated individual profit making is creating another type of criminality. The widespread mentality of money making provides fertile ground for other types of organized criminal gangs that lack the specific regional and national ties of the real mafia. They generally specialize in one specific kind of criminal activity, such as extortion, racketeering, narcotics, private enforcement of business deals, or "protection."

Criminal corporations can develop in a variety of ways. They usually start by finding some profitable but illegal activity that can be organized to furnish a fairly steady flow of illicit gains. One especially profitable illegal activity is smuggling. Early in the post-Soviet period, many small groups engaged in smuggling along Russia's borders, but criminals with ties to custom officials and border troops soon drove out the amateurs. In a short time, illegal border operations had become a highly organized criminal business.

For example, in 1991–1993, numerous smugglers operated along the Estonian-Russian border. Estonia, a very small country with no mining to speak of, became sixth in the world in the export of nonferrous metals (e.g., aluminum, copper). The basis for Estonia's successful export business was the highly organized, illegal importation of nonferrous metals from Russia into Estonia. Since nonferrous metals, unlike diamonds, are bulky and not easy to hide, one can infer that truly massive operations were involved in these illegal border crossings.

Another example is even more striking. Most alcohol sold in Russia in the post-Soviet period is imported from abroad, mainly through Belarus and Georgia (in the Caucasus). There were clear routes of importation across Russia's borders with these neighboring countries. Yet, all attempts to stop these illegal imports (even efforts organized by the army's top officials) and to restore the state's monopoly of the sale of alcohol were unsuccessful until 1998, when the state's monopoly was finally restored and illegal imports dramatically cut. Since perhaps a quarter to a half of the state budget came from alcohol sales in both the tsarist and Soviet periods, illegal bootlegging of alcohol in the new Russia has been a truly big business. Criminal operations on this scale require a very sophisticated organization capable of obtaining raw materials; arranging transportation within the supplying countries, across the border, and again within Russia; distributing and selling it within Russia; handling all money transactions through some sort of banking system; and arranging for protection from the bottom to the top of various law enforcement agencies. Finding ways to get politicians to block the introduction of effective new measures against this lucrative business are surely another part of their criminal operations. This type of illegal business involves a firmly established, well-functioning, huge organization.

The transition to a market economy has affected the respectability of criminals, especially those engaged in criminal businesses as contrasted with crimes against individuals. In a society in which most people must continually struggle to survive, in which legitimate opportunities for success are very few, and in which crime does pay, criminals gain some respect. Indeed, gangsters can even be regarded by some ordinary Russians as educated and talented citizens, with valuable contributions to make to society. (After all, criminal businesses do employ people, and they almost always pay their employees on time.)

Russia has not yet successfully prosecuted any top leader of such criminal organizations or of any politician colluding with them. Charges against the tycoon Boris Berezovsky in 1999 were the first public attempt to deal with this kind of situation. But then Kremlin insiders got the prime minister and the chief prosecutor fired. Soon the investigations stopped, and the charges against Berezovsky were dropped. It is extremely difficult to combat crime when criminals have tentacles reaching into the top levels of the state. Criminal corporations, especially ones with connections in the upper echelons of power, are not easily crushed. Clearly, this form of crime has a very detrimental effect on society.

The only form of criminal activity that damages society more is the spread of **organized illegal activities within the state apparatus.** Marketization in Russia emerged in an environment in which the Soviet party-state controlled virtually all activities with any public significance. In such a social environment, one would expect that state organizations, possibly in some recast form, would become major actors in the new Russia.

Some state organizations were quickly privatized. Arguably the most famous of these is Gazprom, the former Ministry of Gas Production, now the world's largest gas monopoly. Other state organizations began to look for ways to make money. More precisely, those working in state organizations tried to find ways to make money from their official functions. Some of these were legitimate. For example, the State Statistics Office started to sell official statistical yearbooks and census data at high prices.

But not every state organization had some money-making product or service that it could legitimately sell. Sometimes it does not take much to sell some state property or service on the side. For example, Westerners are often shocked that state officials take bribes. But since all state bureaucracies move with glacial speed (even in America), a cynic will ask: Who can complain when the wheels of the state turn faster after crossing someone's palm with a little money? Doesn't everyone gain from this small exchange? However one answers this question, such bribes are certainly the smallest part of the corruption of state officials and of state organizations. This sort of bribery is small-scale, individual, and not highly organized.

Much bigger sums of money could be gained, for example, by finagling "special deals" in the privatization of state property. For example, the Office of Russia's Chief Prosecutor discovered that some corporate actors bought the "right numbers" for their economic activity from the State Statistics Office; that is, they bought the numbers that would reduce their taxes. To give yet another example, city offices dealing with property and ownership rights began to make money in transfers of ownership rights and in licensing of new businesses.

It is impossible to give an exhaustive list of the multitudinous kinds of illegal activities in which Russia's state bureaucrats and state organizations have become engaged. We can confidently say, however, that they have been amazingly inventive in figuring out how to make money from their official functions. One could not fault them for a lack of business ingenuity.

Such mixing of public function and private profit is widespread. Some Russian army officers even handed their enlisted men over to Chechen rebels for money. One can imagine how state organizations beyond the watchful eye of the public and press are functioning. When the operations of state organizations are not subject to public oversight, criminal organizations and mafias recognize and seize new "business opportunities" that are facilitated by corrupting state officials. This process of criminalization of state organizations tends to mushroom as fewer and fewer state organizations remain untainted and vigilantly on guard to protect the public welfare.

The free-for-all nature of the Russian transition to a market economy has resulted in a blurring of the borders between legal and illegal activities and between public and private domains (Lapidus 1995). A weak state with corrupt law enforcement agencies cannot cope with the existing situation.

8.5 SUMMARY

Historically, law was not used much in Russian society. In the tsarist and Soviet systems, most social spheres of activity and most social behaviors were governed by nonlegal means. For example, rulers mainly used direct administrative orders to control the economy rather than laws. Laws were concentrated on forbidding theft and violence against persons (e.g., murder, rape). In contrast, law enforcement agents were always used extensively in Russian society, and fear of the law enforcement system is deeply rooted in Russian society. When an ordinary Russian puts together these two features, he or she concludes that the state uses law arbitrarily to punish people.

To achieve the supremacy of law over orders from above in Russian society is an immense task. The new Russian state has been gradually working to achieve this goal. The greatest accomplishments to date are the development of various new legal institutions. Russia now has a Constitutional Court, and for the first time in Russian history, the constitution is not just a list of good intentions but the actual foundation of law. Courts are gradually gaining their independence from the executive branch. The transformation of the judiciary is occurring primarily at the level of the highest courts because so many judges in lower courts have very low official salaries and depend on side payments from others (from state bureaucrats to criminals) to earn a decent living.

A further and important sign that the legal system is becoming more independent of the executive branch is given by the fact that charges against President Yeltsin were even investigated by the Office of the Chief Prosecutor. Again, at lower levels of the system of justice, changes are happening slowly because prosecutors depend on other state bureaucrats and seek ways to supplement their meager salaries.

Following paralysis during the first years of the new Russian state, law enforcement agencies are again functioning more as they did in Soviet times. One benefit is that orders are starting to be enforced. But a drawback is that the abusive use of force and bullying of the populace by law enforcement agents are on the upswing.

A very important development under way is the transfer of prisons and other correctional facilities to the Ministry of Justice. This change may improve the desperate situation of Russian prisoners, of whom more than a fifth have either HIV or a new form of tuberculosis resistant to antibiotics. In this unhealthy situation, guards' common abuse of their power is a secondary problem.

Another accomplishment well under way is the development of processes to establish new laws. The new Russian state began with a well-developed system of criminal law, but the law dealing with criminal procedures was far behind that in modern Western countries. There is a major effort to develop the civil law, which is needed to deal with issues pertaining to private property. The civil law is literally being developed from scratch since the Soviet state had no need for civil law. In Soviet society, virtually all property belonged to the state, and it could be reallocated and used for various purposes by the state through executive orders. Now civil laws must be drafted and passed. Attorneys and judges must learn civil laws and how to work with them. These changes call for substantial changes in the system of legal education. At the university level, legal faculties and law students have expanded greatly.

A third, rapidly expanding branch of law deals with public administration. Under the Soviet system, phone-call law was the rule of the day, and administrative law barely existed. It was unimaginable that different Soviet agencies would settle their disputes through the courts. As regionalization of Russia has proceeded, it has become necessary to have legal arrangements fixing various rights of governmental units and agencies as well as procedures for implementing these rights.

Law enforcement also has novel features. To declare law supreme and to follow it are entirely different things. For people actually to obey the law is a major problem for Russian society. It requires a certain kind of preparation by the populace as well as by state officials. The practice of obeying the law needs to start in the president's office. In this regard, it is worth noting that Yeltsin used decrees to bypass the Duma. He even conducted the 1994–1996 war in Chechnya without a proper legal basis for the war. Legally established procedures for law enforcement agencies to conduct criminal investigations are also deficient. Many criminal cases fall apart because legal procedures are done sloppily, allowing the defendant's attorney to win. Last but not least, as judges are paid little, deals are made, and money changes hands. But there are also some encouraging signs, such as the three-time refusal of members of the Federation Council to confirm Yeltsin's attempts to fire Russia's chief prosecutor.

The weakest area of law enforcement occurs with civil law. Foreigners make deals and sign contracts after being shown the tip of the legal iceberg. Later they complain that the laws have been changed, but often they were informed of only some of the laws. Laws at different levels of government, from the central state to the local level, are sometimes contradictory, and mechanisms for determining which level's laws hold are unclear. Interpretation of the laws can also be ambiguous. As a result, civil courts sometimes make seemingly mysterious decisions. A situation in which civil law and courts truly oversee the rules for running the economy is still a future prospect.

As in every other post-socialist country, Russia has a problem with rising levels of criminal activity. To attribute crime to Russia's mafia does not really explain much.

The main roots of this new criminal activity do not lie in the past. First, the Soviet Union was a safe place for ordinary people going about their daily lives; the rate of criminal activity was very low by U.S. standards. This safety was achieved by the rough-and-ready control implemented by the KGB, the militia, and other law enforcement agencies. The emerging Russian state initially disregarded those powerful agencies and neglected law enforcement. Law enforcement officers were paid little, and many left the official law enforcement agencies, not infrequently to join new criminal organizations.

Second, the emergence of private business with few regulations and little law enforcement creates lucrative opportunities for enrichment. Criminal and noncriminal behavior in this process is sometimes a matter of interpretation. Legal and illegal businesses are often intertwined.

Third, a majority of Russians were pushed into poverty, and young men in many parts of the country became jobless. In some regions, four-fifths of working age adults are out of regular work. Homeless children and the unemployed are highly visible on the streets of Russia's cities. Such conditions are an ideal ground for organized and unorganized criminal activity when a contract killing might earn a thousand dollars.

Criminals are a major problem in Russian society. They are well organized, and many are well educated. Fighting crime requires a huge effort. It is not a matter of dealing with just street and other ordinary crimes but with very skilled and professional criminal organizations that have accumulated large amounts of money. The Russian state does not yet have enough resources or personnel committed to the battles that are needed to win the war against crime.

Conclusion

As a society with a 1,000-year history, Russia differs from the United States in the deep roots of most of its social patterns. Nobel Prize winner Aleksandr Solzhenitsyn (1995) claims that Russia's present depends at least as much on its past as on its future opportunities.

Russians have expanded their territory and natural resources more than any other nation (ethnicity). Starting from tiny Muscovy in the fifteenth century, Russia grew under the tsars to become the largest country in the Eurasian landmass. It expanded even further under the flag of the Soviet Union. Following the collapse of the Soviet Empire, Russia still has the largest landmass and is indisputedly the world's richest country in terms of natural resources. No other country has both a sizable population (nearly 150 million) and such a large living space for its people. Russia faced formidable obstacles in acquiring such a vast living space; indeed, achieving this expansion required the largest army in the world for the last three centuries.

The price for Russia's centuries-long expansion was high. It meant that Russia entered the modern world with an undeveloped infrastructure. Its deficiencies start with its transportation system, which does not connect large subregions of the country, and run to its economy, which lacks internal integration. The Soviet command economy struck a major blow, building an economic structure that ignored economic efficiency and profitability. Thus, for centuries the institutional development of Russian society was postponed due to concentrating control of its resources in a state with autocratic rulers. Consequently, a civil society with institutions independent from the state did not emerge. Unlike most developed countries, Russia did not forge the kinds of social linkages that help to bridge conflicts of interests, and it did not evolve the sort of cultural norms that allow social and political divisions to be healed through negotiations. The result was two real social catastrophes in the last century: the establishment of a totalitarian, communist regime following the Bolshevik Revolution in 1917; and the collapse of its empire, economy, and living standard in the final decade of the twentieth century.

In all premodern societies, a communal, collectivistic outlook predominated. But at least among Western countries, Russia is unusual in beginning the twentieth century with a highly collectivistic mentality. This mentality, termed collectivism, was elaborated and codified into a Communist ideology that directly challenged the concept of the individual as a free person with private property and as an independent actor who could make choices about his or her own life. The collectivistic ideology suppressed not only entrepreneurship but individualization of the members of society. Individualism and the resulting individualization would have provided a multiplicity of life strategies that would have enriched the potential of the nation to take advantage of the new opportunities provided by the modern world.

The new Russia emerged from the old one in a very complex situation following the collapse of Soviet Union as a world superpower. The Soviet collapse happened as a result of the arms race with the United States and the loss of faith in Communist ideology, but a crucial factor was the bankruptcy of the Soviet party-state political elite. For all practical purposes, the new Russia began without competent leadership. Realizing this, Andrei Sakharov (1975), father of Russia's hydrogen bomb and winner of the Nobel Prize for peace, advised his country to follow the example of the Western world.

The new Russia emerged from a state, society, and ideology that were in many ways opposite those in American society. America's well-functioning, established institutions are a major asset that gradually developed over the last two centuries. Another major plus is the entrepreneurial spirit of the American people, which has been nourished by competition in its market economy. In contrast, the new Russia started with leaders and a population who lacked any experience with either a market economy or democracy and who knew these terms as only abstract ideas. Political leaders and enterprise managers had neither the knowledge nor the skills needed to engage in economic activities profitably. A market economy is a complex phenomenon with many institutions that function as an integrated system; it requires considerable and widely dispersed competencies to operate successfully. As advised by Western experts, Russia's leaders chose shock therapy: the sudden, top-down change in macroeconomic policies. Probably a better way out of its previous command economy would have involved gradual change, first giving opportunities and responsibilities to the masses of peasants and ordinary people, as China did. Russia's shock therapy has brought much hardship and pain to its people, and the transition to a market economy has been neither smooth nor successful.

Linking Russia's weak, unprofessionally run, emerging market economy to the global market economy via financial markets was a questionable decision. The Russian leadership did not understand the basics of the world market: Its main and enduring participants are highly capable business professionals who survive and manage to make profits in an environment of extremely tough competition. By analogy, one could say that Russia's leaders were like the winners of the para-Olympics who came to compete in the Olympic games with the world's best athletes; their failure in this new, world-class competition was predictable. Not surprisingly in retrospect, even Russia's internal markets have largely been dominated by foreign goods and businesses. As a result, Russia's production potential has collapsed. In some areas of Russia's economy, output fell to only a tenth of that in 1990 (see Table 5.2, which is based on *Goskomstat Rossii* 1998). Only in 1999 was there a glimmer of hope that the bottom had been reached and that economic output may slowly be rising.

But the new Russia has had examples of extremes in a positive direction, too. Very successful companies and wealthy people managed to emerge in only two or three years. The levels of profits that a few people achieved in Russia in the 1990s are unimaginable in such a short period in most countries. An unregulated, volatile market and immense natural resources provide unique opportunities for businesses to make profits. The development of the institutional basis for a market economy occurred within a decade. The same is true about political processes: Some political parties and blocs with countrywide support emerged in every parliamentary election.

Despite its economic problems and hardships, there are **some obvious benefits from Russia's transition** to a market economy. First, a multiplicity of actors have emerged in Russian society. For the first time in Russian history, its regional provinces were transformed into independent actors with relatively broad freedom of action and responsibility to their local constituencies. The long-term consequences of this change are hard to overestimate. Second, interests rather than ideologies are driving social processes in Russia. Sooner or later, this change can be expected to have positive effects. Third, more than half of the Russian economy is now in the private sector. Economic theory gives hope that eventually the new private sector will revive its moribund economy. As the capital, Moscow provides a success story even in the sense of the better standard of living of its residents.

All of its rapid economic changes have introduced differentiation of Russians in unexpected ways. First, the gaps between Russia's generations are arguably the deepest of any modern society. The oldest generation, those aged 40 and older, are the biggest losers in the market transition and survive in a most difficult situation. In contrast, young adults who were in their late 20s or 30s in the early 1990s are the biggest winners; they are at the core of the new private economy. But those in their early 20s at the turn to the new millennium are also relative losers because the opportunities available to them are much fewer, having mainly been absorbed by those only a few years older than themselves.

Second, young women in Russia, who are better educated than young men, might have been expected to be more successful in the new labor market than their male counterparts. But, privatization has created a disadvantage for women. Women have not acquired the main new assets in Russian society: property and the social positions that give people the means to amass great wealth. Women's incomes are also much lower than men's, and their unemployment rates are higher. After older generations, women as a group are the second-biggest losers in Russia's transition to a market economy. In the early years of this transition, a university education has also not been a major asset. Although economic returns from a university degree have not yet been substantial, this situation is likely to change as its economy starts to expand.

An important achievement is the openness of the country to Western experience and know-how in diverse areas, but especially in economic affairs. Business consulting, business education, and cooperation with Westerners are flourishing. The expertise and skills brought to Russia's economy by this new openness creates the potential for running its emerging market economy productively.

An enormous achievement was the solution of the financial, social, and political crises that erupted in August 1998 by means of a political compromise between the president and the Duma to form a new government. It was the first major political compromise in the new Russia. It suggests that Russia may develop political processes in which compromise among disagreeing parties is normal. In a society in which those in power were always right and the others wrong, this was a real turning point in the development of effective political institutions in Russia.

Moreover, the Russian Federation managed to solve the thorny problem of a smooth transition from its first president, Boris Yeltsin, to a successor. As most autocrats realize when the end of their power is approaching, their successors may not protect them from retribution for their past abuses of power. Not surprisingly, one of Yeltsin's conditions for resigning from the presidency was his immunity from future prosecution for his misdeeds. His departure signals the end of a dark and dismal period for Russians; they look to the twenty-first century as the start of a new and better era. In an incredibly hopeful sign, Yeltsin's successor, Vladimir Putin, began with something brand new in Russian history: a confession to the Russian people that their leaders should be ashamed for the misery of ordinary Russian people. That Russia's ruler publicly announced the responsibility of the political elite for the country's past troubles, and implicitly for its future opportunities, was unprecedented.

At the same time, Putin is what Russian call a *"gosudarstvennik,"* which means that he advocates a strong Russian state and is a defender of the state's interests. One can hope only that his leanings in this direction do not turn out to mean autocratic leadership and the restoration of a top-down political and administrative system. But Russia's second president at least appears to work hard, to take a pragmatic rather than an ideological approach to solving problems, and to fulfill his promises to the public. These are positive qualities in a country's leader.

Finally, though the rule of law is not yet supreme, law has begun to be taken seriously. In the past, the state bureaucracy was the primary regulator of people's behavior, and within the legal realm, criminal law was dominant. Both of these former patterns can be expected to change as Russia continues on the path of developing a market economy. In a fully developed market society, civil law provides the framework that allows impersonal actors to have productive and largely peaceable relationships with one another. In such a society, civil law not only is more important than criminal law but also takes precedence over the decisions of state bureaucrats. Russia's transition to a rule of law and the dominance of the law over the decisions of state bureaucrats is bound to be slow, but at least it seems to have begun.

For social scientists, Russian society is an extremely interesting object of research. The United States has a well-established society and a state in which almost all changes occur incrementally and gradually. Russia presents social scientists with a society whose subregions are as diverse as those of the United States, but change is manifold and at times sudden. The magnitude of destabilization of society is such that even basic demographic processes veer toward extremes. No modern country not at war has had such low birth rates and such high death rates as Russia. Not surprisingly, the drop in the standard of living has increased suicides and the spread of infectious diseases.

No one now understands well how all of these social processes work together. What are the root causes, and what are their effects? More than a few American and other social scientists (including ourselves) are engaged in research on Russian society in search of answers to these questions. The scientific opportunities for learning about basic social processes are especially great in this kind of destabilized society in which swings in different directions are relatively rapid and sizable.

It is for the Russian people to decide how things will proceed in their great country in the new millennium. In growing numbers, they are engaged in building their own individual and collective future. We are not only social scientists seeking to understand the complex world we live in, we are also fellow human beings who wish the Russian people the best of luck in their common endeavors.

Alberigo, Giuseppe; and Oscar Beozzo with Georgy Zyablitsev (eds.). 1996. *The Holy Russian Church and Western Christianity.* Maryknoll, NY: Orbis Books.

Andrusz, Gregory; Michael Harloe; and Ivan Szelényi. 1996. *Cities after Socialism: Urban and Regional Change and Conflict in Post-Socialist Societies.* Oxford: Blackwell.

Åslund, Anders. 1995. *How Russia Became a Market Economy.* Washington, DC: Brookings Institution Press.

Bartlett, Roger (ed.). 1990. *Land Commune and Peasant Community: Communal Forms in Imperial and Early Soviet Society.* Basingstoke: Macmillan.

Beissinger, Mark R. 1995. "The Persisting Ambiguity of Empire." *Post-Soviet Affairs* 11: pp. 149–84.

Billington, James H. 1970. *The Icon and the Axe: An Interpretive History of Russian Culture.* New York: Vintage Books.

Braudel, Fernand. 1979. *The Perspective of the World. Civilization and Capitalism 15th–18th Century.* Vol. 3. New York: Harper & Row.

Burawoy, Michael. 1997. "The Soviet Descent into Capitalism." *American Journal of Sociology* 102: pp. 1430–44.

Burawoy, Michael; and Pavel Krotov. 1992. "The Soviet Transition from Socialism to Capitalism: Worker Control and Economic Bargaining in the Wood Industry." *American Sociological Review* 57: pp. 16–36.

Chinn, Jeffrey; and Robert Kaiser. 1996. *Russians as the New Minority.* Boulder, CO: Westview Press.

Clem, Ralph S. (ed.). 1986. *Research Guide to the Russian and Soviet Census.* Ithaca, NY: Cornell University Press.

Colton, Timothy J. 1995. "Superpresidentialism and Russia's Backward State." *Post-Soviet Affairs* 11: pp. 83–88.

———. 1996. "Economics and Voting in Russia." *Post-Soviet Affairs* 12: pp. 289–317.

Connor, Walter D. 1996. *Tattered Banners: Labor, Conflict, and Corporatism in Postcommunist Russia.* Boulder, CO: Westview Press.

Conquest, Robert. 1991. *The Great Terror: A Reassessment.* New York: Oxford University Press.

Davies, R. W. (ed.). 1990. *From Tsarism to the New Economic Policy.* Ithaca, NY: Cornell University Press.

Denisova, L. N. 1995. *Rural Russia: Economic, Social and Moral Crisis.* Commack, NY: Nova Science.

Department of Economic and Social Affairs, Population Division. 1998. *World Population Prospects: The 1996 Revision.* New York: United Nations.

Djilas, Milovan. 1957. *The New Class: An Analysis of the Communist System of Power.* New York: Praeger.

Drobizheva, Leokadia; Rose Gottemoeller; Catherine McArdle Kelleher; and Lee Walker (eds.). 1996. *Ethnic Conflict in the Post-Soviet World: Case Studies and Analysis.* Armonk, NY: M.E. Sharpe.

Farmer, Paul. 1999. "TB Superbugs: The Coming Plague on All Our Houses." *Natural History* 108(1): pp. 46–53.

Flakierski, Henryk. 1993. *Income Inequalities in the Former Soviet Union and Its Republics.* Armonk, NY: M.E. Sharpe.

Frank, Stephen. 1999. *Crime, Cultural Conflict, and Justice in Rural Russia, 1856–1914.* Berkeley, CA: University of California Press.

Gellner, Ernest. 1996. *Conditions of Liberty: Civil Society and Its Rivals.* New York: Allen Lane/Penguin Books.

Gerber, Theodore P.; and Michael Hout. 1995. "Educational Stratification in Russia during the Soviet Period." *American Journal of Sociology* 101(3): pp. 611–60.

Gerber, Theodore P.; and Michael Hout. 1998. "More Shock than Therapy." *American Journal of Sociology* 104: pp. 1–50.

Goskomstat Rossii. 1992–1999. *Narodnoe khoziaistvo Rossiiskoi Federatsii.* Moscow: *Goskomstat Rossii.*

———. 1995. *Osnovnye itogi mikroperepici naseleniia 1994 g.* [*Main Results of the Population Microcensus for 1994*]. Moscow: *Goskomstat Rossii.*

———. 1997. *Demograficheskii ezhegodnik Rossii* [*The Demographic Yearbook of Russia*]. Moscow: *Goskomstat Rossii.*

———. 1998. *Rossiiskii statisticheskii ezhegodnik: Statisticheskii sbornik* [*Russian Statistical Yearbook: Statistical Collection*]. Moscow: *Goskomstat Rossii.*

Goskomstat SSSR. 1989. *Nacelenie SSSR 1988: statisticheskii ezhegodnik.* Moscow: *Finansii i statistika.*

———. 1990. *Demograficheskii ezhegodnik SSSR.* Moscow: *Finansii i statistika.*

———. 1990, 1991. *Narodnoe khoziaistvo SSSR.* Moscow: *Ezegodnaia.*

Horowitz, Irving Louis. 1983. *C. Wright Mills: An American Utopian.* New York: Free Press.

Hosking, Geoffrey. 1985. *The First Socialist Society.* Cambridge, MA: Harvard University Press.

Ilin, Vladimir. 1996. *Gosudarstvo i sotsialnaia stratifiatsiia sovetskogo i postsovetskogo obshchestv, 1917–1996 gg.: opyt konstruktivistsko-strukturalistskogo analiza.* Syktyvkar: *Syktyvkarskii Gosudarstvennyi Universitet.*

Interstate Statistical Committee of CIS. 1994, 1995. *Demographic Yearbook.* Moscow: Interstate Statistical Committee of CIS.

———.1998–1999. *Statistical Yearbook.* Moscow: Interstate Statistical Committee of CIS.

Khrushchev, A. T. 1997. *Ekonomicheskaia i sotsialnaia geografiia Rossii.* Moscow: Kron-Press.

Kliuchevsky, Vasili O. 1994. *A Course in Russian History: The Seventeenth Century.* Armonk, NY: M.E. Sharpe.

———.1997. *A Course in Russian History: The Time of Catherine the Great.* Armonk, NY: M.E. Sharpe.

Konrad, George; and Ivan Szelényi. 1979. *Intellectuals on the Road to Class Power.* New York: Harcourt, Brace, Jovanovich.

Kornai, Janos. 1980. *Economics of Shortage.* Amsterdam: North Holland Publishing House.

———.1992. *The Socialist System: The Political Economy of Communism.* Princeton, NJ: Princeton University Press.

Lapidus, Gail (ed.). 1982. *Women, Work, and Family in the Soviet Union*. Armonk, NY: M.E. Sharpe.

————.1995. *The New Russia: Troubled Transformation*. Boulder, CO: Westview Press.

Lijphardt, Arend. 1984. *Democracies: Patterns of Majoritarian and Consensus Government in Twenty-One Countries*. New Haven, CT: Yale University Press.

Lincoln, W. Bruce. 1983. *In War's Dark Shadow: The Russians before the Great War*. New York: Dial Press.

Linz, Juan J.; and Alfred Stepan. 1996. *Problems of Democratic Transition and Consolidation: Southern Europe, South America, and Post-Communist Europe*. Baltimore, MD: Johns Hopkins University Press.

Lipset, Seymour Martin. 1996. *American Exceptionalism: A Double-Edged Sword*. New York: W.W. Norton.

Mattison, Lindsay; and Natalia Alexeyeva (eds.). 1994. *Russian Regions Today: Atlas of the New Federation*. Washington, DC: The International Center.

McAuley, Mary. 1992. *Soviet Politics 1917–1991*. Oxford: Oxford University Press.

McFaul, Michael. 1997. *Russia's 1996 Presidential Election: The End of Polarized Politics*. Stanford, CA: Stanford University Press.

McFaul, Michael; and Tova Perlmutter (eds.). 1995. *Privatization, Conversion and Enterprise Reform in Russia*. Boulder, CO: Westview Press.

Millar, James R. (ed.). 1987. *Politics, Work, and Daily Life in the USSR: A Survey of Former Soviet Citizens*. Cambridge: Cambridge University Press.

————.1990. *The Soviet Economic Experiment*. Urbana, IL: University of Illinois Press.

Moss, Walter G. 1997. *A History of Russia*. New York: McGraw-Hill.

Murrell, Peter. 1993. "What Is Shock Therapy? What Did It Do in Poland and Russia?" *Post-Soviet Affairs* 9(2): pp. 111–40.

North, Douglass C. 1991. *Institutions, Institutional Change and Economic Performance*. New York: Cambridge University Press.

Nove, Alec. 1986. *The Soviet Economic System*. 3rd ed. Boston, MA: Allen and Unwin.

Pospielovsky, Dimitry. 1998. *The Orthodox Church in the History of Russia*. Crestwood, NY: St. Vladimir's Seminary Press.

Ragin, Charles, and David Zaret. 1983. "Theory and Method in Comparative Strategies." *Social Forces*. 61: 731–754.

Rand Corporation. 1996. *Population of Russia, 1993, Annual Report: Russia's Demographic Crisis*. Santa Monica, CA: Rand.

Riasanovsky, Nicholas Valentine. 1993. *A History of Russia*. 5th ed. New York: Oxford University Press.

Roeder, Philip G. 1993. *Red Sunset: The Failure of Soviet Politics*. Princeton, NJ: Princeton University Press.

Róna-Tas, Ákos. 1994. "The First Shall Be the Last? Entrepreneurship and Communist Cadres in the Transition from Socialism." *American Journal of Sociology* 100: pp. 40–69.

Sachs, Jeffrey. 1996. *Reforms in Eastern Europe and the Former Soviet Union in Light of the East Asian Experiences*. Cambridge, MA: National Bureau of Economic Research.

Sakharov, Andrei. 1975. *My Country and the World*. New York: Alfred A. Knopf.

Schapiro, Leonard. 1984. *1917: The Russian Revolutions and the Origins of Present-Day Communism.* Hounslow, Middlesex: Temple Smith.

Shaw, J. Thomas. 1967. *The Transliteration of Modern Russian for English-Language Publications.* Madison, WI: University of Wisconsin Press.

Silverman, Bertram; and Murray Yanowitch. 1997. *New Rich, New Poor, New Russia: Winners and Losers on the Russian Road to Capitalism.* Armonk, NY: M.E. Sharpe.

Smelser, Neil J. 1976. *Comparative Methods in the Social Sciences.* Englewood Cliffs, NJ: Prentice-Hall.

Solzhenitsyn, Aleksandr. 1963. *One Day in the Life of Ivan Denisovich.* New York: Farrar, Straus, and Giroux.

————.1973. *The Gulag Archipelago, 1918–1956: An Experiment in Literary Investigation.* New York: Harper & Row.

————.1995. *The Russian Question at the End of the Twentieth Century.* New York: Farrar, Straus, and Giroux.

Szporluk, Roman (ed.). 1994. *National Identity and Ethnicity in Russia and the New States of Eurasia.* Armonk, NY: M.E. Sharpe.

Tismaneanu, Vladimir (ed.). 1995. *Political Culture and Civil Society in Russia and the New States of Eurasia.* Armonk, NY: M.E. Sharpe.

Titma, Mikk. 1997. *Sotsialnoe rassloenie vozrastnoi kogorty* [*Social Differentiation of Age Cohort*]. Moscow: *Institut sotsiologii Rossiskoi Akademii Nauk.*

Titma, Mikk; and Ellu Saar. 1995. "Regional Differences in the Secondary Education of the Former Soviet Union." *European Sociological Review* 11(1): pp. 37–58.

Titma, Mikk; Brian D. Silver, and Barbara A. Anderson (eds.). 1996. "Estonia's Transition from State Socialism: Nationalities and Society on the Eve of Independence." *International Journal of Sociology* 26(1–3): pp. 3–99.

Titma, Mikk; and Nancy Brandon Tuma. 1993. "Stratification Research in a Changing World." In *Eastern European Societies on the Threshold of Change,* ed. Z. Mach, J. Mucha, and J. Szmatka, pp. 225–54. Lewiston, NY: Edwin Mellen.

Tuma, Nancy Brandon; and Mikk Titma. 1998. "Educational Attainment in the Former Soviet Union: Why Women Outdid Men." Unpublished manuscript. Department of Sociology, Stanford University.

Walder, Andrew G. 1996. "Markets and Inequality in Transitional Economies: Toward Testable Theories." *American Journal of Sociology* 101: pp. 1060–73.

White, Stephen; Richard Rose; and Ian McAllister. 1997. *How Russia Votes.* Chatham, NJ: Chatham House.

Yanowitch, Murray; and Wesley Fischer (eds.). 1973. *Social Stratification and Mobility in the USSR.* White Plains, NY: M.E. Sharpe.

Zhou, Kate. 1996. *How the Farmers Changed China.* Boulder, CO: Westview Press.

Zinoviev, Aleksandr. 1986. *The Madhouse.* London: V. Gollancz.

WORLD WIDE WEB RESOURCES

There are a number websites devoted to Russia, both in English and in Russian. The following are some sites with interesting and informative links and material in English unless otherwise noted.

http://www.lib.utexas.edu/Libs/PCL/Map_collection/commonwealth. html
Maps of Russia and the former Soviet Union.

http://www.departments.bucknell.edu/russian/chrono.html
An extensive chronology of Russian history from 860 to the present.

http://www.departments.bucknell.edu/russian/material.html
Bucknell University's Russian department offers one of the most comprehensive pages of links to Russia-related sites.

http://www.russiatoday.com
Similar to *USA Today, Russia Today* provides news, financial, and cultural information, as well as a number of links to related sites.

http://www.moscowtimes.ru
The *Moscow Times* is the leading English-language newspaper in Moscow.

http://www.sptimes.ru
Under the same ownership as the *Moscow Times*, the *St. Petersburg Times* offers news from Russia's "second capital."

http://www.wrn.org/audio/vor_eng_usa.ram
You can listen to daily broadcasts of *Voice of Russia* radio news from Moscow (in English), provided in Real Audio format.

http://www.ru
Russia on the Net provides links to various cultural, political, business, and entertainment sites, as well as many more areas of interest. Official home pages of many political parties discussed in this book can be accessed through this site.

http://www.moscow-guide.ru
The official guide to Moscow, providing information on travel, entertainment, culture, dining, and more in Russia's capital city.

http://www.spb.ru
St. Petersburg Online is the official guide to the "second capital" of Russia.

http://www.interknowledge.com/russia/index.html

The official site of the Russian National Tourist Office, providing virtual tours of many of Russia's highlights, as well as information on traveling to Russia.

http://www.russianembassy.org

The Russian Embassy in Washington, DC, provides general historical and cultural information, as well as information on visiting the Russian Federation.

http://www.gov.ru/index.html

The official website of the government of the Russian Federation, providing links to the official pages of the Russian president, the Duma, and other official sites. Primarily in Russian.

Kievan and Appanage Periods

862–879	Rule of **Rurik (Hrorekr).**
988–990	Baptism of Vladimir in 988; official conversion of Russia to Christianity in 990.
	(Pagan beliefs still persist among the people.)
1019–1054	Rule of **Yaroslav the Wise.**
1054–1073	*Russkaia Pravda,* first Russian law, drafted.
1240–1480	Period of **Mongol-Tatar** yoke.
1275	Russia's population reaches 10 million.
1380	Victory of Dmitri Donskoi over the Tatars at Kulikovo Field.
1453	Fall of Constantinople to the Ottoman Empire.
1547–1584	Rule of **Ivan IV, the Terrible.**
1560s	Publication of *Domostroi,* a book on the principles of family life.
1582	Yermak and the beginning of the conquest of Siberia.
1652	Foreigners in Moscow required to live in a certain district, *Nemetskaia Sloboda.*

The Imperial Period

1689–1725	Rule of **Peter I, the Great.**
1703	Founding of **St. Petersburg.**
1708	Establishment of the *guberniias* (provinces).
1722	Table of Ranks established.
1741	Vitus Bering discovers Alaska and the Aleutian Islands.
1755	Lomonosov founds Moscow University.
1762–1796	Rule of Catherine II, the Great.
1773–1775	Pugachev's Rebellion.
1812–1814	Napoleon invades Russia; Alexander I pursues Napoleon to Paris.
1825	Decembrist Revolt.

1851	St. Petersburg–Moscow railroad opened.
1861	Emancipation of the serfs.
1864–1865	Conquest of Central Asia.
1867	Alaska sold to the United States.
1869	Publication of Tolstoy's *War and Peace*.
1870	Publication of Mendeleyev's *Principles of Chemistry*.
1878	Tchaikovsky's *First Piano Concerto* takes Paris by storm; his opera *Eugene Onegin* opens; Tolstoy's *Anna Karenina* published.
1880	Publication of Dostoevsky's *The Brothers Karamazov*.
1897	First census covering all of Russia counts 128,907,692 people.
1904–1905	Russo-Japanese War, which ends in Russian defeat.
1905	1905 Revolution.
1906–1911	Stolypin's land reforms.
1914–1917	World War I.

The Soviet Period

1917	**1917 Revolution** (February 23–March 8).
Nov. 1917	**October Revolution** (October 25–November 7).
1918–1921	Russian Civil War.
1918–1924	Vladimir Ilyich **Lenin** rules as head of Communist Russia.
1921	**New Economic Policy (NEP)** begins.
1924	Lenin dies; USSR constitution ratified; USSR recognized by Britain, France, and Italy.
1927–1953	Josif Vissarionovich **Stalin** rules as head of the USSR.
1929	Collectivization and industrialization begin.
1932–1933	Famine in Ukraine.
1933	United States recognizes USSR.
1936	Stalin promulgates a new constitution.
Dec. 1936	"Show trials" of Zinoviev, Kamenev, and other leading individuals.
1937–1941	*Stalinshchina* (Stalin terror).
Aug. 1939	Nazi-Soviet nonaggression pact signed by Molotov and Ribbentrop.

1941–1945	German invasion of USSR and Great Fatherland War (World War II).
1945	Soviet troops enter Vienna and Berlin, and control Austria, Czechoslovakia, East Germany, Hungary, Rumania, Poland, Bulgaria, Yugoslavia, and the Baltic states.
1945–1949	Soviet Union helps Mao Zedong to gain control over China.
1949	USSR tests atomic bomb.
1953	Stalin dies.
1956	Twentieth Party Congress; Khrushchev gives "secret speech" denouncing Stalin; Lenin's testament read to the Congress.
Nov. 1956	Hungarian revolt crushed.
1957	Launching of the **Sputnik** satellite, the first satellite in space.
1961	Yuri Gagarin of USSR becomes the first man in space.
1962	Publication of Solzhenitsyn's *One Day in the Life of Ivan Denisovich.*
Oct. 1962	Showdown between Khrushchev and Kennedy in the Cuban missile crisis.
1964	Khrushchev ousted; Brezhnev becomes first secretary of the Communist Party.
1968	Czechoslovakia briefly liberalizes in the "Prague Spring" but ends when the USSR sends tanks.
1975	Andrei Sakharov wins Nobel Prize for Peace.
1979	Soviet Union invades Afghanistan.
1985–1991	Mikhail **Gorbachev** serves as general secretary of the Communist Party; introduces glasnost and perestroika.
1989	Berlin Wall comes down; East and West Germany reunited.
June 12, 1990	Congress of People's Deputies of the RSFSR passes Declaration of State Sovereignty of Russia (Independence Day).
June 1991	Boris **Yeltsin** elected president of the RSFSR of the Soviet Union.
Aug. 1991	Coup d'etat directed against Gorbachev but thwarted.

| Dec. 1991 | USSR disbanded and replaced with the Commonwealth of Independent States (CIS). Gorbachev resigns. |

The Post-Soviet Period

1992	Gaidar government formed and starts macroeconomic marketization.
Oct. 1993	Yeltsin orders troops to fire on the White House where the Supreme Soviet sits.
Dec. 1993	New constitution of the Russian Federation approved in a popular referendum.
Oct. 1994	Value of ruble plummets in a single day.
1994–1995	People elect governors of regions for the first time in Russian history.
1994–1996	Secession of Chechnya leads Yeltsin to send troops, who are unsuccessful.
Dec. 1995	First election of Duma; Communist Party wins a plurality of the seats.
June 1996	Yeltsin reelected president of the Russian Federation.
Aug. 1998	Russia's default on government securities triggers panic in Western financial markets.
Fall 1999	Terrorism blamed on Chechens; Russian troops sent to Chechnya and are fairly successful.
Dec. 1999	Second election of the Duma.
Dec. 31, 1999	Yeltsin resigns as President; Vladimir **Putin** becomes acting president.
Mar. 26, 2000	Putin elected president of the Russian Federation.

GLOSSARY

APPARATCHIK   A member of the Communist Party apparatus.

ASSIMILATE, ASSIMILATION   A social and cultural process in which the identity of a person or group is partly or fully changed to the identity of another country, ethnicity, or culture.

BLACK MARKET   The unofficial, private sale and trade of goods, commodities, and services; also a place where such trade takes place. Under the Soviet regime, the black market was a way to get goods and services not readily available by official means. A gray market is like a black market, except that its existence is tolerated (if not condoned) by the state.

BOLSHEVIKS   Meaning "majority" in Russian, the Bolshevik Party was the group of socialists led by V.I. Lenin that took power in the October Revolution of 1917. In March 1918, the Bolshevik Party officially changed its name to the Russian Communist Party.

BOURGEOISIE   The entrepreneurial class that arose out of the Industrial Revolution. It was this class of people that Marx and Lenin saw as the oppressing class of the PROLETARIAT, and thus Lenin set about eliminating the bourgeoisie as a social class.

BYZANTINE EMPIRE   Established by Constantine in the fourth century as the new center of the Roman Empire, home of the Orthodox version of Christianity adopted by Russia in 988. In 1453, Byzantium fell to the Ottoman Turks, and the center of ORTHODOXY moved to Moscow.

CAUCASUS   The mountain system and region lying between the Black and Azov Seas (west) and the Caspian Sea (east). Russia, Armenia, Azerbaijan, and Georgia have territory in this region.

CENTRAL COMMITTEE   In theory, the highest official organ of the Communist Party of the Soviet Union (CPSU), the Central Committee had little power in reality. Convening only once or twice a year, this large body approved only decisions already made by the POLITBURO or the GENERAL SECRETARY OF THE COMMUNIST PARTY.

CHAUVINISM, CHAUVINISTIC   Extreme nationalism held by a large nation (ethnic group). Russian chauvinism is characterized by antagonism and even hatred toward minorities.

CHECHNYA   A republic in the North Caucasus that seceded from Russia in 1991. In December 1994, Yeltsin sent Russian army troops into Chechnya to suppress the Chechen rebels. The ensuing bloody war lasting until 1996 was a disaster for Russia and further eroded Yeltsin's already diminished popularity and political support. In the summer of 1999, terrorist bombings and kidnappings, which Russians blamed on Chechens, allowed Russia's leaders to send troops into Chechnya again. On this second occasion, Russian troops were much more successful.

CIS (COMMONWEALTH OF INDEPENDENT STATES)   A voluntary association formed in December 1991 of all post-Soviet states, minus the three Baltic states of Estonia, Latvia, and Lithuania.

CIVIL SOCIETY   The structure of a society that functions relatively independently from state control.

CLASS DIVISIONS   The division of a society into different social and economic classes. In Marxist theory, class divisions would one day cause the PROLETARIAT to rise up against the oppressing classes to create a new classless society.

COHORT   A collection of people who share some feature that gives them similar experiences and differentiates them from others in their society. A birth cohort is a collection of people born around the same time. An age cohort is a collection of people who are approximately the same age at a given time.

COLLECTIVE FARMS (KOLKHOZES)   Large plots of state-owned land that were communally farmed by people living in a nearby village or town; created by Stalin's COLLECTIVIZATION of agriculture. Collective farms were notorious for their extreme inefficiency and low productivity.

COLLECTIVISM   A cultural pattern encouraging individuals to think and behave in ways that put a collectivity or group above an individual. For the contrast, see INDIVIDUALISM.

COLLECTIVIZATION   Joseph Stalin's move to bring all agriculture and production under control of the state. It began in 1928.

COMMAND ECONOMY   An economy in which all natural, technological, monetary, and productive resources are under state control. In it, state-controlled resources are distributed by a state structure of ministries, divisions, and work organizations (e.g., factories, retail stores, hospitals). While a command economy tries to estimate the resources needed to meet predetermined production goals and to allocate resources according to estimated needs, in practice needs are not estimated well and resources are not allocated efficiently.

COMMUNISM   According to Karl Marx, communism was the final stage of historical development in which the state would "wither away" and all class divisions would cease to exist after the "proletariat revolution." Under communism, everyone would be equal, and wealth would be distributed according to each person's needs. Lenin's version of communism was claimed to be purely Marxist, but in fact his implementation of it in the Soviet Union differed in many ways. The term often used for his version is "state socialism."

CONGRESS OF PEOPLE'S DEPUTIES   In 1989, it superceded the SUPREME SOVIET as the highest legislative body of the USSR. It was the first time since 1917 that Russian voters were allowed to choose among multiple candidates in an election.

CONSTITUTIONAL COURT   The highest court in the Russian Federation; its duties are to interpret and decide legal issues pertaining to the Russian Constitution and in this respect is analogous to the United States' Supreme Court.

COSSACKS   A group of Russians with a tradition of independence who assisted in the southeastward expansion of the Russian Empire in the sixteenth century. The Cossacks remained relatively independent of the Russian state but were eventually crushed by the communists.

COUP D'ETAT   The often violent overthrow of an existing leader or political regime. Russia has experienced a major coup d'etat twice in the twentieth century: the Bolshevik's successful seizure of power in October 1917, and the failed attempt by Communist hard-liners to oust Gorbachev from office in August 1991. The failed coup d'etat in 1991 ultimately led to the collapse of the Soviet Union.

CPSU   The Communist Party of the Soviet Union (also known as the BOLSHEVIK Party) was the ruling force in Russia from the October Revolution of 1917 until the collapse of the Soviet Union in August 1991. The CPSU dominated all aspects of life in Russia, including political, economic, and social matters.

DEMOGRAPHICS   Demographic means literally "of the people" or "of the population." In social science, demographics pertain to basic statistics describing a population, such as births and deaths, marriages and divorces, and in- and out-migration.

DIASPORA   A group of people living away from their ancestral or cultural homelands. With the collapse of the Soviet Union in 1991, many Russians were left in former Soviet republics, thereby forming a Russian diaspora.

DISSIDENTS   Those openly opposed to the Soviet regime. Though KHRUSHCHEV'S THAW allowed some dissidents to express their views (though even then to only a very limited extent), many dissidents spent the Brezhnev era in prison and were released only during Gorbachev's PERESTROIKA. Famous dissidents included Aleksandr Solzhenitsyn (author of the anti-Stalinist *GULAG Archipelago*), Boris Pasternak (author of *Doctor Zhivago*), and Andrei Sakharov (physicist who helped create the first Soviet hydrogen bomb and later turned against the Soviet regime).

DUMA   The lower house of the Russian parliament established by the 1993 constitution; comparable to the U.S. House of Representatives. This 450-member body is relatively weak compared to the vast powers of Russia's president, though it does have the right to accept or reject the president's nominations for prime minister and other cabinet positions.

EDUCATIONAL ATTAINMENT   The level of education that someone has achieved.

EMERGING MARKET ECONOMY   A concept characterizing the departure from a previous COMMAND ECONOMY and the attempt to develop a functioning MARKET ECONOMY.

ETHNICITY   Features that are socially and culturally characteristic of members of a certain group who typically are associated with a particular homeland. NATIONALITY is the most common form of ethnicity, but it may also be associated with a particular clan or tribe.

EXCHANGE MOBILITY   SOCIAL MOBILITY that remains after STRUCTURAL MOBILITY is taken into account.

FEDERAL SECURITY BUREAU **(FSB)**   The FSB is the successor to the KGB.

FEDERATION COUNCIL   The upper house of the Russian parliament, comparable to the U.S. Senate. This 178-member body gives equal representation to each of Russia's 89 republics and regions.

FIVE-YEAR PLAN   Originally created by Stalin in 1928, these plans were designed to industrialize the Soviet Union and build its COMMAND ECONOMY in five-year increments. Stalin's Five-Year Plans were successful in achieving industrialization quickly, but they created a great shortage of consumer goods.

FREE MARKET SYSTEM   An economic system in which the terms of exchanges are largely governed by the free choices of potential partners to exchanges and, in particular, are not coerced or fixed by some superordinate authority, such as the state.

GAZPROM   Russia's monopoly in natural gas, formed when the resources of the former Soviet Ministry of Gas Production were privatized under Viktor Chernomyrdin, then Russia's prime minister.

GENERAL SECRETARY OF THE COMMUNIST PARTY   Originally created in 1922 as a bureaucratic post for Joseph Stalin, it allowed him to assume control of the Communist Party and thus the USSR. After Stalin's death in 1953, the position of general secretary of the CPSU remained the most powerful position in the CPSU and the USSR.

GEOPOLITICS   The view and study of countries in terms of their competitive political and economic relations with their geographical neighbors.

GLASNOST   Mikhail Gorbachev's term describing his aim of liberalizing and opening up Soviet society.

GNP (GROSS NATIONAL PRODUCT)   The total value of all goods and services produced in a country in a given year.

GREAT FATHERLAND WAR   World War II, one of the defining historical events for Russians. Over 27 million Soviet citizens lost their lives defending their motherland from Hitler's invasion.

GULAG   Stalin's vast system of Soviet labor camps where political prisoners and criminals were detained. Lasting from the 1920s until the mid-1950s, the GULAG held millions of prisoners at its height in the 1930s and 1940s. The total deaths in the GULAG's three decades of existence are estimated to be from 15 to 30 million.

HUMAN CAPITAL   A term, made famous by American economist Gary Becker, referring to the resources embedded in a person that enable him or her to be productive. Aspects of human capital include a person's intelligence, education, work experience, health, strength, and so on.

INDIVIDUALISM   A cultural pattern of encouragement of free and independent thinking and behavior in individuals. For the contrast, see COLLECTIVISM.

INDUSTRIALIZATION   The process of converting a society based on agriculture to one based on industry. For most European countries, industrialization took place during the Industrial Revolution of the late eighteenth and nineteenth centuries. Russia, however, did not become industrialized until the 1930s, when Stalin's FIVE-YEAR PLANS "did in a decade what it took Europe 50 years to do."

INOVERTSY, INOZEMTSY   *Inovertsy* is the Russian word for one who is not a follower of the ORTHODOX CHURCH; *inozemtsy* is the Russian word for an ethnic non-Russian. Both words carry a heavy negative connotation, and those bearing such labels are considered inferior by Russians.

INSTITUTION   An enduring social process or tradition within a society that most members of the society take almost for granted. For example, the system of checks and balances is a political institution in America. Sometimes it means a formal organization.

INSTITUTIONALIZATION   The transformation of something into an institution. In Russia, political, judicial, and legislative practices have not yet been institutionalized, making them weak and hard to predict.

INTELLIGENTSIA   The term used to refer to the educated social STRATUM in France, Italy, and Russia in the nineteenth century, which the Soviet Union continued to use.

INTERGENERATIONAL, INTRAGENERATIONAL MOBILITY   Intergenerational mobility refers to the social position of adult children relative to their parents. Intragenerational mobility refers to the changes in social position that occur within a single individual's lifetime. See SOCIAL MOBILITY.

KGB (NKVD)   Under the Soviet regime, the KGB was the strongest and most important security organ of the USSR. Not only engaged in espionage and counterintelligence abroad, it also served as a powerful domestic force, engaging in manifold activities designed to protect the state; these included everything from censorship, to antidissidence efforts, to security for political leaders. It also had significant internal security troops.

KHRUSHCHEV'S THAW   The period of relaxed political and social control under Nikita Khrushchev, beginning with his secret speech to the Twentieth Party Congress (1956) in which he denounced the crimes of Joseph Stalin. During this cultural thaw, some dissidents such as Aleksandr Solzhenitsyn were allowed to publish anti-Stalin material (i.e., Solzhenitsyn's *One Day in the Life of Ivan Denisovich*, 1962). This thaw also shaped younger generations, giving rise to future reformers such as Mikhail Gorbachev.

KIEVAN Rus   The cradle of Russian civilization, Kievan Rus was a kingdom in present day Ukraine that prospered through trade on the Dnieper River. The grand era of Kievan Rus ended in 1240 when Kiev was sacked by invading Mongol forces and became part of the Golden Horde.

KOLKHOZES   See COLLECTIVE FARMS.

KOMSOMOL   The Communist Youth League in the Soviet Union. It spread Communist teachings among its members (ages 14–28) and prepared them for activity in the CPSU when they got older.

LUKOIL   Russia's privatized oil monopoly, formed out of the former Soviet oil ministry.

MACROECONOMIC MARKETIZATION   The process of developing a MARKET ECONOMY through the top-to-bottom establishment of an appropriate legal and institutional framework. Historically market economies develop gradually through the largely individual efforts of a multitude of individual entrepreneurs.

MARKET ECONOMY   An economy in which there are multiple buyers and sellers of various goods and services, and prices are established by the law of supply and demand. See FREE MARKET SYSTEM.

MILITIA   The Russian term for the ordinary police.

MUSCOVY   The principality of Muscovy (Moscow) was founded in the thirteenth century; over time it grew in size and strength until it became the dominating force in Russia. Using Moscow as their power base, future Russian leaders would eventually expand the empire to the Pacific Ocean and along the Pacific Coast of North America.

NACHALNIK   A Russian word meaning someone who decides and commands. It is typically used to refer to the head or chief of an office or department. Ordinary Russians use this word to refer to their boss at work.

NATION   A group of people who share a societal organization, usually based on a common origin, tradition, and language. *Ethnic group* is an American term with a similar meaning. When a nation also possesses a defined territory and government, it is considered a *nation-state* (e.g., France, Germany).

NATIONALITY   See ETHNICITY.

NEAR ABROAD   The term among Russians for the territories not in the Russian Federation but formerly in the Soviet Union and in the Russian Empire under the TSARS.

NEW ECONOMIC POLICY (NEP)   Lenin's NEP, begun in 1921, was a temporary retreat from the building of socialism in Russia. Measures such as allowing peasants to cultivate private land for profit while paying taxes to the state allowed the USSR to recover from the devastating effects of the Civil War of 1918–1921.

NOMENKLATURA   The list of people eligible to hold positions in the Soviet PARTY-STATE apparatus. A selection system was established in every party-state organ to control the vast pool of possible candidates for promotion into the ranks of the *nomenklatura.*

NORM   That which is culturally or traditionally normal within a society.

OBLAST   Similar to a state in the United States. The Russian Federation has 49 *oblasts,* along with 21 republics, six *krais* (border lands), two federal cities (Moscow and St. Petersburg), one autonomous *oblast,* and 10 autonomous *okrugs* (national districts).

OCCUPATIONAL STRUCTURE   A sociological concept referring to a society's division of labor in terms of occupations.

OLIGARCHS   The popular name among Russians for the very few beneficiaries of marketization in Russia, who have become a major economic and political force.

ORTHODOXY, ORTHODOX CHURCH   In the fourth century, the Christian Church split into an eastern branch (the Orthodox Church) and a western branch (the Roman Catholic Church). The division had political as well as theological aspects. The Orthodox Church developed in the eastern part of Europe and was centered in Byzantium until the tenth century. Thereafter, the western branch of the Christian Church became dominant. The Orthodox Church has been more conservative than the Roman Catholic Church and has avoided reform for centuries. It is divided into various national Orthodox churches, of which the Russian Orthodox Church is the largest.

OTTOMAN EMPIRE One of the strongest states in the world in the sixteenth and seventeenth centuries, based on Muslim Turks. In its heyday, it included not only Turkey and Greece, but also parts of southeast Europe, the Middle East, and northern Africa.

OUTER EMPIRE East European countries formerly in the Soviet bloc (e.g., Hungary, Poland).

PARTY-STATE A state such as the Soviet Union in which a single political party dominates and controls the state.

PERESTROIKA Mikhail Gorbachev's initiative to reform and restructure the Soviet PARTY-STATE.

PHONE-CALL LAW An extralegal system of justice in which orders passed down from higher party or state officials (usually via telephone) take precedence over the laws themselves.

POGROMS Mob attacks, which were usually condoned by the state, carried out against Jews or other minorities in the Russian Empire in the late nineteenth and early twentieth centuries.

POLITBURO The highest organ of the CPSU; comprised of a small group of powerful party members. After Stalin, the Politburo led not only the CPSU, but also essentially the Soviet state itself.

POSTINDUSTRIAL The stage of economic development after industrialization in which a service-based economy is dominant.

PRIVATIZATION A process in which state-owned enterprises are transferred to private owners.

PRIVATIZATION OF LAW ENFORCEMENT Due to the lack of adequate protection by the official security organs in Russia (the MILITIA, the FSB, etc.), many private law enforcement agencies have sprung up, offering wealthy clients services ranging from personal protection to contract negotiation and debt collection.

PROLETARIAT The working class that Karl Marx envisioned would one day rise up against its bourgeois oppressors; the basis of BOLSHEVIK support.

PUTSCH The word used by Russians for the attempted COUP D'ETAT against Gorbachev in August 1991.

REFUSENIK An American term for Soviet DISSIDENTS.

REVOLUTIONARY JUSTICE After the October Revolution in 1917, formal laws that matched Lenin's radical goals had not yet been established. Revolutionary justice, meaning decrees by BOLSHEVIK leaders, solved this problem. Such "justice" often meant the violent elimination of opposition and gave rise to the famous Red Terror.

ROSSIIANIN   This word indicates one's citizenship or civic status as Russian, meaning a person lives within the Russian state. Thus, one who is Rossiianin is not necessarily an ethnic Russian (RUSSKII).

RUSSIAN ORTHODOX CHURCH   The version of Christianity chosen for the Russian people by Vladimir, Grand Duke of Kiev, in 988. The Russian Orthodox Church remained the official state church of the Russian Empire with Russia's tsar as its head.

RUSSIFIED, RUSSIFICATION   To give something a Russian character or make it Russian. During Soviet times, Russification of nationalities was used as a means to increase state control throughout the Soviet empire. By enforcing Russian as the official language, as well as by importing ethnic Russians into areas dominated by different nationalities, Soviet leaders hoped to create a distinct "Soviet [wo]man" who would be more easily controlled.

RUSSKII   The word for an ethnic Russian, as contrasted with one who is a citizen of the Russian state (ROSSIIANIN).

SERF   Under feudalism, a serf was a tenant farmer who was bound to a hereditary plot of land, as well as the will of his landlord. While serfs were not slaves (they could not be bought or sold), they were forced to give a portion of their crops to the landlord and to perform certain duties that the landlord demanded of them. They often received brutal treatment. While most of Europe had abolished serfdom by the fourteenth and fifteenth centuries, Russia did not do so until 1861 when Tsar Alexander II emancipated the serfs.

SHOCK THERAPY   The method of marketization followed by Russia after the USSR collapsed in 1991. Its proponents included Swedish economist Anders Åslund and Harvard economist Jeffrey Sachs, as well as Russian reformers like Yegor Gaidar and Anatoly Chubais. It involves large-scale, rapid economic reforms that start at the top and are supposed to work downward.

SOCIAL CLASS   The term used by nineteenth century French historians to characterize large groups of people in terms of differences in their work relations. The division of society into the nobility, BOURGEOISIE, PROLETARIAT, and peasants began to be the basis of political, social, and economic relations in Europe and later in other parts of the world.

SOCIAL DIFFERENTIATION   A social process in which people or social groups come to be socially different from one another in institutionalized ways. For example, people may be differentiated in terms of the work that they do, in their social roles, or in the social rewards they are given.

SOCIAL MOBILITY   A sociological term referring to differences between people's social position at one point in time and either their parents' social position (INTERGENERATIONAL MOBILITY) or their own social position at an earlier point in time (INTRAGENERATIONAL MOBILITY). Movement to a higher social position is called upward mobility; movement to a lower social position is called downward mobility.

SOCIAL STRATIFICATION   The durable, institutionalized ordering of members of a society (or social organization) in terms of power, wealth, prestige, and other scare social values.

SOCIAL STRUCTURE   An institutionalized system of social arrangements (e.g., positions) in a society.

Soviet Council of Ministers The powerful council in the Soviet state structure whose members were the heads of the various state ministries.

spatial division A country's territorial division, usually corresponding to its administrative structure.

state apparatus The state along with all of its executive structures. In Russia today, the state apparatus is largely a holdover from the Soviet regime; most government agencies and employees carry out the same state functions as in Soviet times.

stratum A sociological term coming from the Latin word for "layer," meaning a group of similar people who are in a certain layer of a social hierarchy.

structural mobility Social mobility that results from changes in the occupational structure.

Supreme Court The court that reviews and oversees the actions of other courts in the Russian Federation. Except for Russia's Constitutional Court, it is the highest court in the Russian Federation, but it does not deal with constitutional issues.

Supreme Soviet Formally the highest legislative body in the USSR, the Supreme Soviet's importance was largely symbolic. Its primary function was to approve decisions already made by the Politburo. During most of the Soviet era, "elections" to it meant the affirmation of unopposed CPSU candidates.

Tatar-Mongol yoke The occupation of Russia by Tatar-Mongol forces lasting from the mid-thirteenth century until the sixteenth century. During this time, Russians were forced to pay heavy tribute or taxes to their oppressors.

Third Rome Moscow was regarded as the Third Rome because it gradually assumed the leadership of Orthodoxy world after Constantinople (the Second Rome) fell to the Ottoman Turks in 1453.

totalitarian, totalitarianism A political system that allows no personal freedom and subordinates all aspects of society to the authority of the state. Usually a totalitarian regime is characterized by a strong dictator and powerful police forces; it lacks a civil society. The father of modern totalitarianism is usually considered to be Joseph Stalin, whose iron hand ruled the USSR from 1924 until his death in 1953.

tsar Originating from the word "caesar," the Russian tsar (sometimes spelled czar) was historically the head of the Russian state as well as the Russian Orthodox Church. Ivan IV (the Terrible) became the first tsar of Russia in 1547. The last tsar, Nicholas II, was executed along with his family by the Bolsheviks in 1918 after having been ousted from power in the Revolution of 1917.

Urals The mountain range separating European Russia from Asian Russia. During Stalin's industrialization, many new factory cities were built throughout the Ural region. This proved to be a wise move because these factories, many of which were essential to the defense industry, were beyond the range of Hitler's air force in World War II. Nonetheless, the heavy emphasis on industry as well as the harsh climate has made the transition to a market economy difficult for the Ural region.

urbanization The process in which a rural population moves to cities and becomes city dwellers.

INDEX